I0794358

First Timers and Old Timers: The Texas Folklore Society Fire Burns On

First Timers and Old Timers: The Texas Folklore Society Fire Burns On

Edited by Kenneth L. Untiedt

Publications of the Texas Folklore Society LXVIII

UNT PRESS

University of North Texas Press
Denton, Texas

© 2012 Texas Folklore Society

All rights reserved.
Printed in the United States of America.

10 9 8 7 6 5 4 3 2 1

Permissions:
University of North Texas Press
1155 Union Circle #311336
Denton, TX 76203-5017

The paper used in this book meets the minimum requirements of the American National Standard for Permanence of Paper for Printed Library Materials, z39.48.1984. Binding materials have been chosen for durability.

Library of Congress Cataloging-in-Publication Data

First timers and old timers: the Texas Folklore Society fire burns on/edited by Kenneth L. Untiedt. — 1st ed.p. cm. — (Publications of the Texas Folklore Society; 68)
Includes bibliographical references and index.
ISBN 978-1-57441-471-4 (cloth : alk. paper) — ISBN 978-1-57441-483-7 (ebook)
1. Folklore—Texas. 2. Texas—Social life and customs—20th century. 3. Texas—Social life and customs—21st century. 4. Texas—Biography. 5. Texas Folklore Society. I. Untiedt, Kenneth L., 1966– II. Series: Publications of the Texas Folklore Society; no. 68.
GR110.T5F5 2012
398.209764—dc23
2012032712

First Timers and Old Timers: The Texas Folklore Society Fire Burns On is Number LXVIII in the Publications of the Texas Folklore Society

CONTENTS

III. *Legends in Their Time—and Ours Still*

IV. *Everything But the Kitchen Sink: Ghosts, Legends, Language, and Other Lore*

PREFACE

The Texas Folklore Society has been around for over a hundred years now, and in terms of printed scholarship pertaining to the lore of Texas and the Southwest, we've produced more than any other organization in the state. In fact, I think it's safe to say that we've contributed more to folklore scholarship in general than any state folklore organization in the country. This is the 68th full-length book in our regular Publications of the Texas Folklore Society series, and we've assisted with the publication of dozens of other books in our Extra Books series and other related works. But what is the future of the Society? In this "information age" of the Internet and social networking sites and trying to keep up with constantly changing technology, what is the future of an organization that focuses on trying to maintain its culture through the oral tradition?

It's right here. This book, as is the case with most of our publications, is composed of papers that have been presented at the organization's annual meetings. Half of the articles in this volume exemplify what the Society has offered its members consistently throughout its history—namely, folklore research from some of the most respected folklorists in the state, including Lora B. Garrison, James Ward Lee, F. E. Abernethy, and Kenneth W. Davis. The last four decades of the Texas Folklore Society meetings have benefitted immeasurably from these prolific members. But we're not stopping there. We're not even slowing down. With the rest of the articles coming from newcomers such as J. Michael Sullivan, Lori Najvar, Acayla Haile, and Ken Baake, you can be sure that we'll keep on doing what we've done for over a century. These members, some of whom were still teens when they presented a paper at a meeting, provide fresh perspectives on topics, but still examine them for their folkloric elements.

Janet Simonds, my office secretary and the Society's Treasurer, did well to point out to me something from the preface of the very first PTFS, eventually titled *Round the Levee.* In that initial volume, George Kittredge shared his thoughts on the contributors and ways to collect lore:

> Everybody can help. A few items, jotted down in a leisure hour, and sent to the secretary, become part of a treasury of manuscript material which may soon grow to surprising proportions. There is not toil involved in such casual collecting. It is pure sport, and serves to while away many a fragment of idle time that otherwise would pass but laggingly. Yet the results will count for much in the aggregate. The serious student will bless the amateur who was not too lazy or too indifferent to send his contribution to the common store. (1)

That's what this book is all about—the members, young and old, who've taken the time to jot down a few observations and share them with the rest of us. They are preserved here, and presented for the benefit of all.

Besides thanking the many contributors featured in this book, I want to acknowledge a few other people who help make these publications possible. As always, I thank Karen DeVinney and all the folks at the UNT Press who help us put these books together each year. I thank the administrators at Stephen F. Austin State University who support the TFS; Mark Sanders, the Chair of the English Department, has been especially generous this past year in providing a Graduate Assistant who helped catalog and organize our extensive collection of folklore books and other materials. I also thank Brian Murphy, the Dean of the College of Liberal and Applied Arts, and the many other supportive colleagues who make us glad to call SFA and Nacogdoches home.

Finally, I thank Janet Simonds, who does more than I can mention to help get from an idea to a finished manuscript; sometimes those ideas start off in pretty rough fashion, but the final product always seems to come together just the way we want it. Janet is intimately involved in every phase of the process—from the mechanical things, such as formatting submitted papers and scanning photos, to helping make more critical decisions, such as offering analytical suggestions regarding which papers to select and ways to phrase things. I could probably put out a book without her, but I don't even want to consider that possibility. Janet, it is a pleasure and an honor to work with you.

This book is dedicated to those members who are being published in a PTFS for the first time. We all appreciate your efforts, for you are keeping the fire alive.

Kenneth L. Untiedt
Stephen F. Austin State University
Nacogdoches, Texas
May 21, 2012

"BACK IN THE DAY":

REFLECTIONS ON TIME PASSED

World War II poster

USE IT UP. WEAR IT OUT. MAKE IT DO. DO WITHOUT.

by Linda Wolff

Use it up. Wear it out. Make it do. Do without.

I heard these refrains day in and day out in my youth, primarily from my mother. I'm surprised she didn't make me and my brother repeat the entire chorus each morning before we left for school. Later, I learned that these phrases were the text from a World War II poster, illustrated by American artist Ben Shahn, who worked at the Office of War Information from 1942 to 1943. I have not, however, been able to determine who wrote the slogan. But I would bet that the writer for that poster had a frugal mother. I certainly did.

Now I do want to note here—up front—that my mother was not miserly. Tracey McBride, author of *Frugal Luxuries*, says it well. Miserliness, she says, is the "absence of generosity. A miserly person will spend money reluctantly and deprive himself of all but the barest of essentials, *for the sole purpose of hoarding* money."[1] My mother reminded us often that money saved in one area was money that could be *better spent* for something else. Lord knows that she and her siblings—and many others growing up in the 1930s—had to "make do" or "do without."

She grew up with lye soap made from saved grease. Store-bought soap was a luxury not to be wasted. When the bar was reduced to slivers, she put a handful of them into a net bag so that all of the soap could be used. Shampoo was watered down, and still is when I visit her home today. She *does* buy liquid soap to wash dishes today. When I was growing up we used a small spoonful of laundry detergent. She still washes her dishes by hand because in her view a dishwashing machine is wasteful of soap, water, electricity, and time when there are dishes for only two people to be washed.

Apparently, the turning of worn collars and cuffs on shirts has been a frugal practice for generations. James D. Patton, the Walker County Historical Commission chair, told me everything his mother could get from a shirt. Buttons were removed because buttons were never thrown away, even if you had a gallon jar filled with them. The button facing would be cut from the edge of the shirt because it could be used to tie together dogwood branches to make a broom. The front panels of the shirt were stitched together with the back panel to make an apron. The pocket was as useful on the apron as it had been on the shirt. The elbows, of course, were worn thin, but two long strips could be cut from the inside of each sleeve. These became apron strings. The back panel of shirts could also be cut and hemmed to become dish towels. Cuffs, opened wide, with some quilt batting between them, made hot pads.

I remember dresses made with ample hems and side seams so that they could be altered as I grew. A row of rick-rack would cover the former hemline. Embroidery or a row of lace might be used to conceal a stain on a bodice. Also remembered by many are dresses, shirts, and even underwear made from feed sack fabric. Many a farmer or rancher's wife would accompany her husband to the feed store so that she could pick the fabric for her next sewing project. Sometimes women would collect different designs and trade them with their friends. Underwear for an especially active toddler might sport a familiar advertising logo. A floral design would be used for a dress, stripes or a plaid would become a man's shirt to be worn to a Saturday night dance, and a border print was destined to become a kitchen curtain or towel.

Feed sacks were also used to make quilts. Today, bidding can be fierce for quilts made from vintage feed sacks because they are considered "shabby chic." Lillian Lau of Victoria has one from the annual quilt auction sponsored by the Lutheran Church at Colletoville. Collectors on-line pay as much as $100 for vintage feed sacks that are barely one yard by 43 inches in size. Imagine!

When we made our beds with clean sheets we alternated between having the wide hem at the top and having it at the bottom of the bed. We always bought flat sheets—not fitted—so that their use as a top sheet or bottom sheet could be swapped. This evened out the wear. My mama took sheets that were worn in the middle, split them in half, turned the worn edges to the outside, and seamed the good edges together at the middle. Recently, I learned from Jean Schnitz of Boerne that her grandmother, Dora Scnudder, did the same. Shirley Spies of Victoria told me that her grandmother stitched feed sacks together to make the sheets for her guest beds. "I loved our visits to grandma," Shirley told me, "but I hated sleeping on all those seams."

Speaking of bed linens reminds me of some other ways that people "made do." Layers of newspapers were placed between the bed coils and the mattress to offer some insulation on cold winter nights. Typically, houses were not heated during the night. Many a bed has also been warmed with a hot water bottle, a technique I used when I discovered that the furnace in my Port Lavaca home was not adequate during the coldest nights of the winter. A hot water bottle is a much cheaper option than a new furnace. Sometimes it is best to do without.

Henry Wolff, Jr., my spouse, recalls his family moving into a sharecropper house that had been vacant for some time and was infested with bed bugs. His father placed cans of kerosene under each bed post. There was no Orkin man to call. Sometimes you just have to make do.

Socks were darned. That is, they were mended by weaving darning thread over the hole. In and out, wear it out. Darning thread isn't manufactured anymore. We used a burned out light bulb as the darning egg. Mama was quick to remind us that a small hole was easier to mend than a larger one. I think there's a life lesson there.

Pots and pans with holes were repaired with a Mendet kit, another product that is no longer made. This was piece of metal clamped to the side of the pan so that the hole would be plugged and the pot could be returned to service. You *might* find a Mendet kit at an antique shop, but it will cost you more than the original 15 cents.

Mendets metal repair kits

Do you remember when purchases made at the store were wrapped in paper and tied with string? That was a bit before my time, but Henry tells me that his mother saved every bit of string, even when the ball became too large to fit into a drawer. Patsy Hand of Victoria has a lovely counterpane that was crocheted from market string. Audrey Dornburg of Yorktown told me that saved market string was also used to tie-off sausages. I remember the heavy brown sacks that our groceries were packed in. These were used to wrap packages to be shipped, and to duplicate sewing patterns shared by a friend.

When my mother was growing up her family didn't have money to buy lunch meat. So they "made do." Her mother mashed beans leftover from the meal the night before and spread it on two slices of bread. In between she added a generous layer of sauerkraut. The sandwiches my mama carried to school were wrapped in newspaper with an apple in the middle of it. Her

Common items were used for multiple purposes

mother didn't buy sandwich bags. And apparently most families didn't. Lunch was generally carried to school, or work, in an empty lard bucket. A good example of "Use it up. Wear it out. Make it do. Do without."

Henry remembers his mother preserving sausages in a jar by pouring grease over them. These sausages were then used to make the sandwiches that he carried to school in a paper bag and stored in the cloak room. By noon the grease would be dripping through the bag, but his buddies were happy to trade their peanut butter and jelly sandwiches on white bread for his sausages wrapped with home-made bread. I carried my lunch to school in a paper bag, but I knew that I had to bring that bag home so that it could also be used for Tuesday's lunch, Wednesday's lunch, and then on Thursday and Friday.

After my mother was widowed she was invited to attend a brown bag lunch for singles that was held on a Saturday at the church. Out of habit she packed her lunch in the same paper bag she had used the previous five days. The fellow seated across from her observed her lunch bag then leaned over to his friend to say, "Well, at least we know she's frugal."

For a long time my mama would not buy plastic wrap. We had circles of plastic with elastic edges that we stretched over our bowls, washed, and then reused again and again. She also saved the paper wrappers from the butter cubes in the refrigerator. These were used with a dab of shortening to grease pie pans, or casserole dishes. Use it up.

There were ways to be frugal outside the home, as well. Henry says his father never threw away a piece of leather because it could be used as a door hinge. Every farm or ranch had a scrap pile for odd bits of lumber, plywood, hardware, baling wire, latches, screen, window frames, and shingles—anything that could be used again. After all, they weren't completely worn out. "Use it up. Wear it out. Make it do. Do without."

Henry recalls used crankcase oil from farm equipment being used as a beauty treatment of sorts for pigs. Burlap bags were soaked with the used crankcase oil and these were wrapped around a cable stretched between two posts so that pigs passing under the cable could lubricate themselves with the oil, keeping their skin soft. It may have also deterred parasites. My father kept a bucket of sand in which he would pour used oil from our car. Before he put his gardening tools away he would thrust them into this mixture to clean and protect them from rust.

I remember once as a child seeing a garden path made by sinking beer bottles upside down into the ground. I smiled when I saw that again—decades later—at the home of Mrs. Jonathan Pierce in Blessing. At the Pioneer Museum at Fredericksburg upended wine bottles are used as edging around a garden, apparently a common practice at one time.

Gardens made from old tires were once common, but not so anymore. Often the tires were turned inside out and were cut with

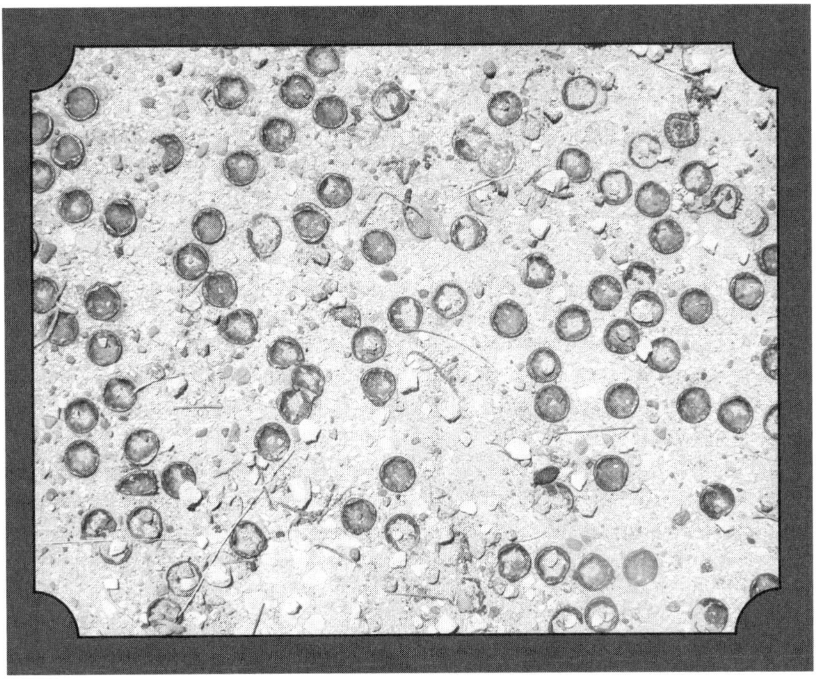

Why throw it away? Bottle caps mixed in with concrete

a zig-zag edge, perhaps to deter cats from entering the garden. Henry and I could not find a tire garden in Victoria, but we did find a half dozen in Kenedy. Bottle caps from opened bottles of beer, or soda pop, were once used in parking lots of almost any tavern or dance hall, like the remnant in front of a café at Weesatche. How long has it been since you have seen that?

My mother used empty tin cans to bake bran bread and to mold cornmeal mush that was fried and served with syrup. With scraps of pork or sausage this was sometimes known as scrapple, or panhas if you were from a German-ancestry family. Cans were also used over fence posts to protect them from rain water.

During the time I did research at the lower Indianola Cemetery, I admired the horseshoe that someone had welded onto the gate to make a latch. It's now gone—stolen, I suppose by vandals who didn't have a scrap pile, and certainly no understanding of "Use it up. Wear it out. Make it do. Do without."

I find buying children's gifts at Christmas a frustrating experience because everything is made out of cheap plastic and invariably requires batteries. The toys I remember best are the ones that didn't break: monkey dolls made from socks, Lincoln Logs, dominos, and my bicycle. Did my parents buy me a new bicycle? No. My father went to the junk yard and brought home three bicycles in various states of disrepair. With his welding torch he combined two frames into one and was able to salvage three wheels, tires and tubes. He taught me how to mend a tire tube so that I would always have a ready-to-mount wheel hanging in the garage if I had a flat tire.

My friends and I spent hours with a loop of string making string figures. I can still do Crow's Foot, Teacup and Saucer, and Jacob's Ladder.

Patsy Hand recalls making paper dolls from the pages of a Sears & Roebuck catalog. My brother and I colored the Sunday comic pages that were still printed in black and white. Sometimes we colored the fancy borders around the car ads.

An old inner tube from a tire—too patched to be used again—could be cut into strips to make a sling shots. I read recently that Ernest Hemingway carried a sling shot with him during his early years in Paris to bring down small birds that he cooked for his meals. I bet he, too, had a frugal mother.

Fishing trips were another common pastime. Henry recalls cotton wagons loaded up with blankets and picnic baskets taken down to the river for an overnight fishing excursion. Left-over chicken guts were used for bait. Toothpaste tubes made of zinc were cut into strips to make sinkers. Use it up. Make do.

When I was too young to get a job to earn spending money my mother advised me to plant tomatoes in the garden. I sold them for 50 cents a bag and had regular customers until the season was over. I gave them the tomatoes but kept the sacks. Later, I bought watermelons from a truck and sold them at my father's service station. Can't get a job? Make do.

This paper would be incomplete, of course, if I did not describe the frugal practices of WWII. Since I'm a Baby Boomer, that was a bit before my time, but I heard enough from family stories.

We know, of course, that tires and fuel were rationed. Used grease was collected for the war effort, to be used in the manufacture of munitions. Scrap drives picked up almost anything made of metal: obsolete farming equipment, parts replaced when a tractor was overhauled, and broken tools.

Aluminum foil might be used to cover a casserole, then wrap a canning jar to be used as a vase for flowers picked from the garden. Then it was carefully unwrapped and used to bake a potato. And then smoothed out and used to protect the crust of a chicken pot pie. Finally, it was washed, and then sent to the scrap drive. Even the tin foil used to wrap chewing gum was added to the scrap pile.

Sugar was rationed. My great aunt, Esther Dickens, put in a row of bee hives in Gage, Oklahoma. She converted her baking recipes from sugar to honey and had extra honey to sell to her neighbors. She generously shared her recipes and had no problem selling her honey. Meat was rationed, so housewives learned to make casseroles so that every bit could be stretched into extra servings by adding noodles, rice, or beans. Eggs were rationed, so city folks who didn't have chickens eagerly clipped recipes for "One-egg Cake." Make do or do without.

Vegetables were in short supply, so home gardening and canning became common practice. Likewise, cans were needed for the war effort. How many young people today know what a Victory Garden is? Henry harvests collard greens from our garden that are much better than the frozen ones purchased at the store. And we all know the luxury of home-grown to-MAY-ters.

Left-over mashed potatoes became potato croquettes. Dabs of left-over vegetables became soup when they were combined with vegetable water, plus broth made by boiling bones and the bits of meat that were still on the bones. Henry's mother even ate chicken feet. I'm so glad my mama never served me chicken feet.

Henry recalls gathering cattle and sheep bones during WWII because they could be crushed to make bone meal. It was used in animal feed and to make fertilizer, commodities that were in short supply.

Hemlines became shorter during WWII to conserve on fabric. Fabric was rationed because it was needed to make military uniforms. Older clothes were taken apart and then remade into newer styles. Old sweaters with moth holes could be unraveled and knitted again into a new garment. Patsy Hand recalls that her mother even saved the sewing thread that she picked from the seams of worn-out garments that were stitched.

During WWII, while my mother was attending high school, she had one skirt, one sweater, and two blouses. Each night she would hand-wash a blouse or sweater, her undies and socks, so that she would always have clean clothes to wear. Today, she is incredulous that anyone would pay to wear clothing with advertising printed on it.

Shoes made of leather were rationed, and it's a safe bet to say that people probably took better care of the shoes they had, and repaired them with heel taps or new soles as needed. Due to the shortage of leather, Henry recalls a softball that was shared until the hide was literally knocked off of it and the elastic had become unwound from its hard rubber center. I recall re-stitching at least one softball with dental floss because the seam had split, *and that was a decade after WWII.* Today it would just be tossed into the trash.

Some in the younger generations might think that we were disadvantaged because we were frugal. I think not. I think we learned to be creative and self-reliant. We learned that the small things in life bring the greatest pleasure.

And the art of being frugal is still practiced by some. Tracey McBride's book *Frugal Luxuries*, published in 1997, is still in print. I see *Simple Living* magazine prominently displayed on the magazine rack at the grocery store, and there are a multitude of websites dedicated to "frugal living." Just Google it.

And then there is the success of eBay. It's clear that there are still people out there looking for a bargain, who are not opposed to owning something that is not yet used up and worn out. If the national debt continues to climb, and the price of gas continues its upward spiral, I suspect Americans will rediscover the art of being frugal and better understand the slogan, "Use it up. Wear it out. Make it do. Do without."

Endnote

1. McBride, Tracey. *Frugal Luxuries: Simple Pleasures to Enhance Your Life and Comfort Your Soul.* New York: Bantam, 1997. 4.

John Allen Davis with prize winning Angora goats, circa 1940

GROWING UP IN THE GOAT PEN

by Lora B. Davis Garrison

We children—in my family—all grew up in the goat pen, which was our way of life and our livelihood. Our lives could no more be separated from the goats than our bodies could live without the food we ate. From daylight to dark and often longer during kidding season we were never far from the goat pens. The whole family was dedicated to this industry. Many times little kids (baby goats) had to be taken into the house and warmed behind the wood stove, to help them make it through the night.

I was reminded of how it used to be when I went to visit with my brother John Allen, and found him in the goat shed awaiting the arrival of twins (he suspected). The nanny was getting old and had produced twins in the past. She was stock from some of the old line Papa had, and John Allen was very proud he had gotten some of that bloodline back. We talked about the goats while we waited. Sure enough, in about forty-five minutes two beautiful little nanny kids were on the ground. But not without difficulty, resulting from breach births and the sack being over the face of the firstborn. With a sigh of satisfaction John Allen commented, "See there, if I hadn't been here I would have lost them." That was the third set of twins his flock had produced in the past twenty-four hours. We both agreed that to witness and be a part of such a beautiful miracle was near to holiness.

My grandpa's cousin, Dr. James Davis of South Carolina's Agriculture Department, went to Turkey in 1847 to teach them how to grow cotton. When he returned to the United States he brought with him two pair of Cashmere goats, a Tibetan buck, and two pair of Turkish goats. It was through this cross breeding that the Angora goat we know today was begun.

James Davis's brother Nat went to Turkey with him. Uncle Nat, as my family knew him, took two of the Turkish nannies in an ox wagon with one kid and one billy tied behind the wagon to California. This was during the Gold Rush in 1849.

My father Bob was born in Brown County, Texas, in 1880, a fifth generation Texan. He was the son of John Henry Davis and Nancy Susan Blanton Davis. The Davis family moved first to Nolan County, then to Edwards County in 1888, on the headwaters of the Nueces River. They brought with them a tent, a wagon, a few cows, a bull, and four children. That year Nancy Susan helped organize the first church in the Bullhead community, now called Vance, Texas. Meetings were first held in a brush arbor, typical of the times. That same year a cattle drive stopped to overnight there. During the night two baby calves were born, and being too young to travel the next morning, the trail boss gave the calves to Bob. The next year he traded these two yearlings to Johnny Brown for eleven old nanny goats. About that time Uncle Nat came to the Nueces River with his flock of one hundred-seventy goats. He was still living in his wagon, and the goats were following him. Uncle Nat had been living in California all those years. The goats, being raised for several generations around the wagon, were trained to stay with it. When the wagon moved to a new range the goats followed.

In 1893, Uncle Nat sold his entire herd to Johnny Brown, except for thirty head that he gave to Bob for the help he had given him in caring for his goats. Brown accused Nat of coaching Bob on which goats to choose. Uncle Nat declared, "Bob knows those goats just as well as I do." Bob acquired more Angoras, and soon he earned more money from the newly introduced Angora goats than his Father did from cattle.

My grandpa moved to the West Prong of the Frio River, on land he bought from Alex Auld. Bob stayed with Johnny Brown to herd goats, until his mother told him he had to come home and go to school or he wouldn't ever amount to anything. Bob moved his Angora herd to the ranch on the West Prong of the Frio River. His late teens and early twenties were spent at what is now called the Prade Ranch. Between 1892 until 1907, Bob owned a herd of twelve hundred Angoras.

Bob received his education at ranch schools. He had only four years of formal schooling before taking the exams to enter St. Louis College (now St. Mary's University) in San Antonio, Texas. It was here Bob and Annie Auld became acquainted, although they were neighbors back at the ranch. Annie was attending San Antonio Female College (now Trinity University), where she was studying music. Three years later Bob and Annie eloped; they rode their horses from the ranch to Leakey, where Justice Sansom married them October 7, 1903.

In 1907, Bob and Annie bought the Arthur Kelly homestead of 640 acres on Cherry Creek in Uvalde County, between Rio Frio and Utopia, Texas. The Davis Ranch expanded to include Blanket Creek and Bear Creek, increasing to 4,000 acres, and ran a herd of 2,500 Angora goats. This terrain was ideal for raising goats; much of the Texas Hill Country is too mountainous for cattle. It's not as easy as it sounds to build up a herd of goats. Bob, my Papa, had a "die-up" in 1908; he lost more than 1,000 head of goats. Men came with wagons and knocked all those pretty little kid goats in the head and piled them in the wagons to haul off. There were 400 to 500 of those little kids in the lot, without their mamas. About all the goats Papa had left were the yearling nannies. I have never seen a disaster to compare to that.

Dovie Caddel Howard of Concan, Texas, told me of a "die-up" the Caddel family had with their goats. Several hundred nannies got cut off, across the river from the shed when there was a big rain, and the nannies all drowned. Fresh sheared Angoras will drown if rain gets into their hollow hair follicles. Dovie's parents were down with the flu and couldn't do anything; she and her little brother were told to destroy all the little kids. Dovie said she held the little kids with their heads on the chop block while her brother chopped their heads off with the axe.

Kidding is the most important time in the life of the goats. For two or three days after the kids are dropped they must be given good care, if they are to survive. A newborn kid is very delicate, more delicate than a lamb of the same age. The kid arrives in the early spring, about the time the leaves on the trees start budding out. At that time there will also be tender weeds for the nannies to browse. Hopefully, it will be almost warm enough to favor the kids. In cold or wet weather, it will be much more difficult for the kids to survive. A few days before a kid is due the nanny should be separated from the rest of the herd. We always liked to have a very small stall for each nanny, but it was not always possible. Even in a pen of twenty nannies some kids would get trampled to death or injured. Also, there would be more difficulty in getting the nannies to own her kid. It's most important at this time to make sure the nanny owns her kid.

If a kid was dropped in the pasture we had to find it and carry it to the shed or pen and make sure the nanny owns it; many times they will refuse. A lamb will follow its mother soon after it's dropped, but a kid goat doesn't have the strength. The mother will hide it in the brush or behind a log, and leave it expecting to find it when she returns. This often lets the helpless little one fall prey to wild animals, or eagles. If a nanny wouldn't claim her kid after being shut up with it, and she was really stubborn and kicked it away every time it tried to suckle, Mama would take a rope and tie the nanny to a rafter, lifting the nanny's front feet off the ground. She couldn't kick the kid away because she had to stand on her back feet. After twenty-four hours in this position she would be mighty glad to claim her kid when she was let down.

If a little kid had wrinkled or crooked ears Mama always cut a triangle of cardboard and taped it onto the back of the ears. After two or three days it could be removed and the ears would be beautiful and stand up like they were supposed to.

One of the things we did was to stake the kids with a soft cotton string. We used old, soft sacks and tore them into strings to make a toggle that let the kids go only about fourteen to twenty inches from the stake. Each day the toggle had to be untied and put on a different leg to keep from injuring it or cutting off the circulation. The kids had to be carefully watched with this method as long as they were tied, which would be from seven to ten days.

If the little kids were out in the middle of the big lot where there wasn't any shade, little A-frame houses were built for each one to sleep under during the hot part of the day. The nanny goats were put out to pasture every morning while the kids remained staked. At night the nannies came back to the same spot to find their kids. This went on for about three weeks. Later, the kids were kept in pens where the nannies could climb a ramp or bridge into the pen; the end of the bridge would be twenty inches off the ground. Nannies could come and go as they pleased, while the kids would then be free to run loose in a large lot. When the kids were big enough to go out with the herd, they would jump up onto the end of the bridge and follow their mothers out to the pasture.

We had to watch for wormies (screwworms), where blowflies would lay eggs in cuts and wounds. These places had to be doped with tar. I don't remember a vet being called in those days. This ceased to be a problem after the government program to drop sterile flies onto ranches. Once the Angoras were in the pasture they

A-frame shelters protect newborn goats

had to be guarded against coyotes, eagles, and mountain lions. The coyotes were trapped at one time; now ranchers keep donkeys or dogs with the herd. Sometimes a llama herds the angoras. Coyotes are getting bad again. This is the main reason many ranchers are getting out of the Angora goat business. I've heard coyotes at night fighting over their kill and the sound is frightening.

The Show goats had to have special care. When an Angora was selected to save for a Show goat their hair was never cut. I remember one Show goat standing on a table and its hair hung all the way to the floor; these days the hair has to be cut six months before it's shown. Many hours were spent braiding their long hair and tying it up. Then a coat of canvas that Mama made was put on them to keep the hair clean. My older sisters remember taking the goats to the front porch to braid the hair. It would have been a cleaner, cooler place to work. But I remember braiding the goats' hair out in the pen. Perhaps the difference was a labor shortage. It would have taken two or three children to carry a grown goat from the pen to the front porch.

Bob Davis strove diligently for the improvement of the Angora goat breed. It was 1915 when he purchased some registered Angoras from Mrs. Armer in New Mexico. Later, he had one hundred of his old original does registered by inspection, thus commencing his internationally known line. I remember men coming from South Africa and Australia to buy billies from my Papa. In June of 1921, to improve mohair (hair from the Angora) quality, Bob paid the record price at that time of $3,080 for a John Allen Ward buck. He considered the pearl-like luster of mohair to be its single most important quality.

Bob and Annie were always progressive ranchers. They bought one of the first Stewart Shearing Machines, units operated by hand crank for power. They used hand shears to shear their own goats and sheep before that. Bob said, "Annie was the best and steadiest turner I ever had." Annie was a true pioneer ranch wife, an outdoorswoman by choice. She fed her large family and hired hands from her large garden. She managed the ranch when Bob was away buying wool and mohair in New Mexico, Texas, and Arizona during the Depression for mills in Boston, and later while he was tending to his duties as Uvalde County Judge, from 1939 to 1951.

Shearing crews came twice a year to cut the hair from the Angoras, which sold for very good prices until the market dropped in 1993. This was due to the production of synthetic fibers. Mohair was used for fire insulation in the first Space Shuttles, because the hair follicles were hollow and it would not burn. Mohair was also used for carpets, upholstery, sweaters, suits, and coats; these garments are lightweight, and warm in winter and cool in the summer.

The most beautiful sign of spring is a lot full of newborn baby Angora goats, romping around. I always loved to watch them at play, climbing up on logs and jumping off. They love to climb. I remember a sunny day when the pen was full of baby Angoras, and my little brother John Allen was curled up in the corner of the lot, on a pile of leaves with a baby kid in his arms to snuggle, and they were both fast asleep.

The Angora goat raising tradition carries on into the third generation. John Allen Davis, Jr. known as JAD, is preserving the same bloodline from the Bob Davis flock with one hundred fifty registered Angoras, on the land settled by Bob and Annie in 1907.

[Thanks to: my brother Robert K. "Bob" Davis for sharing his memories with me and for his account in the *History of Real County*. —*Garrison*]

Marguerite Hill and little sister Althea driving a Model T, 1913 or so

THE WHEELS OF OUR LIVES

by Scott Hill Bumgardner

Apparently Gronk, the caveman, was inspired when he observed a round rock roll down a hill. This mystery man's invention really, well, to use a bad pun, "started the ball rolling." The wheel revolutionized the world of transportation and machines. It simplified the moving of materials and people with carts, chariots, and wagons. Its use in virtually all machinery, with the coming of the mechanized age, eventually gave us trains, automobiles, and much more. My life has been greatly enriched with not only the use and misuse of automobiles, but with the stories of my family's wheeled past.

The value of wheeled transportation really struck home when I discovered the stories of my ancestors' flight from their home in the "Run Away Scrape" during Texas' revolt against Mexico's tyranny. In April of 1836, my fourth great-grandmother, Lucy Thomson Kerr, was left in charge of the family at Gay Hill near Brenham. She was confronted with the frightening news that Santa Anna's troops were approaching. The Mexican Army's approach was accompanied by rumors of death and devastation to all who were in the area. She gathered the children and servants to quickly load most of their worldly possessions into a wagon that was hitched to several yoke of oxen. The path of escape was made difficult by storms and flooding streams. Lucy and family finally had to abandon the wagon and team to reach safety away from the approaching army. Once fate had smiled on the Texas Army, the family made preparations to return to their home. In order to secure a wagon for the return trip, Lucy had to sell a half-league, or twenty-two hundred acres, of prime Texas land. Now, I think those were some expensive wheels!

Jumping forward to the Christmas season of 1914, we find Lucy's descendant, Marguerite Ruth Hill invited for a ride in another set of expensive wheels. Marguerite's friend, Bess

Reynolds, and her brother Bill Reynolds were delivering live Christmas turkeys to the needy in their family's 1912 Packard. This top-of-the-line, fine set of wheels seems to be an unlikely livestock delivery vehicle, and perhaps that is why a turkey escaped, leading the young folk on a merry chase. It was this exhilarating time that was remembered as the event that sparked a relationship, eventually leading my grandparents, Bill and Marguerite, into a lifelong marriage.

My grandfather Bill also told tales of how he traveled north to buy a locomotive for the family business, the Livingston Lumber Company. He traveled to Pennsylvania where he handed over cash to purchase the H. K. Porter engine number one hundred. Upon completion of the purchase, Bill piloted the locomotive from Pittsburg back to Livingston, Texas, at the ripe old age of sixteen. Even in his mid-eighties, he would smile in remembrance of that engine and the pride he took in having the most powerful locomotive in that neck of the woods. Grandfather often told of helping push the railroad carriers' cars over steep hills that their less powerful engines couldn't negotiate.

H.K. Porter engine purchased for the Livingston Lumber Company, 1915

This all took place when wagons were still in common use. The lumber company employed two thousand workers, many of whom used livestock to snake the timber down to the mill or loading areas. This was also around the time that Bill's future wife, Marguerite Hill, was hitching the family horse to a buggy each morning at their home located at the intersection of Caroline and Anita Streets in Houston for her dad's trip to work at Peden Iron and Steel, on the northern edge of the downtown area. Grandfather William Lafayette Reynolds would remain tied to the wheeled world; this Aggie engineer would later build a career working for Ford Motor Company at their Houston plant.

The other side of my family also had their stories of wheeling around. Dad, J. C. Bumgardner, was a bored wander-lusting kid from Abilene during the height of the Depression. He tells of hitchhiking all over West Texas. At eighty-seven years of age he still has vivid recollections of some of the people that picked him up. He recalls the founder of the Frito Company, which is now Frito-Lay, picking him up in a Model A panel truck, where he was allowed to dine on the crunchy treats to his heart's delight. Dad remembers the fellow who asked, "Have you ever been in a car, going one hundred miles per hour?" The subsequent ride was frightening and the vehicle shook and shimmied violently. Upon stopping, a tire blew out immediately.

He even traded for his own car at an early age. It was around 1937, a time before driver's licenses were required. At the age of fourteen, Dad was looking at some cars in a sales lot in Abilene, when a salesman approached. The man asked if he wanted to buy a car. Of course, Dad had no money. The salesman was determined, though, and took him over to a 1927 Model T. Dad drove that car home after swapping his .22 rifle. The next morning, with four flats and numerous other problems, he found out why the man wanted to get rid of the old car so badly. With a lot of sweat and the advice of some adults he fixed the car, at least well enough to use for awhile. Ultimately, though, he just abandoned it broken down on the side of a lonely Texas highway.

During his high school days, specifically his sophomore and junior summers, Dad snuck onto freight trains and rode out to California. The destination was San Bernardino, California, where both work and adventure were available. The trips were long and hard, with the grit and soot pouring from the smoke stack stinging and blackening the roof-top riders. Sometimes the train car would have a flat spot on a wheel that would jolt the car with each rotation. The thumping vibration hurt after a while, so the riders rose to stand precariously for some relief. Out of Abilene the train was a Texas and Pacific; in El Paso they changed trains for the final leg on the Southern Pacific Railroad.

On the first trip a friend, Don Coffee, went with Dad. They worked toting wheel barrows full of concrete for a few weeks. Ultimately, they found good paying work as caddies at the Chino Country Club. Toward the beginning of the school year Dad took the long, hot trip back to Texas, but Don stayed in California. Dad never saw him again.

I can remember most of the vehicles that my family has owned, at least in my lifetime. I even remember my grandfather's love of trains and the awful trip we took on one. Unfortunately, I was mighty hyper when I was little, and what began as an adventure turned into a grueling, never-ending journey. Mother, grandmother, grandfather, and I climbed onto the beautiful instrument of torture at the depot in Houston. Man oh man was it great—for a while. Surely, many of y'all remember little kids asking, "Are we there yet?" Well, I never thought we would get there. I must admit that our trip did have the comfort of Pullman cars with our own rooms and pull down bunk beds. Our trip turned out to be the grand tour of the west, looping up through Colorado, along the Pacific coast, to San Francisco, and finally across miles and miles of nothing, back to Houston. Here it is fifty-plus years later, and I still cringe at the thought of it. The only bright spots I recall on that trip were seeing a meteor light the sky in Arizona and watching Lyndon Johnson from our San Francisco hotel room as he campaigned. I sure am glad I never rode the top of a boxcar for hundreds of miles like my father.

My journey into the world of driving automobiles began like it did for most folk my age. Those first lessons when you were all scrunched up tight against your father or mother were great. Finally, after a lot of practice, a teenager is licensed and released as a menace to society. Thankfully, the angels allow the majority of us to live. They protected me as a young adult driving everything from that first 1966 Volkswagen, to the Vette with a 454 engine, and a variety of police cars. My friends, Mark and Mike, were with me in that Volkswagen as we approached a tight curve in a country road. We were just too cool in that Beetle with the racing stripe down the side. It seems like I had on my Australian bush hat with the side brim folded up. One of the guys said, "Don't you think you are going a little fast for this curve?" My response was, "Nah!" We were mighty lucky, and I am glad those cars have strong roofs and roll well. We were fine, but that put me afoot for a long while.

When I was a teenager, back in the late sixties and early seventies, gas could sometimes be found for twenty to twenty-five cents per gallon. Now, we have entered a time when even diesel fuel has risen to prices well above four dollars per gallon. In most states, hitchhiking is illegal, you must have a driver's license to drive, and you had better have that liability insurance. Automobile design and mechanics have advanced to the point that few adults and certainly very few fourteen-year-olds can fix a modern car. It would certainly be an unusual event for a kid to swap a rifle for a car. But, we are still a wheeled society and, despite the changing times, "adventure happens."

A very young Archie P. McDonald

BACK THEN

by Archie P. McDonald

Some time ago management at Red River Radio, a National Public Radio-affiliated network with headquarters in Shreveport that broadcasts to Louisiana, East Texas, southern Arkansas, a smidgen of Oklahoma and Mississippi, and as the announcer says, "streams around the world"—which is internet-ese for the benefit of those whose hair is the color of mine—let me have five minutes of a Friday morning to comment on whatever bemuses me.

From the beginning most of these brief pieces addressed the way people lived "back then." We turned some of those memories into a slender volume with just that title—*Back Then*—and I understand that State House Press has plenty of them left, in case you are interested.

Anyway, here are some samples of the way we lived, Back Then. I got started in November 1935, but real memory commenced a few years later, about World War II time. The first of the "Where were you when..." questions I can answer concerns the Japanese attack on Pearl Harbor, December 7, 1941.

I had just begun the educational process at Averell Elementary School in Beaumont. That big Philco radio that focused our living room prior to the advent of television told us that war had found us. I remember my grandmother crying softly and the strained countenances of my mother and aunt, though I really did not understand why.

The next four years provided more vivid memories of WWII. Do you remember:

Ration books issued by the OPA necessary to purchase such commodities as shoes and sugar. No ration stamp, no purchase—at least legally, but of course some unscrupulous individuals participated in a "black market." The purchase of meat required "red points," dime-sized red plastic disks that equated to so many points per pound allowed;

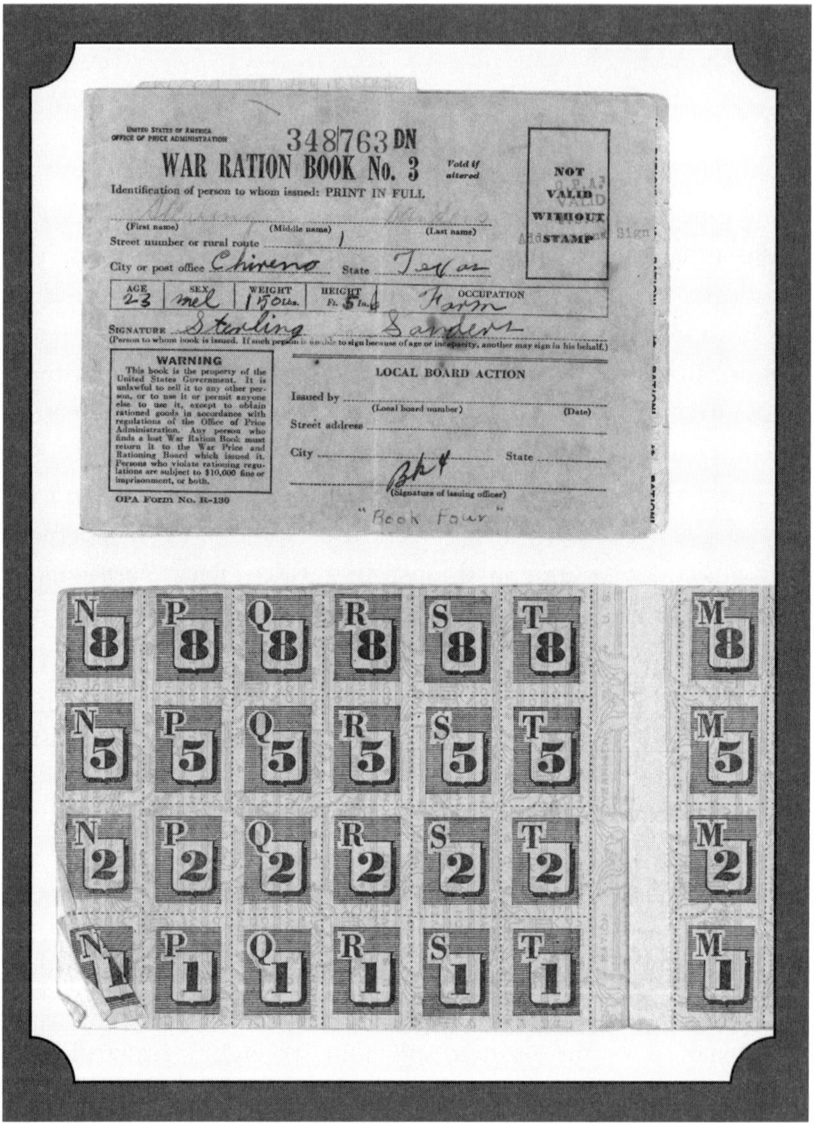

War ration book and stamps

"A" or "T" stickers in auto or truck windshields, indicating the amount of gasoline allowed for that vehicle. And gasoline cost about 15 cents per gallon;

War Bonds, Series "E," the $18.75 deducted from Daddy's paycheck that purchased a document worth $25 in ten years, and the little books we school kids filled with a savings stamp every week, ten cents a stamp, until we, too, had helped pay for the war and put a little nest-egg aside. We didn't care that this was the government's way to finance the war and slow inflation, but we did anticipate the agonizingly slow compounding of the interest;

V-Mail, or victory mail, letters received from servicemen overseas that had been photographically diminished to lessen the load of hauling so many letters from America's millions of men in far-flung duty stations. And marvel of marvels, traveling all that way without a postage stamp;

Scrap drives of everything from rubber—the first—to all metals, newspapers, even animal fat saved from cooking. I remember pulling my wagon door-to-door collecting newspapers for reprocessing, but I don't remember ever hearing the word "recycling." I also remember searching for discarded cigarette packages so we could separate what we called "tin foil" used to seal the pack for freshness, roll it into balls, and turn it in. I also remember lines outside stores on the one or two days per week that cigarettes were available for purchase;

Blackouts—when the siren sounded, lights were "cut off" and if any had to be illuminated, blankets covered windows lest the air-raid warden, usually a neighbor empowered to patrol the area, knocked to issue the warning that we were aiding feared but never-appeared German bombers.

What I don't remember is much complaining about these inconveniences. America had a different vision, then.

* * *

For a kid, the last day of school seems a thing of joy. This is more social suggestion than a genuine feeling of relief, at least for elementary school scholars who mostly *like* school and their schoolmates. Still, every year now in May I see youngsters on the news who swarm out of the schools as if they had just been released from a dentist's chair. I think they stage these escapes for the benefit of TV camera operators who wish they could have the summer off from work. Within days, kids across America will be complaining that "there's nothing to do."

War bonds

Back in time a ways, there was. It was called Vacation Bible School, and every church in town promoted these summertime, weeklong, activity-filled enterprises that occupied youth just fine. We didn't know that the Baptist, Methodist, and Church of God preachers even talked to each other, but they must have because their churches held Vacation Bible Schools in *succession*, not in competition. This was a wonderful conspiracy. Each congregation welcomed us all, and I don't recall any high-pressure denominational proselytizing. All, however, were intent on saving our souls and keeping the Devil at bay by occupying as much of our summer time as possible.

I was introduced to the world of Vacation Bible School in Burkeville, a sawmill community located in Newton County, Texas. I spent the week with Aunt Thelma and Uncle Bill, and my cousins Eleanor Lois and Kathryn. Just how it worked out that I would visit the very week the Baptists held Vacation Bible School, I do not know, but probably there was more conspiracy involved.

We walked to the church each morning for assembly. We had Bible drills (for the unwashed, this was a contest to see who could locate a particular verse first); we sang hymns, the good ones that everyone knew; we had craft lessons—I remember making a sharp pair of bookends by splitting a section of oak limb, nailing boards on the bottom of one end of each half, and shellacking them to a fine luster; and, of course, we had cookies and punch with a sandwich lunch. I had so much fun getting the Devil chased out of me that I stayed on for the Methodist and Church of God versions. Even got to sing in a quartet at the Church of God for which I learned shape notes. I can still identify the notes from their location on the staff, but I have forgotten what the shapes mean.

For a few years afterward my summer visits to Burkeville were timed by my elders to coincide with Vacation Bible Schools. I am the better for it. I expect that I learned something about the Bible. I know I learned to love to sing, how to make bookends, and a lot about ecumenicalism. I hope rural churches still do this. We need to learn, somewhere, that Methodists don't really have horns, no matter what Aunt Thelma said.

* * *

Add a few years, and here is an experience of puberty with which some may relate.

Fairs, especially county and state fairs, originated in medieval times. I know this because of that great song from the musical *Camelot* about escorting Lady Guinevere to the fair. And I know enough American history to enable awareness of these exhibitions of agricultural and domestic skills and their centrality to fun and competition in rural areas, usually held after crops were "laid by."

I haven't attended a fair in a long time, but none could equal the South Texas State Fair in Beaumont in 1951, when my Uncle George let me show a Hereford calf in the livestock competition. I had to join the 4-H Club to qualify, but they were lax and didn't make me attend meetings. What I did was bond with that dumb calf. He taught me how to lead him around the show ring, not to stand within range of his hind foot—which kicks *forward*—and to try to look nonchalant when his body eliminated its wastes in public places.

I survived. Finished 11th in field of thirty or so competitors, and that blamed steer sold for about $1,000—remember now, this was more than a half-century ago. And there were other benefits: I skipped school a lot during fair week—had to care for the calf, don't you know—with permission from the ag teacher. And this: I was introduced to the wonders of human female anatomy. Don't forget, I was about fifteen years old and bestirred by the natural hormonal revolution of adolescence. So, some of us under-agers broke the law and attended a tent show that featured "Evelyn West and Her Million Dollar Chest," and Evelyn educated us about why King Arthur's knights all wanted to take Guinevere to the fair.

I have always believed that fairs offer a variety of educational opportunities.

* * *

Dr. Arthur Speck, a Nacogdoches urologist with whom my prostate is intimate, and I, upon the occasion of cooling ourselves on an August evening in his swimming pool, amused ourselves by reviewing the transformation of the world during our lifetime, which spanned about two-thirds of the last century. Our parents began with real horsepower for transportation, yet lived to see, on television, Neil Armstrong walk on the moon. Our first telephones required the assistance of an operator to complete calls. We learned to dial our numbers on a rotary wheel. Then Touch-Tone sped the process, and a while ago I rode in a car accessorized with a voice activated and operated communications system, and I'll bet every one of us has a cell phone. All this, folks, is progress.

I am not so sure I can agree that is the case about what has happened to drug stores. Remember those emporiums, if you are old enough, the way Norman Rockwell painted them? If you don't remember Norman Rockwell, I'll paint the picture for you.

They were not all on the corner, but we remember them best that way. There is a soda fountain, a gathering place where morning coffee is shared by merchants, retirees, or others without much to do. At lunch, another crowd gathers for ham sandwiches and chips or maybe chili and crackers, accompanied by a Coca-Cola drawn from a fountain that mixed the syrup and carbonated water into a glass so familiar you could identify it blindfolded by touch. They always tasted better than the bottled kind.

All kinds of wares line shelves located along the walls or in short aisle-islands: patent medicines, jewelry, beauty aids, toys for the youngsters, walking canes for the old folks, paint, guitar strings—you were likely to find almost anything. Newspapers and magazines, which one could review without buying, occupied a rack. And in the back, usually elevated a bit, was the pharmacist who filled your prescriptions and gave advice on their use. Hundreds of bottles of liquids and pills of various colors and configurations—capsules, tablets, and powders—with mysterious healing properties, all in an order he understood thoroughly, surrounded him.

The pharmacist was a familiar, reassuring figure. You trusted him as completely as the doctor whose prescription you delivered because you had grown up seeing him there, behind his counter. He had lagniapped a peppermint for you when you visited with your parents, sent you home with his nostrums for ailing family, kept an eye out for your safety if a rough crowd dropped by after school. Later, you appreciated his service on the school board, town council, or some similar civic service.

And when you were grown, and *married*, and it was entirely proper unless you were Roman Catholic, you approached this trusted old friend, with some trepidation, and whispered, "Some prophylactics, please." Without a word or look of judgment, he fetched the product and presented it to you in a plain, non-plastic, non-transparent sack so the whole world didn't know your business.

I'll not forget the first time, in the 1980s, after the sexual revolution, when I first saw condoms hanging out there for selection between the foot powder and the Band-Aids. That meant, I suppose, that one in the market for such had to haul it to the checker—probably a teenager—so the barcode could be scanned. God help you if she had to call on the loudspeaker for a price check.

Norman Rockwell and I do **NOT** regard this as "progress."

* * *

"When I was a young man," begins a song written in 1938 by Kurt Weil and Maxwell Anderson for a musical titled *Knickerbocker Holiday*. You know this "September Song," because I'll bet most of the folks here have sufficient years to appreciate the metaphor of September.

Measuring our lives by the calendar, we who make it to September hope we are lucky enough to *have* an October, November—and December. Even if we do, we concede that our race is three-quarters run. We are retired, or planning on doing so when we can afford it, if by "afford" we include the caveat of trying to imagine what in the world we will do to fill our lives.

> When I was a young man..., I played me a waiting game.
> [And if things did not work out at first, well....]
> I let the old world take a couple of whirls,
> and as time came around, it came my way....
> Oh it's a long, long while, from May to December,
> but the days grow short, when you reach September.

There is melancholy in that confession, for "when the autumn weather, turns the leaves to flame, one hasn't got time [left] for the waiting game." Those bright hopes of May, career dreams that led so inevitably but too often misleadingly to owning your own company or a big house on the hill, or whatever goal upon which youth focused, are, by September, actualized or forgotten amid daily struggles that make Friday a more attainable goal than any December.

We who live this song think about health more than wealth, unless it is to worry that we will outlive the nest egg set aside for our December. We wonder if the kids, who never seem sufficiently responsible or mature, will "make it" in a world without us to assist them.

We who have worked at the same job long enough to know how to do it well, picking up that calf every day and building up the strength to keep on keeping on, no matter the exponential growth of the work, now realize that we are not indispensable and that *someone*, someone with greater technological skills and fewer years can do it faster and maybe better, and that is unsettling.

Right now, in September, we are at the top of our game, but the game changes, and we know not whether to let loose or hold on. Future fear is fearsome indeed. Time was, things came easily to us; now they are complicated and sometimes we are afraid of the dark, in these "days [that] dwindle down to a precious few"... This is one of those precious days, and I am grateful to spend part of it with you.

[The portions of this article on the drug store and vacation Bible school appeared in the author's book *Back Then: Simple Pleasures and Everyday Heroes*, published by State House Press, 2005.]

Jack Duncan as a young boy

I'M HERE TO TELL YOU!: FAMILY VIGNETTES FROM THE DEPRESSION ERA

by Robert J. (Jack) Duncan

I was born in Pilot Point, in Denton County, Texas, on December 7, 1941, just a few hours before the Japanese planes attacked Pearl Harbor. Before 1941, more Texas babies were born at home than in hospitals; after 1941, more were born in hospitals. That year was the break-over year when it was about half-and-half. I was born at home. I was an only child, and I was the seventh grandchild on each side of the family, so some family members felt that I somehow lent a certain balance and symmetry to our family tree.

We lived in Pilot Point for a while and then moved about five miles north, to my paternal grandparents' farm in the Liberty Hill community east of Tioga, in the southwest corner of Grayson County. My dad (who earlier had worked as a grocery store clerk) helped his father with the farm work during the war, or at least during much of it, when labor—like virtually everything else—was scarce.

My grandparents and my Aunt Pat, who was just six years my senior, lived up the road in a two-story farmhouse that—in my child's memory—seems as big as a mansion, although I know, in reason, that it was nothing very large or elaborate. But for the purpose of oral "shorthand" we all referred to it as the "big house," that contrasted it to the farm's other house, the one that my parents and I lived in, which we called the "little house." My earliest memories—at around the age of two—are of that time, and they are so sketchy they seem almost like grainy snapshots, or perhaps tableaus caught, illuminated, and frozen in time by a strobe light.

One of those memories is of my parents and me waiting for the rural mail carrier, and then seeing his car come up the road to deliver to our roadside mailbox a letter from the local draft board. Daddy came extremely close to being drafted, but he was granted an exemption at the last minute, probably because of his farm worker status, an occupation necessary to the war effort.

Most of the things that I want to tell you about, though, happened *before* I was born, and likewise, of course, before the war. I learned about one of them just a couple of decades ago. Sometime around 1989, I had driven my dad somewhere, and we were on our way home, going south through the eastern edge of Pilot Point. Dad was eighty, give or take a year.

"See that barn over yonder, and that row of trees?" he asked.

I thought I knew what he was getting at. My parents were married ten or twelve years before I was born. For as long as I can remember, I have known that Daddy and Mama had lived on that place for a year or two as a young married couple. It was "Uncle" Jim Ledbetter's home place; he was an aging bachelor who had hired them, Daddy to do much of the farm work, Mama to cook and keep house. The honorary title "Uncle" was a prefix used simply to convey respect and affection, not kinship.

I remembered that my folks said that Uncle Jim sometimes kept late hours visiting a "widow woman" in Gunter. One night Uncle Jim came home pretty late, and he had lost his house key. Daddy had to get out of bed and unlock the door to let him in.

Daddy seized the opportunity to kid the old man. "Good God, Uncle Jim," he said, "If you don't quit tom cattin' around, you're liable to have to marry that ole gal."

Uncle Jim's face turned red, but then he took Daddy's warning as a compliment and chuckled. (Ironically, eventually he *did* marry the woman, and my parents moved back to town.)

"Did you hear what I said?" Daddy asked me. "See that barn over there?" That jarred my mind back to the present. I nodded.

He said, "That's where you were conceived."

I don't think I had ever heard him use that word before. "You mean in the two-story house that used to be there," I said, to correct him.

"*Nosir*, I mean in that barn, up in the hayloft. I know, in reason, that's when it was. Anyhow, your mama always thought that was when it happened. It's just something I thought you might like to know, so there it is."

That was one of the few times in life when I've been literally speechless. I could have said *something*, I guess, but there was too much running through my mind. It was a revelation and an epiphany. It was also the best thing he could have told me at that late date: my creation, pinpointed in space as well as time, right then and there.

Can conception location have anything to do with that impish grin?

So that's how it was, I thought. Maybe knowing that would shed some light on my irreverence, my informal outlook about a lot of things. It was something I would always remember. A few times when I was young and I left a door open, someone would ask the rhetorical question, "Were you born in a barn?" But no one had ever said anything about conception.

Whether we get it from reading Einstein's Unified Field Theory, watching a rerun of the film *The Incredible Shrinking Man*, or just stargazing on a clear night, we learn that there are worlds within worlds, that our solar system is more or less the structure of the atom *writ large*. That makes everything insignificant, but somehow conversely, it simultaneously makes everything significant. Whether we're at the very center of the universe or on some forgotten galactic outpost spinning dangerously out of control, each of us is significant; we all matter, if only to one another.

I knew that, as I said, my parents had been married several years before my birth, but I never really imagined what their life had been like before I existed. I guess the capital "I" had distorted my view. All things had been relative—relative to me. Regardless of what I knew, I had never really *felt* that life had gone on before my birth, or that it would continue after my death. That's a very egocentric and shortsighted perspective, of course, especially for a fifty-year-old person. At some point, each of us needs to accept his own mortality. Now I began to think about the things my parents had gone through when the immediate family consisted of just the two of them, during the decade that the Great Depression was a blight upon the land.

I knew that my parents had attended the Texas Centennial in Dallas in 1936. It was one of the high points of their lives, a bright spot always remembered. They had saved the brilliant full-color souvenir tickets for the better part of a lifetime.

They used to tell about buying a mug of root beer at the Centennial. Mama thought the mug was interesting in its design. In examining it, she pointed out to Daddy that the bottom of the mug was recessed about an inch. They were just curious, innocent young folks off the farm for a day, unsuspicious of their fellow man. The vendor overheard Mama's comment and misinterpreted it as criticism about the capacity of the mug.

"Lady," he said, exasperated, "What do you expect for a nickel?"

Daddy used to tell a story on himself about a bad earache that he had at some point in the 1930s.

He said to Mama, "Hon, pour a little coal oil in my left ear."

"Why, you don't want me to do that!" she warned him. "That would set you on fire."

"It won't do no such of a dang thing," he said. "Now go ahead and pour it in there. I've got to have some relief. This pain is killin' me."

Against her better judgment, Mama finally did as Daddy asked.

Their little house consisted of just four rooms, each with a doorway connecting it to the two adjacent rooms. The coal oil started burning Daddy's ear almost immediately. He jumped off the bed and started running in circles through the house—through those four rooms. Instead of running around the bed—which was in his path—each time when he came through the bedroom, he ran right across the top of the bed. He was screaming, praying, and promising. He didn't later report that he had used any profanity, but I suspect that there might have been a little bit of that, too. Eventually the pain subsided somewhat, but it was still a lot more intense than the earache alone had been.

Daddy would tell that story on himself and laugh so hard he would be wiping away tears. "This world and one more!" he would say. "This world and one more."

One day fairly early in their marriage, Mama realized that Daddy was getting ready to plant potatoes. She was horrified. "You can't do that!" she said—Daddy was instantly mad even before he heard the rest—"The moon's not right," she continued. She said that her father, who was known as a fine farmer, always timed his planting according to the almanac and the proper sign of the moon. "If you don't do it that way, the crop won't make," she said.

"Good God a-mighty *dang*!" Daddy yelled. He didn't have a superstitious bone in his body. "*I'm* the one that's doin' this! And there's another little verse right under that: I ain't plantin' my p'taters in the moon; I'm a-plantin' 'em in the ground!"

Well, they did grow a few potatoes that year, but it was far from a bumper crop. By the way, the almanac that my grandfather used was the *Ladies' Birthday Almanac*, which was in major disagreement with the *Farmers' Almanac*.

Throughout the Great Depression, Mama and Daddy never owned a house. For years they always lived in one rented house or another. Some were no better than sharecropper houses, the outer walls consisting of just a single thickness of boards, so when a norther blew in, the wind would literally whistle through the house. Over and over Mama and Daddy, following a nesting impulse, would fix up a house they were renting, decorate it with wallpaper and paint, and about the time they got it, as Mama would say "looking decionable"—meaning *decent*—for one reason or another they would move on to another rent house and start over.

It was a matter of pride to never move out and leave the empty house dirty in any respect. They would load their furniture on a truck, then work like Trojans to leave the house "spic and span." It was something along the lines of being sure you wore clean underwear in case you were in a wreck. They would sweep and mop until the world looked level to make the shack scrupulously clean for the next tenant family. They wouldn't have dreamed of leaving it in any other condition. Not something you see a lot of these days.

At one of their residences, my parents' nearest neighbors were habitual borrowers. The couple would frequently send their children to ask if they could borrow a cup of sugar or flour or corn meal, a spool of thread, or some other commodity. And they never repaid any of it. During those financially gloomy days of the Depression, my parents were lucky if they had enough for themselves, and they finally had to resort to little white lies, claiming that they, too, just happened to be out of whatever was the commodity of the day. The man of the family took offense and broadly

Elmer & Viola Duncan, 1944

hinted that Daddy was not generous, but Daddy just chuckled at him and coolly recited the old axiom that charity begins at home. Somehow they remained friends and good neighbors.

One time Daddy was helping his father with a major repair project on the farm's windmill near the "big house." Daddy was standing on the ground at the base of the windmill, and my grandfather was at the top. My grandfather was handling a long, heavy length of pipe. It slipped out of his hands and fell, hitting Daddy in the head. Daddy was looking up, so his face was pointed toward the sky. The pipe hit him a staggering, but fortunately a glancing, blow on his chin. It knocked him unconscious for a few minutes and cut a deep gash in his chin. They had to rush him to the doctor, but he was pretty lucky. If the pipe had hit him in the upper part of his head or anywhere on his face other than his chin, it probably would have killed him. When the pipe hit his chin, his jaw dropped open, of course, and that allowed the pipe to fall right on past his chin. And the scar turned out not to be a defacing one; in fact, it gave him a dapper look.

In the fall of 1932, Mama and Daddy were picking cotton one day when the calf of Mama's leg began stinging. Then it started swelling. They thought it might be a snakebite, but Daddy couldn't see any fang marks. By then the pain was growing intense, so Daddy put her in the car and drove her to town to see the doctor. Doc examined her. The swelling and pain were getting worse by the minute.

"I'm sending her to the hospital in Sherman," Doc said, looking Daddy in the eye. "She's been bitten by a black widow spider. It must have happened early this morning. If she's not lucky, she might lose that leg. In fact," he said, looking down at the floor, "that could be the least of our worries."

"Good Lord!" Daddy said. It was all he could say. Mama began crying.

They checked her into a private room in the Sherman hospital, St. Vincent's Sanitarium, on one of its upper floors. The hospital was an imposing six-story structure that had been built in 1902. It was located several blocks southeast of Sherman's downtown square.

Mama was in the hospital for two or three weeks but finally recovered. Daddy stayed in the room with her. At night he slept in a chair. From a window in the room, he could see the corner grocery store across the street. Several times while Mama was resting or sleeping, Daddy would go downstairs and across the street to the store. That gave him a chance to stretch his legs a little. He would buy a pack of cigarettes or maybe sardines or cheese and crackers for a meal. He got casually acquainted with a couple of the men who worked in the store, just passing the time of day, shooting the breeze. One can speculate that they probably discussed, at one time or another, the weather, the economy, politics, and music: in other words, probably more specifically the lack of rain, the hard times of the Depression, the former governor (and current gubernatorial candidate) "Ma" Ferguson, and musician Bob Wills and his band, the Light Crust Doughboys. From what Daddy later told me, I don't think they had yet got around to discussing crime, more specifically Bonnie Parker and Clyde Barrow's bizarre crime spree that was underway.

On Tuesday evening, October 11, at about 6:30, Daddy was lounging and dozing in his chair. The window was up, and Daddy heard several pops coming from the direction of the grocery store. At first he assumed that the noise had been a backfiring car. He stood and looked out the window. There was a Buick sedan parked on the street near the store, and that more-or-less fit with his supposition that he had heard an automobile engine backfire a few times. Then he saw three men jump into the Buick and drive away very fast. A few minutes later, Daddy learned that Howard Hall, the grocery store's butcher, had tried to stop a young man from robbing the store, and Hall had been shot several times. Three eyewitnesses later identified the leader as none other than the notorious Clyde Barrow. Daddy was still twenty-two-years-old in October of 1932; he and Clyde Barrow had both been born in the same year: 1909.

Initially Howard Hall was still alive, and several men carried him across the street to the hospital, but he died about an hour after the shooting. The owner of the grocery store, Mr. Sidney Little, was not there at the time of the robbery and shooting. The holdup occurred shortly before closing time; a few minutes earlier, Mr. Little had removed most of the money from the cash register and taken it off the premises, except for approximately $60 to be used for making change that evening and the next morning. Homer Glaze and Lester Butler were clerks who were employed by the store, and Howard Hall was the butcher and meat market manager. Hall was fifty-seven-years-old.

Clyde Barrow entered the store at about 6:30 p.m. According to published accounts, Homer Glaze was behind the counter at the front of the store. Glaze saw the young man, who seemed a bit nervous, come in the door, but he did not recognize him as the notorious robber. Clyde grabbed a loaf of bread and took it to the cash register. Homer Glaze asked him if he needed anything else. He answered yes, that he wanted half a dozen eggs and some lunchmeat. After he got those two items, he handed Homer Glaze a dollar bill in payment. Glaze opened the cash register and looked down to make change.

When Homer Glaze looked up again with the change in his hand, Clyde was pointing a pistol at him. Clyde shoved Glaze out of the way, stepped in front of the register, and took the money from it. Howard Hall, working in the meat market at the back of the store, saw what was happening and called out to Clyde, "Young man, you can't do that!" Undoubtedly he had absolutely no idea who he was talking to.

Clyde was instantly infuriated. He ordered both men toward the store's side door and commenced cursing while he was hitting and kicking Howard Hall. A customer, a Mrs. Butler, entered the store, saw what was happening, and hid in one of the far corners of the store. As the three men got near the side door, Clyde hit Hall in the face, knocking Hall's glasses out the door and onto the sidewalk. As Clyde drew back his arm to hit Howard Hall again, Hall tried to grab Clyde's arm. Barrow fired three bullets into Hall's chest. Hall fell out the door and onto the sidewalk. Clyde stepped over Hall and shot him again. Clyde then focused his attention on Homer Glaze, who was standing horrorstricken just inside the doorway. Clyde pointed the gun at Glaze and pulled the trigger, but fortunately somehow the pistol failed to fire. Clyde ran down the street several steps to the Buick sedan. He and two accomplices escaped Sherman via Highway 82 East. A few days later he rendezvoused with Bonnie Parker in Denton. They would survive for another eighteen months.

As I was contemplating this story, suddenly a shiver ran through my body. It had just dawned on me that if Daddy had been in that grocery store at the wrong time—or if Mama had not survived that poisonous spider bite—they couldn't have got together in that hayloft later on. And that would have had dire implications for yours truly. But I'm thankful that everything turned out okay for our family, and I'm very happy that *I'm here to tell you.*

The author in more recent times

Jim Najvar, Helen Najvar, and salesman

A CZECH WAY OF BUSINESS

by Lori Najvar

In the early 1870s, Czech immigrants from the Moravian region of the Austro-Hungarian empire began settling on and cultivating the rich blacklands found throughout Central Texas. Years passed and many second-, third-, and fourth-generation Texas-Czechs were born and became prominent citizens. This story is about a mid-twentieth century Lavaca County grocery store run and co-owned by my aunts and uncle, second-generation Texas-Czechs, Helen Najvar and her brother and sister-in-law Václav (Jim) and Pauline Najvar.

Living was simple in Hallettsville, "the City of Hospitality"—population 2,200. The seat of Lavaca County and a thriving town with a prosperous agrarian community had charm. Historical buildings surrounded the town square and were shadowed by the towering courthouse. Because of the county's demographics, adult conversation was mixed with German and a Czech-Moravian dialect.

Location and Surroundings

The year was 1965. Walking southeast of the 1897 county courthouse, the sidewalk led you to the three important food establishments: Chovanetz City Bakery, Novasad's Meat Market, and Najvar's Store. These Czech-owned businesses catered to the community at large, but also offered traditional Czech food and life essentials. Chovanetz City Bakery offered *kolaches* (fruit filled pastries), *klobasniky* (pigs-in-blankets) and *chleb* (rustic country bread). Novasad's was a local butcher shop that provided seasonal meat products like *klobasa* (sausage), *jelita* (blood sausage), and *jitrnice* (liver sausage).

Double Bubble pink bubble gum sold for a penny apiece. There were also Orange Crush and RC Cola sodas and Big Hunk and Baby Ruth candy bars. Sandwich meat was sliced before your eyes, and they had truly fresh produce from the farm. In the mid-sixties, the small grocery store was more than a place to pick up a quart of milk. It was a neighborhood place where kids were sent to pick up a last-minute forgotten item for dinner. It was a no-frills, compact store where everyone could buy everything they needed in just a few minutes. Children weren't carded for buying tobacco for their parents. You could be short fifteen cents and were trusted to make up the difference later.

Najvar's Store offered all the nourishment and essentials for a household. One could special-order items by dialing a simple five-digit phone number and add the transaction to one's personal monthly charge account. Several decades and a generation later, this type of store is non-existent in Hallettsville today.

Vendors and Deliveries

Salesmen (no women at the time) had their regular visits. Deliveries were made and carried to the back of the store where there was a storage area. The salesmen always greeted Helen as Miss Helen. They were often amazed that she did all the heavy lifting in the store herself. She was a single, independent woman who cared deeply for her parents and extended family. She never hesitated to help her customers, and extended her trust and kindness to her business associates as well.

Deliveries were made every day. Some vendors had more character than others. The Buttercrust Bread man, "Shorty" Leopold, stood tall as he carried four crates of white and wheat sliced bread stacked and carefully balanced over his shoulder. Shorty towered at a height of 5'4". With a half-chewed King Edward cigar in one corner of his mouth he managed to mumble a greeting out the opposite corner: "How's everything this morning? *Dobry den* (good day) Miss Helen," as he leaned to one side and straddled the narrow isle. Shorty managed to change out the bread in no time. After taking the older bread back to his truck, he rushed back into the store and pulled out the "bookkeeping system" he had attached by a leather chain to his belt. He grabbed his pencil from behind his ear, scribbled numbers, tore out the sheet, handed it to Helen, moved the cigar to the opposite side of his mouth, and zoom—he was gone. Helen placed the invoice in a special green metal tackle box beneath the register. What I didn't see is how quickly she scanned (with her eyes) the amount of bread delivered. "Trust" was not something one had to think of . . . it was a given.

First Job and Learning Retail

Aunt Helen invited all her nieces and nephews to come and work. If we came—we worked. When I was in elementary school, I had the opportunity to work at Najvar's Store. The experience and memories are worth more to me than the pay of 75 cents per day plus a Dreamsicle ice-cream.

My first tasks were to sweep the floor and dust the shelves. Once I mastered those tasks and didn't appear bored, I was asked to price products with the "high tech" hand-held metal stamper. Aunt Helen carefully lined up numbers on the moveable rubber-stamp belts; she handed the stamper to me and I became a diligent pricing machine. I positioned the stamper in the middle of the lid, and with the right amount of pressure . . . presto!—a 25-, 35-, or 40-cent purple pricemark appeared. I gained power with each can, box, and case in a day's work. Once the cans were marked, I placed and arranged them on the shelves. I became a true stocker of the store and my job had meaning. It sure beat playing make-believe store in an empty refrigerator box.

Helen took the empty boxes that the cans had been delivered in, used a twelve-inch butcher knife and cut down the packaging into small pieces. It wasn't until my early adult life that I realized that cutting anything with the blade *toward* one's own body was not the safest practice.

Money and Mannerisms

Helen's accounting system was simple. At the checkout counter sat a rather large manual cash register. A small adding machine was nearby, but I was more impressed by the large adding machine in Helen's head. The counter height required a stool for all of us young employees to step up to the cash register, punch the numbers, pull the long lever and open the register drawer.

With customer purchases, I learned to give change by counting backwards, and as the last coin was handed out, I was encouraged to add a greeting: simple phrases of the time like "Please, Come again!" "Enjoy the butter!" "See you soon!" and the Czech phrase "*Sponem Bohem*" (May God be with you!).

Helen trusted me to take the weekly deposit to the Hallettsville National Bank in the rectangular bank bag. As I walked the half-block distance to the bank, I made sure the zipper was shut and kept my course. To my knowledge, little crime occurred in the town—no bank robbers—just A. J. passed out from drunkenness in the gazebo and periodically taken to jail to sleep it off. Regardless of the peaceful setting, I always felt relieved after passing off the bank deposit to the teller, receiving the deposit slip, and making my way back to the store. There may have been as little as $300 in the pouch, but in my mind I could have been carrying thousands of dollars.

Take-home pay was distributed at the end of the week. Making my own deposit was quite a different experience. My parents set up a Sacred Heart Credit Union account. I was anxious to get my hard-earned pay of $5.00 into the black safe and logged in my account passbook. This was not the usual procedure, for there wasn't a physical bank building to visit. Instead of steel bars on the windows and door, there was the hand-painted haircut price signage on the glass. Instead of a regal bank sign, there was an old-fashioned barber pole. You see, the credit union president, Mr. Zaveski, was a barber. The credit union safe sat in the back of his barber shop business. I patiently waited, watching him complete the current customer's haircut, shave, and side-burn trim. Being the only girl in the shop, it was obvious I was there to make a deposit. Mr. Zaveski walked me to the back of the shop, took my money, and placed the bills in a small wooden box. I witnessed him carefully making the deposit entry in my passbook, and then he placed the money in the safe. Somehow, this transaction had an impact on my ability to manage money for the rest of my life.

LANGUAGE CONVERGENCE

A great number of German immigrants settled in Texas in the mid-1800s, almost three decades before Czech immigrants arrived. Most Texas-Czechs, speaking little English, if any, came to America with a Moravian dialect and adapted their native tongue by adding German words for new objects and experiences. This was true for foods, crops, or items that did not exist in the old country. The local Germans also learned to converse in Czech while they socialized or conducted business.

The band stage and dance floor is where the two languages united. Weddings and social dances were the weekly entertainment and gathering spots. Czech and German bands played old and new polkas and waltzes for the community. Everyone sang in their native tongue, but German bandmembers learned to play a Czech song or two, and the Czech musicians learned a few German songs. And there was plenty of *pivo* (beer) flowing regardless of which group was the host.

Another example of shared language usage was in local business transactions. A story my ninety-two-year-old father still loves to tell goes like this:

> One day, bank teller Leo Fredrick was aspiring to speak Czech phrases to share with Czech-speaking customers. Helen made a bank deposit, completed her transaction, and Leo said to her, *"Prd' zas"* (Fart again). Helen gave him a stern look and thought he was crazy. Leo repeated, *"Prosim, prd' zas"* (Please, fart again). He'd meant to say, *"Přijde zas"* (Please, come again)! Helen's face read confusion and she was rather appalled. By the end of the day, everyone around the town square had heard the story.

Homemade Goods and Conveniences

Produce in the '60s was the true meaning of the words *fresh and organic.* Jim and Pauline raised chickens and had milk cows, so they provided eggs, milk, butter, homemade cottage cheese, homemade sausage, molasses, and homemade soap to the store. "Fresh poultry" meant the hens were caught that morning, butchered, de-feathered, cleaned, and brought to the store by 8:30 a.m. each Friday morning. No pasteurizing, no labels, no FDA involved. In the winter, Jim made homemade molasses. Since everyone else sold larger jars of molasses with an unaffordable price, Jim offered the product in much smaller jars. It embodied the true meaning of consumer packaging specifically for the special customers.

Cheese (called orange, rat, or *syr*) was sold by the pound and freshly cut and sliced if you desired. Large jars of fresh lard, odd-shaped chunks of homemade lye soap, one-pound bags of raw poppy seed, two- to three-yard pre-cut pieces of fabric, individual floral wrapping paper, three-pound bags of chicken feed, balls of string, large cooking roasters, simple toys, school supplies such as Big Chief tablets, ice-cream bars, and Shinola shoe polish were main staples. The 35 × 60 square foot size of the store was part of the charm. In retrospect, this old fashioned store was on the cutting edge in that it resembled what a contemporary ethnic store in Chicago, New York City, or any newly developed urban neighborhood might look like. It had much more to offer than a modern 7-11 store. Instead of the annoying convenience store buzzer, a tiny bell hung on the Buttercrust Bread door handle. The screen door would bounce open and slam shut with each customer entering. No Muzak or sophisticated sound system or intercom. There was just a constant hum from the Blue Bell ice cream freezer and produce refrigerator case, and an occasional polka played on the local radio station.

Cigarettes and tobacco were stored behind the checkout counter. I remember the older women buying Scotch Snuff; older men purchased Brown's Mule chewing tobacco and unfiltered cigerettes such as Camels and Lucky Strikes—customers below the age of fifty bought Marlboro cigarettes—"a man's cigarette" was the Marlboro Man campaign!

The vertical toy rack stood alone. It spun around as if it was a toy itself. Cork guns, balsa wood airplanes, and bags of jacks hung on the rack. Rolls of gift-wrapping paper placed on the top shelf barely cleared the pressed-tin ceiling where electrical wires and plugs were suspended. Every square inch of the walls was filled from top to bottom. The concrete floor was cold and needed no care. The aroma of soap and sometimes bread filled the air. Handwritten signs were taped to the special-of-the-week items.

For 75-cents-a-day wage, along with my Dreamsicle ice-cream treat, I learned the basics of retail, and hard work was the reward. I believe this has been true for my whole life! And in this current day, I often chuckle to myself and wonder if the Walmart greeter in Hallettsville has learned any Czech phrases.

Al Lowman

SOME RECOLLECTIONS OF DEFINING EVENTS

by Al Lowman

When I remember bygone days

I think how evening follows morn;

So many I loved were not yet dead,

So many I love were not yet born.

Ogden Nash—"The Middle"

When I entered this world my parents were living on a Nueces County cotton farm south of Violet on the road to Petronila. It was the era when women gave themselves and each other home permanents, when green olives were stuffed with real pimiento, when toothpaste came in metal tubes—not plastic. And when you rolled them at the end they by Jove stayed rolled. People were being told that they should worry more about halitosis and constipation, for which the remedies were Listerine and Post's Bran Flakes.

I was born at Fred Roberts Memorial Hospital in Corpus Christi on Ground Hog Day 1935. According to the *Corpus Christi Caller-Times*, the weather was cloudy with brisk northerly winds. The Lindbergh kidnap case dominated the newspaper headlines, but five thousand miles away a Hungarian expatriate in Argentina had just perfected a technique for grinding a tiny, ink-dispensing metal sphere that made the ball-point pen feasible and the decline of Western civilization inevitable.

The hospital in which I was born had been named in memory of a one-time secretary of the local Ku Klux Klan chapter. His assassination by the Nueces County sheriff in 1922 had brought famed Texas Ranger Frank Hamer to restore calm. He had the situation well in hand by the time I got there thirteen years later.

My earliest memories are of Aladdin lanterns, battery-powered radios, treadle sewing machines, and mud roads. I remember the roads because in rainy seasons Daddy would put mud lugs on the Farmall tractor in order to haul Mama to her teaching job at the Oso School three miles east. The rural letter carrier was widely acknowledged as an expert mud driver, so if a shopping trip to Robstown were contemplated in such circumstances Daddy's response was, "Let's wait awhile and let Humphries cut the ruts." Our conveyance in those days had been a tan Model A coupe with a rumble seat, until it was swapped out in 1935 for a two-door Ford sedan that was gun metal gray. So, Humphries cut the ruts and life inched forward. The fecund black earth extended from our house in all directions. Four hundred years before my time Cabeza de Vaca saw part of Nueces County and described "vast and handsome pastures, with good grass for cattle, and . . . it strikes me the soil would be very fertile were the country inhabited and improved by reasonable people." Nothing waits more patiently than the earth itself.

The house in which we lived was a nondescript, white frame structure that faced east; two bedrooms and a bath on the south were separated from the kitchen and another small bedroom on the north by a combination dining and living area that opened up the midsection. A screened-in front porch extended nearly the width of the house. Despite its single-wall construction, that dwelling kept us dry, if not exactly secure, through several late summer hurricanes. The inside walls were bare boards painted white, but no amount of paint ever concealed the half-moon indentations where hammers had gone wide of the mark.

That house, and others of its vintage, had advantages not duplicated in contemporary structures. They seemed to respond to, to come alive from human habitation in a way that modern dwellings with their cement foundations do not. One could walk across the floor of our living room to the accompaniment of dishes rattling in the china cabinet. This gives inhabitants a comforting sense of being at one with their surroundings, and such feelings are reinforced when winter winds blow. No matter how carefully cracks and crevices are stuffed with rags, there is always that furtive movement in one or more curtains giving witness to a living presence. They don't build houses like that anymore.

Grandpapa Lowman had bought the farm in 1915, and in the summer of the following year had sent three teenagers—Daddy, his older brother Quincy, and their black friend W. C. Hunt—to construct a house on the property. As they pounded nails, they were mindful of Mexican bandito raids on surrounding ranches, but in his nineties Hunt swore to me that they weren't in the least apprehensive. Ah, the bravado of youth. One rather imagines that the boys were just as happy to return to their central Texas home at Staples, about a dozen miles downstream from the San Marcos River headwaters. Although from his mid-twenties to his death thirty years later Daddy lived in other locales, he never left Staples in spirit. And from my earliest childhood I was subjected to an endless barrage of stories about the characters who lived there; only in the last fifty years have I appreciated what a fine legacy he gave me.

Long before Daddy died in the mid-fifties I had noticed that his memory seemed to improve with age. He could remember everything—whether it happened or not. Not only was he an exceptional storyteller, he knew another art as well; he knew how to listen *for* stories, which is different from listening to them. He had grown up before the development of transportation and television, when people relied on their own wit and ingenuity for entertainment. Traditional folk tales, ghost stories, buried treasure legends and the like never took root in Staples. Doc Hunt once explained to me that "Them people in Staples was either too good or too mean to be scairt of ghosts." People made up their own yarns from the simple ingredients of their everyday life. In format they were mostly anecdote, personal experience narrative, and artfully contrived tall tales. While their church orientation taught them the limits of civilized behavior, they seldom took time to memorize the "thou-shalt-nots." To say "thou shalt not bear false witness" did not mean that one couldn't tell a tall tale about one's friend or relative. Daddy's stories may have been exaggerated at times, but he sure as blazes knew how to bring the dead to life.

Some years ago I was visiting with Daddy's youngest brother, Horace, in an attempt to verify certain details of what had become a family legend. Uncle Horace exuded the weariness of a man who had waged a life-long crusade on behalf of truth and justice. He had his hands full; truth has always been elusive in the family, and the younger members allege there was no justice, either. I wasn't especially astonished when Uncle Horace responded passionately: "Your Daddy could make 'em up faster than anybody could deny 'em. About half the stuff that's been passed off as authentic history was the result of your Daddy's imagination. An honest man would wear himself to a frazzle just trying to keep the record straight." Uncle Horace, a one-time school teacher with a master's degree, would have done well to recall Samuel Butler's admonition that "God cannot alter the past, but historians can."

Daddy's stories nearly always involved people with roots in Staples, and from the outset of my childhood I seemed surrounded by persons displaced from there. Our closest neighbors in Nueces County were the Merritt clan, which consisted of three brothers with families and their maiden sister—Joe, Arthur, Thomas, and Miss Margaret. The Lowman and Merritt families had first made acquaintance a couple of generations earlier when the Merritts lived on a farm between Cottonwood and Byler Pool southeast of Staples. The Merritt men were of medium height and build, with high cheekbones, piercing eyes, and a distinguishing aquiline nose that in each case supported steel-rimmed glasses. At first acquaintance one might have thought that they suffered some sort of congenital anhedonia, but actually they got most of their looks from Grandma Merritt.

I recall a photograph made when she was about eighty—a doughty old lady in a high-collared black taffeta dress, fixing the camera with unflinching gaze as if the devil himself were working the shutter, and she wasn't about to be compromised. It is quite possible the picture was made about the time she was staying with her youngest son, Thomas, and his wife Ruth. One Saturday noon, during a late summer cotton harvest, the pickers had cleaned the field next to the house, collected their weekly wages, and headed for town to grocery shop. The place was deserted except for Mr. Thomas, Aunt Ruth, and Grandma. Hardly had the last picker departed when Grandma's keen eye observed that a single row of cotton beyond the driveway remained untouched. She lost no time reporting this carelessness to her son, who responded that the row could be gathered in a matter of minutes on Monday morning.

"But, Thomas, it might rain," the old lady protested. "I think you'd better get out there and pick it. Now."

Gazing into the withering heat, Mr. Thomas advised her that the profit from a single row of cotton was hardly worth the effort. When Grandma remonstrated one last time, she was told not to worry about it in language that carried unmistakable overtones of finality. Mr. Thomas climbed in his car and drove away on business of his own, leaving wife and mother alone in the house.

For the next hour or so Aunt Ruth was busy at her sewing machine. Suddenly, and for no apparent reason, she began to feel uneasy about Grandma. Before she could move from her chair to investigate, she heard the screen door at the back of the house tap closed. Aunt Ruth reached the kitchen as the old lady plopped a cotton sack on the floor and wiped her forehead with a handy apron.

"There," she exclaimed, "I don't have that to worry about anymore. Now I can take my nap." She disappeared into her room. The afternoon lengthened into an eternity for Aunt Ruth, who wondered if her mother-in-law would ever wake up. Two hours later Grandma emerged in quiet triumph.

The old lady was dead before my time. But she truly typified the Staples breed. Indeed, she was pioneer Staples stock, her family having arrived in the greater metropolitan area well before the Civil War. Settling nearby at about the same time was the Stanfield family. Their daughter, Dora, married Tom Anderson in 1880, and they made their home in downtown Staples, surrounded by a vegetable garden, milk shed, and other farmstead detritus.

"Granny" Anderson was a remarkable individual of such formidable personality that her spouse scarcely existed outside her shade. Tom Anderson was once justice of the peace, but his main job was to sit on the front porch, rock, and look neat-as-a-pin while

Granny did all the work. For most of the day she gave him the sharp edge of her tongue as she bustled about. Then, at day's end, she would pull a stool up to his easy chair and sweet-talk him for a while before going in the house to fix supper.

A single episode in Granny's long life became *the* watershed event in the community's history. Everything in Staples happened either before or after she was gored by the old milk cow. As long as they lived—and as late as the nineteen-eighties there were a handful yet living—the witnesses knew exactly where they were and what they were doing when Granny was gored. So many of them claim to have been "right there" when it happened that I am convinced that half the town was sitting around waiting for it to happen.

This awful event seems to have occurred early on a weekday afternoon in the fall of 1911, as Granny was trying to separate her milk cow from its newly born calf. The nervous cow unexpectedly charged Granny, who was unable to swerve aside fast enough to avoid being totally disemboweled by one of the horns. Jim Sherrill, who lived across the road from the Andersons, heard the poor woman's blood-curdling screams for help, came running, and was first at her side. Others heard the screams as well and never forgot them. Someone ran to fetch young Doctor Wilburn Williams, whose office was three houses away. Robert Lowman, Daddy's cousin, had been at the store only a few minutes when a distraught Ed Anderson, one of Granny's sons, appeared in the doorway. Ashen-faced and in tears, he implored the bystanders, "The old cow has just about killed Mama. Can some of y'all help us get her to the doctor?"

Instantly a half-dozen men ran to assist. When they reached the Anderson cow pen they found the stricken woman, perfectly conscious, lying with her intestines strewn on the manure-covered ground beside her. Dr. Williams had already arrived. He now supervised her removal to a stretcher, improvised from a barn door panel, and led the way to his office. Robert Lowman told me he carried her intestines in his hands, as the litter bearers marched along. When they reached Williams' office Granny was laid gently on the only feasible surface, which happened to be a dining room table.

Years later Dr. Williams confessed to his foster daughter, Myrtle Tarbutton, "I was never so scared in all my life. There was the woman's husband and a couple of the big kids depending on me to do something. They sure as hell didn't know what to do and neither did I. So I washed the cow manure off her guts as best I could, stuffed 'em back in place as best I could, and sewed her up as best I could. There was no use saying a prayer because she didn't have one." (Indeed, there was so much cleaning to be done that the doctor is reported to have used tap water. The Staples water supply was not approved by the State Health Department until the early sixties.) Robert Lowman remembered that when the doctor had finished, he remarked to onlookers in the jam-packed operating room, "I haven't done a very good job here, but there's no way she could live anyway." At this time Granny was in her late fifties, Dr. Williams in his early thirties. Just like an Anderson to make a liar out of somebody. She lived to 105, surpassing the doctor by a decade. Granny was holding court at Staples reunions well into my lifetime.

If Granny Anderson's goring was the defining event in Staples history, then there were two events that defined the history of the south Texas community where I first lived, events that are even now fondly recalled by those who experienced them. At this point I want to move ahead of my story to relate the second most memorable event of my childhood. Aside from the play that I invented for myself, looking at books and having them read to me was my principal diversion—as it was for most farm children of my era. Christmas was the book-buying season, and rummaging under the tree in search of them was unalloyed delight. The most perfect Christmas present I ever received was *A Picture Almanac for Boys and Girls* by Nisenson and Kohl, the gift of Aunt Jewell for Christmas 1942. Each page was devoted to a single day of the calendar year with concise accounts of persons, places, and events related to that day, plus other miscellany that remains fixed in my mind even now. All these childhood books disintegrated years ago—to my everlasting regret.

I was four years old when, one early summer morning in 1939, a strange panel truck came crunching into our driveway. Stranger yet, the sole occupants of the cab were two women utterly unknown to me. Nor could I read the lettering on the side of the truck. I ran to Mama in the kitchen with news of this arrival. She peered through the window over the sink, and I detected a note of delight and excitement in her voice when she said, "That's the bookmobile!"

Hot damn! I didn't know what it was, but it sure sounded promising. And certainly this was one of the few experiences of my life that offered more than it promised. The only drawback was the rationing policy, "because other little boys and girls want to read those books, too." I doubted it. But I made do as best I could from one week to the next, and always eagerly anticipated my next selection. The bookmobile continued in operation until the gasoline and tire shortages of World War II led to its premature demise, but I had started school in the fall of 1941 and was no longer quite so dependent upon the bookmobile for entertainment.

But the bookmobile story has an interesting aftermath. I never forgot one of those two women drivers. Her name was Ard, Katherine Ard. She went on to a distinguished career in Texas library service, becoming President of the Texas Library Association right after World War II. Much later she was director of the Montgomery County Library at Conroe, and then about 1970 she was named a division chief of the Texas State Library in Austin. One day I walked into the office of the director, who happened to be Dorman Winfrey, and there she sat, conversing with him. Her back was to me when I entered. As I approached, Dorman jumped from behind his desk and said, "Al have you met Katherine Ard, the new director of our field services division?" Without missing a beat I said airily, "Oh, Dorman, I've known Katherine Ard thirty years and more. She used to drive the bookmobile in Nueces County when I was growing up down there. It's good to see you again, Miss Ard." At this point she proffered a somewhat reluctant hand, knowing that I wasn't mistaken but wondering who the hell *was* I.

The next time I saw her around the State Library, perhaps a month later, she remembered. Boy, did she ever remember. "I have you placed now," she said in a tobacco-cured baritone. Had I been alert I would have noticed the mischievousness in her countenance that I learned to watch for later. "I recall the day I drove up in the bookmobile and you came running out the front door to meet me, wearing a brand new pair of boots that your parents had bought for you at Lichtenstein's department store in Corpus. You threw your arms up wanting me to hold you, and then you began calling my attention to those new boots by kicking me with them."

The conversational ball was now in my court. I quickly explained to Miss Ard that she was the last librarian I had ever kicked or even thought of kicking because, I explained, there were two other influences in my early life that were as significant as any of the treasures in her bookmobile. And what might those influences have been, she wanted to know.

"My father's belt and my mother's hairbrush."

As I said, the bookmobile was the second most memorable event of my childhood. I have kept the best for last, like the best piece of candy in the sack, to be savored with total concentration after all else has been consumed. No event in our lives ever had more profound impact than rural electrification, which came to Nueces County in 1938. Prior to that event all our heating, cooking and night lighting were done with kerosene. Refrigeration depended on an icebox that had to be restocked every other day by the ice man, who drove from Corpus Christi.

Washday at our house came around every Saturday, and Daddy did it, the only man in the neighborhood who did. Water was not to be wasted because it had to be run through a hose under weak pressure from a distant faucet. Mama brought the dried clothes in from the line, sprinkled them lightly with water to facilitate ironing, and then pressed them with a sad iron. It had to be heated on the stove, and, because it retained heat poorly, Mama owned at least three—two to heat while she ironed with the third. If moisture from the sprinkled clothes had remained on the iron's surface as it reheated, any smoke from the stove would create a dirty film on the bottom. This film—soot, actually—made a mess of whatever it touched next, so Mama would quickly wipe the freshly heated iron across a folded towel kept next to the ironing board before touching clothes with it.

The absence of electricity meant that Mama cooked our meals on a kerosene range. At night she struggled to finish her housework, and Daddy to read his *Caller-Times*, by the light of an Aladdin lantern. On long winter evenings Daddy would settle in his rocker, adjust the faltering lantern light and read O. Henry's short stories. Many of these tales had settings in the south Texas cattle country, which the author knew firsthand. Wintertime would also bring out the kerosene space heaters. Neither Mama, nor my aunts, nor the neighbor women, were bashful about backing up to one of those heaters and hiking their skirts to bask more fully in the warmth. The Atwater Kent radio was used sparingly so as to save wear on the batteries. It was kept tuned to the NBC affiliate in San Antonio and was turned on for newscasts at seven in the morning, noon, and ten at night. On weekdays it stayed on for the farm market reports at 12:15.

Electricity, given its availability, could revolutionize life on the farm. Daddy and other neighbors appealed to the Central Power and Light Company to provide electric power. CP&L agreed to do so, provided the farmers would pay five hundred dollars per mile to build the lines and then pay double the rates charged to its customers in Corpus Christi. In these Depression times such a "deal" was out of the question; these farmers didn't have that kind of money. The power company countered that service to individual farms was uneconomical—but farmers now had an ace up their sleeves.

In 1935, President Franklin Roosevelt signed an executive order creating the Rural Electrification Administration, and later that year Congress allowed the REA to make self-liquidating loans to cooperatives established by the farmers themselves. Having spent much of 1937 in futile negotiation with CP&L, Mama, Daddy and the neighbors decided to form a rural electric cooperative and to try for an REA loan. To guide them through this uncharted territory, they hired a twenty-three-year-old attorney freshly graduated from the University of Texas Law School. His name was Cecil Burney; he was the son-in-law of Clyde Hunsucker, who had grown up with the Lowmans and Merritts at Staples. They figured young Burney was hungry for work, and he happened to be well acquainted with an up-and-coming young congressman who was similarly engaged in trying to get an electric co-op established in his own Texas Hill Country constituency. Burney, later president of the State Bar of Texas, laid some of the groundwork for the Nueces County Electric Cooperative in the Washington office of Lyndon B. Johnson, whom he had met when Johnson was head of the Texas office of the National Youth Administration.

Burney's perseverance resulted in a four-hundred-thousand-dollar loan to the newly formed co-op, and electricity seemed on the way. CP&L officials made a last-minute effort to derail the co-op by offering to build the lines and charge rates comparable to those afforded its urban customers, but the farmers would not now be dissuaded.

So, all that summer and fall of 1938, hole diggers, pole setters, spike men, and stringers constructed power lines while farmhouses were wired for electricity and farm wives cautiously bought washing machines, refrigerators, and newfangled irons. By mid-December everything was ready, waiting only for the lines to be energized. Our Christmas tree stood framed in a living room window to the right of the front door. Mama had decorated it with something I had never seen on any tree of ours: colored lights.

And so it came to pass that on an unusually mild December morning it was suggested, somewhat pointedly, that I go sit on the front steps and watch for the co-op service vehicle that would soon appear on the horizon. The men in that truck, I was told, would flip a switch that would give us electricity. I'd been seated on the steps only moments when I saw a pickup moving west on the Corpus road. It turned north at Uncle Joe Merritt's house and headed our way, stopping near the entrance to our driveway. There, by the mailbox, stood a utility pole with a transformer attached at the top. From the transformer two electrical wires connected to the house. It was obvious to my not-quite-four-year-old mind that whatever was about to happen was going to take place out front. When I saw Daddy walking down the driveway toward the parked vehicle, I ran to join him.

As we reached the mailbox a lineman had finished putting on spikes and was ready to climb the pole to the transformer. With my right arm around Daddy's left leg, I watched the lineman's ascent. When he reached the transformer, Daddy said, "Son, look yonder at the house. You see the Christmas tree in the window?" Suddenly the lineman flipped a switch in the transformer. The lights on the tree came to life.

It was a moment of sheer magic. Nothing else in my experience has even come close. Nothing.

I stood for a few brief seconds totally mesmerized by the sight, then suddenly let go of Daddy's leg. The last thing I can remember is running toward the house as fast as I could go.

Al Lowman turning over the TFS Presidency to Kenneth W. Davis, April 14, 1990

TEXAS

MUSIC

"Still Hunting Buffaloes on the Northern Range," by J.H. Moser. (Found at The Project Gutenberg EBook of *The Extermination of the American Bison*, by William T. Hornaday, http://www.gutenberg.org/ebooks/17748.)

"HELL IN TEXAS": CROSSING BETWEEN SIN AND SALVATION IN TEXAS FOLK SONGS

by Ken Baake

Stories of development from childhood to adulthood or of journeying through a life-changing experience to gain new knowledge are replete in oral and written tradition, as exemplified by the Greek epic of Odysseus and countless other tales. The theme of travel, hardship, and eventual spiritual or intellectual awakening is perhaps one of the most common. Often the hero journeys naively to an alien land and then with great difficulty, returns home, wiser, but forever scarred. The journey can take the hero to terrible places, from which he may escape physically, but from which he can never escape emotionally.

Recall the narrator of Joseph Conrad's late 19th century novel, *Heart of Darkness*, who pilots a ferry boat over the Congo River in search of Kurtz, a European ivory trader made bestial by his travels. This narrator, Marlow, survives the journey but is plagued by his knowledge of human savagery. Kurtz fares worse, of course, dying on the boat while muttering about the horror of human nature. Implicit in this novel is the message that there exists some line, geographical, psychological, or otherwise, which cannot be crossed without forever transforming the traveler.

Not surprisingly, this theme of crossing a line between innocence and the awareness of life's horrors is the essence of much folklore and many musical folk ballads. Because the story of American history is a story of travel into and across frontiers, this theme is especially strong in folklore of the American West. The song "Bury Me Not on the Lone Prairie," for example, tells the lamentations of a settler from the East whose dying wish is to be buried on the sylvan hillsides of his native Virginia amidst his family members rather than on the desolate prairie. But alas, as with many characters in these travel tales, he cannot return home even in death, but instead is buried in a "narrow grave just six by three," an insignificant mound on a vast plain where the coyotes will howl over him.[1]

The Great Plains in the late 19th and early 20th centuries were often described as an area that was expansive and intimidating, "non-irrigable" as the U.S. Geological Society report from Willard D. Johnson proclaimed in 1900. Somewhere around the 100th meridian the trees, lush grasses, and the life-giving waters of the great river valleys yield to short grasses, parched land, wild animals, and an unending canopy of relentless sun. Color choices on maps of the Great Plains subtly convey this warning even today. One example is found in the Web page of the Great Plains Network Consortium, a computer software group, in which a clear line exists between the Edenic green of the East and Hellish deep red of the interior lands.[2]

Thus, we see the repeated theme or rhetorical commonplace in these folk songs of Westward migration where—like Adam and Eve—the adventurer will pay for the sin of crossing over into forbidden land and, in essence, be banished to Hell. Or he may create his own physical and emotional hell in the new land—as Kurtz did in *Heart of Darkness*. For example, one folk song that goes by as many names and settings as there were frontier lands in the 19th century reveals that the traveler clearly found a hell he wasn't bargaining for—in this case, it was the Dakotas:

> We've reached the land of desert sweet,
> Where nothing grows for man to eat;
> The wind it blows with feverish heat
> Across the plains so hard to beat.[3]

Alternate endings to these stories provide salvation and rebirth for the protagonist who is lucky enough to be able to venture into the wild and return. These variations recall Samuel Taylor Coleridge's *Rime of the Ancient Mariner*, the 19th century British Romantic poem where bad luck befalls the sailors after they shoot the albatross, leaving only the narrator who did the shooting alive at the end to return and offer his tale as a warning against such misdeeds.

One example of a narrator transgressing but escaping with his life is the traditional cowboy song "The Buffalo Skinners." Here the narrator joins the hunting team sometime in the 1870s in the

Texas town of Jacksboro—presumably located just this side of Hell. The song depicts the savage extermination of the buffalo and was adapted from earlier versions where Hell was the Maine forests where lumberjacks toiled or, even earlier, the Atlantic Ocean that European settlers crossed to the mysterious New World.

In "The Buffalo Skinners" the other side is across the Pease River, where death lies waiting as it does across the ancient River Styx. The men face hardships of rancid food, fleas, gypy water, flesh wounds and, ultimately, betrayal by their leader. Only after killing him and "leaving his damned old bones to bleach" are they able to hobble back from the range of the buffalo, forever chastened not to cross back over again. In this story the only salvation is to try to return from Hell scarred, but wiser and ready to confess one's sins to others who might be so tempted to cross to the other side:

> Oh, it's now we've crossed Pease River, and homeward we are bound,
>
> No more in that hell-fired country shall ever we be found.
>
> Go home to our wives and sweethearts, tell others not to go
>
> For God's forsaken the buffalo range, and the damned old buffalo.[4]

In an African-American spiritual found in Texas in the 1940s titled "Travelin' Shoes," the river of death actually pursues the narrator, rising first to his ankles and eventually to his chin. The narrator escapes after pleading he hasn't fulfilled his duty on earth, has not yet earned his "travelin' shoes." His mother, however, has her shoes and is ready to make the journey in his place.[5]

Travel and crossing over, of course, is a prominent theme in the spiritual and secular folk songs of African Americans, who were forcibly carried across the Atlantic in slave ships from the 16th through 19th centuries. The weary narrator in "Swing Low, Sweet Chariot" implores a band of God's angels to carry the narrator home to heaven, which sometimes is associated with freedom back in

Africa, far away from the hell of slavery. Other songs in the African-American folk tradition welcome the test of faith that comes with a journey over into dangerous lands. Echoing the story of Christ's temptation by Satan, the slave song "Go in the Wilderness" asserts that "If you want to find Jesus, go in the wilderness."[6]

Modern folk music of Texas continues using the story line of traveling from safety to danger and back. In the song "Shades of Gray" by singer songwriter Robert Earl Keen, the line is the Red River separating Texas from Oklahoma. Three teenage boys drive into Oklahoma with whiskey and home-grown marijuana on an escapade that has them stealing a cow and selling it, only to be tracked down and then released by state police who take pity on their "sorry" state. Chastened and presumably wiser, they cross back to safety in Texas. As in the *Bildungsroman* genre where a young person grows up over the course of the novel, these characters are now prepared to meet their fate like men:

> They left us by the roadside
> Down hearted and alone
> Randy got behind the wheel
> Said boys I'm going home
> We turned around to face our fate
> Hung over but alive, on that
> Morning in late April, Oklahoma, '95.[7]

This song recalls the great era of the railroad ballad where journeys on train often carried an allegorical meaning of a crossing into dangerous or forbidden lands.

Like the characters in Keen's adventures, the Texas cowboy who is passed out on the barroom floor rides "The Hell-Bound Train," barely escaping with his life. With a boiler filled with beer and "the devil himself" as the engineer, the train careens further and further into a wild country as sulfur fumes scorch the passengers' faces. The cowboy awakes from his horrible drunkard's dream that has culminated with the Devil's threats, and like Keen's characters, promises never to sin again:

Your flesh will scorch in the flames that roar
And my imps will torment you forevermore.
Then the cowboy awoke with an anguished cry.
His clothes were wet and his hair stood high.

Then he prayed as he never had prayed before,
To be saved from his sins and from hell's front door;
His prayers and his pleadings were not in vain,
For he never rode on that hell-bound train.[8]

In some cases, however, Texas is not the safe haven to return to after a near-fatal adventure in the wild. The song "Hell in Texas," said to have been collected by the proprietor of the Buckhorn Saloon in San Antonio in 1909, is a whimsical tale of the Devil's negotiations with God for a plot of land that would be even more hellish than Hell itself, a place "where he could torment the souls of men." The Lord offers him an unwanted tract of sand that he doubted even the Devil could use, "down on the Rio Grande," where the water causes dysentery and "smells like bad eggs," the trees and cattle all have outsized thorns, the rattlesnakes and scorpions lie waiting for victims, and food is unpalatable because of Mexican spices.[9] "Hell in Texas" seems to advocate a sense of humor and good-natured acceptance of life's hardships rather than any quest for deliverance from them.

Like death's waters in "Travelin' Shoes," Hell sometimes finds the narrator of a folk song. The only thing to do is flee, as we see in Woody Guthrie's well-known 1940 Dust Bowl song, "So Long It's Been Good to Know Yuh." Here, presumably the narrator is innocent of any sin, but a victim nonetheless:

I've sung this song, but I'll sing it again,
Of the place that I lived on the wild windy plains,
In the month called April, county called Gray,
And here's what all of the people there say:

So long, it's been good to know yuh;
So long, it's been good to know yuh;

So long, it's been good to know yuh.
This dusty old dust is a-gettin' my home,
And I got to be driftin' along.[10]

Alas, escape from life's trials that can often approach the hellish is not always possible. Like the dying pioneer who wants only to be buried back home rather than on the lone prairie, the narrator in West Texan Butch Hancock's story of lament on the Texas Plains of today can only dream of escape from his privations. He is not as fortunate as his churchly brethren, most likely not because of his sins, but because of his bad luck as a dryland farmer:

There's some big ol' Buicks at the Baptist church
Cadillacs at the Church of Christ
I parked my camel by an ol' haystack
I'll be lookin for that needle all night
There ain't gonna be no radial tires
Turnin' down the streets of gold
I'm goin down to the railroad tracks
And watch them lonesome boxcars roll.[11]

Thus, we see many folk songs where the narrator is tormented in a hellish land. In many, the trip to the forbidden land is an allegory of sin, payback for the free will of the fallen narrator. In others, the onset of Hell is inevitable, perhaps a test of the character's spirit and righteousness. But in some cases, a life of suffering is simply borne at the hand of fate. The options are to flee with only your newfound wisdom and chastity, laughing it off, or if all else fails, dreaming it away.

Endnotes

1. Traditional. Silber, Irvin, ed. *Songs of the Great American West.* (1967). New York: Dover, 1995. 200–202.
2. *Great Plains Network*, home page. Accessed 29 Aug., 2008. http://archie.csce.uark.edu/gpn/.
3. Dean, John A., via Carl Sandburg. "Dakota Land." In Silber, Irvin, ed. *Songs of the Great American West.* (1967). New York: Dover, 1995. 233–234.
4. "The Buffalo Skinners." In Lomax, John A. and Alan Lomax, eds. *Cowboy Songs and Other Frontier Ballads* (1938). New York: Collier Books, Macmillan, 1986. 335–338.
5. "Travelin' Shoes." In Owens, William A. *Texas Folk Songs.* 1950. Texas Folklore Society Publication XXIII. Dallas: SMU Press, 1967. 172–173.
6. Traditional. Allen, William Francis, 1830–1889, ed. by, Charles Pickard Ware, 1840–1921, ed. by, and Lucy McKim Garrison, 1842–1877, ed. by. *Slave Songs of the United States.* New York: A. Simpson & Co., 1867. Electronic edition http://docsouth.unc.edu/church/allen/menu.html
7. Keen, Robert Earl. "Shades of Gray." On *Picnic.* (1995) RCA, 1997, CD.
8. "The Hell-Bound Train" (Smiling Ed McConnell version). In Cohen, Norm. *Long Steel Rail: The Railroad in American Folksong 2nd ed.* Music in American Life Series. Urbana: University of Illinois Press, 2000. 638–644.
9. "Hell in Texas." In Lomax, John A. and Alan Lomax, eds. *Cowboy Songs and Other Frontier Ballads* (1938). New York: Collier Books, Macmillan, 1986. 317–319.
10. Guthrie, Woody. "Dusty Old Dust (So Long, It's Been Good to Know You)." On *Dust Bowl Ballads.* Buddha Records, 2000. CD.
11. Hancock, Butch. "Boxcars." On *Eats Away the Night.* Sugar Hill, 1995. CD.

Works Cited

Allen, William Francis, 1830–1889, ed. by, Charles Pickard Ware, 1840–1921, ed. by, and Lucy McKim Garrison, 1842–1877, ed by. *Slave Songs of the United States.* New York: A. Simpson & Co., 1867. Electronic edition http://docsouth.unc.edu/church/allen/menu.html

Dean, John A. "Dakota Land." In Silber, Irvin, ed. *Songs of the Great American West.* (1967). New York: Dover, 1995. 233–234.

Great Plains Network home page. Accessed 29 Aug., 2008. http://archie.csce.uark.edu/gpn/.

Guthrie, Woody. "Dusty Old Dust (So Long, It's Been Good to Know You)." On *Dust Bowl Ballads.* Buddha Records, 2000, CD.

Hancock, Butch. "Boxcars." On *Eats Away the Night.* Sugar Hill, 1995, CD.

"Hell in Texas." In Lomax, John A. and Alan Lomax, eds. *Cowboy Songs and Other Frontier Ballads* (1938). New York: Collier Books, Macmillan, 1986, 317–319.

Johnson, Willard D. *The High Plains and Their Utilization.* U.S. Geological Survey, 1900.

Keen, Robert Earl. "Shades of Gray." On *Picnic.* RCA, 1997, CD.

Silber, Irvin, ed. *Songs of the Great American West.* (1967). New York: Dover, 1995.

"The Buffalo Skinners." In Lomax, John A. and Alan Lomax, eds. *Cowboy Songs and Other Frontier Ballads* (1938). New York: Collier Books, Macmillan, 1986, 335–338.

"The Hell-Bound Train." In Cohen, Norm. *Long Steel Rail: The Railroad in American Folksong 2nd ed.* Urbana: U of Illinois P, 638–644.

"Travelin' Shoes." In Owens, William A. *Texas Folk Songs.* 1950. Texas Folklore Society Publication XXIII. Dallas: SMU Press, 1967, 172–173.

Ken Baake performing at the TFS meeting in Lubbock, 2008

Buddy Holly statue in Lubbock, Texas (Courtesy Southwest Collection/Special Collections Library, Texas Tech University)

BUDDY HOLLY, BEETHOVEN, AND LUBBOCK IN THE 1950s

by Paul H. Carlson

I love the music of Beethoven—Ludwig van Beethoven. I also like Buddy Holly's high energy songs, Waylon Jennings's rebel sounds, Virgil Johnson's doo wop, and, in part because I grew up in Minneapolis, I love Sonny Curtis's theme song to the once-popular *Mary Tyler Moore* TV Show.

We know—those of us gathered here know [at the 92nd annual meeting of the Texas Folklore Society, in Lubbock, Texas]—that Lubbock is a college town. It is not Ann Arbor or Palo Alto or New Haven, but it is a college town. We know that Lubbock is a sports town. It is not Chicago or Boston or New York City, but it is a sports town. We know—those of us gathered here know—that Lubbock is an agricultural community. It is not a meat-packing center or an implement manufacturer of any great renown, but it is an agricultural community.

Outsiders don't know this. Outsiders, rather, know that Lubbock is a music town. It is not a Boston Conservatory of Music town—although Texas Tech University and South Plains College have strong music departments—but it's a music town. To outsiders, Lubbock's music image is not the easy genius of a Mozart. It is not that kind of music town. No, Lubbock's music image is that of the working man: the sweat, the hard work, the energy, and the fire of a Beethoven—and it is a Buddy Holly kind of town.

You cannot doze, daydream, or chitchat during Beethoven's "Ode to Joy." Nor can you doze during Buddy Holly's "Rave On" or "Peggy Sue" or "That'll Be the Day." Beethoven, said Bill Holm, interferes with the daily dullness of one's life; he paid attention to the world, writes Holm, and he makes you pay attention to his music.[1] Beethoven, writes Holm, is "the composer-laureate of blue collar life, of manual work, of fence-fixing and hole-digging"—or in Lubbock, I suppose, of cotton picking.[2]

Lubbock's music tradition is often full of energy. And like Beethoven's music it has often been composed only through hard labor and hard thinking. Beethoven's music has more to do with the milk barn and Sears & Roebuck than, say, to do with the country club; similarly, Lubbock's music has much to do with the cotton field and Wal-Mart or the oil patch and J. C. Penney. It is hard-working, plain-folk music—like Terry Allen's "Amarillo Highway." That's the point. Beethoven and Lubbock music do not always behave well at the—well, at the local country club. You don't sing the shirt-sleeve vulgarity of Roy Orbison's "I Drove All Night" or Holly's "Oh Boy" at the country club.[3]

Buddy Holly, Waylon Jennings, Sonny Curtis, Roy Orbison, and many others from West Texas have produced exceptional music. The list includes, for example, Mac Davis, Pat Green, Virgil Johnson, Tommy Hancock, Jimmy Dale Gilmore, Butch Hancock, Joe Ely, and most recently Natalie Maines of the once-again wildly popular Dixie Chicks. It is music, such as Mac Davis's "It's Hard to Be Humble," that is full of energy and grabs your attention. It doesn't bore you, although sometimes it may irritate you.

Holly and Orbison, particularly, give you goose bumps, stiffen your spine, and light a roaring fire in your soul. It's Beethoven's kind of music. Sometimes it's lovely music and sometimes it isn't. But a passive "It was OK, I guess" will never do. "It's, like, you know, like cool, dude" won't work either. You can't describe Holly's "True Love Ways" as "cool"—well, "way cool," maybe.

Why is it that Lubbock and the South Plains region of West Texas have contributed to the American music canon to the great extent that they have? Particularly, what was the cultural milieu of Lubbock in Buddy Holly's time? What role, if any, did that cultural mix play in the formation of Holly's music—or Virgil Johnson's music—or the music of Mac Davis? In a socially and culturally conservative Lubbock, how was it possible for young musicians like Holly, Waylon Jennings, Terry Allen, and Mac Davis to produce their special music so full of shirt-sleeve energy and attention-grabbing lyrics?

Well, Lubbock in the 1950s was in a boom period of growth. It was energetic, self-confident, and prosperous. It had two high schools, but three more would be built in the next decade. It had a bulging university in Texas Tech and a fledgling college in Lubbock Christian, which was established in 1954, one year before Buddy Holly in 1955 graduated from Lubbock High School.

In Buddy Holly's high school days, one of Lubbock's newest and perhaps most fashionable housing subdivisions was O'Neil Terrace, located west of Ave. Q and north of 34th Street—sort of across Ave. Q from present O. L. Slaton Jr. High School. People of wealth and position still lived along West Broadway. Nineteenth Street across from Texas Tech was attracting attention from people who wanted large homes. In 1955, Buddy lived at 1902 24th Street, but his family moved often—very often.

In Buddy Holly's high school days, Lubbock's downtown district was still viable and busy, but 34th Street was attracting attention as an important shopping area. Fiftieth Street in 1950 "was an unpaved, rutted street being considered as the outer loop for the city."[4] South

Downtown Lubbock, 1942 (Courtesy Southwest Collection/Special Collections Library, Texas Tech University)

of 50th Street spread cotton fields, empty lots, and playa lakes. In 1959, however, Monterrey and Caprock shopping centers opened along 50th near Boston and Flint, and housing stretched several blocks south of there. No Loop 289 existed in the 1950s, Slide Road was far out in the country, and plans for the South Plains Shopping Mall were not yet on the drawing board. In the late 1950s, high school students drag-raced their cars along a dirt- and gravel-based 82nd Street westward from University Avenue.

In Buddy Holly's high school days, Lubbock retained "a certain small-town atmosphere of friendliness and [sociability]."[5] Its citizens preferred informality of dress and habit, a circumstance still evident at any fine restaurant in the city.

In Buddy Holly's high school days, the dam at Buffalo Springs Lake was begun, and in 1960 Buffalo Springs as a public recreation area opened. Of course, high school and college students, perhaps including Buddy Holly and Jerry Allison's heart throb Peggy Sue, had for years gone out to the Buffalo Springs and present-day

Postcard of early "Buffalo Springs Park" (Courtesy Southwest Collection/Special Collections Library, Texas Tech University)

Ransom Canyon areas to swim, to test their automobiles on the area's winding, hilly roads, to drink some beer, to hold hands, and to listen on the car radio to Chuck Berry, Muddy Waters, Bill Haley and the Comets, or maybe some other early favorites, whose boogie beats and bluesy voices seemed like a sound from nowhere.

In Buddy Holly's high school days, teenagers gathered at the Hi-D-Ho on 3rd and University and at the Village Mill, once located across from Jones AT&T Stadium in the old Town & Country Shopping Center. Guys, mainly, but some girls as well, drove their cars north on University to the Hi-D-Ho, turned right into the famous drive-in and drove around it and back out to University; a Burger King is there now. They crossed University Avenue and drove through the alley behind the Town & Country and followed the alley west to the Village Mill. Or, they drove through the Town & Country Shopping Center parking lot to the Village Mill. Around the mill they went—or, they stopped to visit with friends—before heading east through the shopping center to University and then north again to the Hi-D-Ho.

No Lubbock Civic Center existed in Buddy Holly's high school days. Thus it was that in the mid-1950s the Fair Park Coliseum on the South Plains Fair Grounds and the Cotton Club on 50th and Southeast Drive attracted large, receptive crowds to hear the touring musicians who performed in Lubbock. Elvis Presley was among them. Presley played at both the Fair Park Coliseum and the Cotton Club in 1955, and Buddy Holly and Bob Montgomery opened for him. At least twice more Buddy and Bob, who were more country than rock at the time, opened a Presley concert in Lubbock.

The Presley events changed music on the South Plains. Not only did Presley introduce his southern-style rock music to West Texas, but also he got Buddy Holly to shift toward "race" music, as it was then called, or "rhythm and blues," the beginning of "Shake, Rattle and Roll." In the spring of 1956, Presley played again before an over-flow crowd and receptive audience at the Fair Park Coliseum.

The original Hi-D-Ho Drive-in (Courtesy Southwest Collection/Special Collections Library, Texas Tech University)

Before Elvis's historic visits, music on the South Plains generally followed two forms: country and gospel. Both styles had already produced local stars. In the 1930s, Roy Rogers and the Sons of the Pioneers spent several weeks in Lubbock singing on the local radio station (KFYO) and shaping the music that was to make them famous in Hollywood. Also in the 1930s, fiddler Bob Wills played for South Plains' dances before gaining national fame with his "San Antonio Rose" in 1940. Wills played many Friday nights at the Cotton Club.

After Elvis Presley's visits, music in Lubbock and on the South Plains transformed itself. It joined trends that were popular elsewhere in the country where rhythm and blues and jazz mixed with gospel ballads and country swing. Until Bill Haley, Elvis Presley, and Buddy Holly, it was basically African-American music dominated by Louis Jordan, Big Joe Turner, Ruth Brown, Chuck Berry, and Muddy Waters.

In Buddy Holly's high school days, the roots of modern rock and roll were sending down deep shoots. Thus, in the 1950s a younger generation (teenagers) turned to the black American

The Cotton Club (Courtesy Southwest Collection/Special Collections Library, Texas Tech University)

sounds of bop, rhythm and blues, and ultimately rock and roll, particularly after Elvis, Bill Haley, and Buddy Holly adopted the genre.

About the time of Elvis Presley's visits to Lubbock, or just afterward, Buddy Holly and some of his teenage friends formed the Crickets. Within three years Holly and the Crickets had skyrocketed to international fame. Inspired by their success, Lubbock's Mac Davis packed his guitar and his wit, left behind his good buddy Fat Boy Pruitt, looked at Lubbock one last time in his rear view mirror, and headed for California. There he became famous for his songs, his singing, and his short-lived television show.

Others followed. As we know—as those of us gathered here know—few other regions in the United States can claim so much music talent and so many high-level stars. Included are those who played with Buddy Holly: Bob Montgomery, Joe B. Mauldin, Glen Hardin, Jerry Allison, Sonny Curtis, Nicki Sullivan, and Waylon Jennings. Others who climbed to national recognition include Virgil Johnson, Tanya Tucker, Jimmy Dean, Bobby Keys, Mac Davis, Ralna English, Jimmy Dale Gilmore, Tommy Hancock, Don Williams, Buddy Knox, Terry Allen, Snuff Garrett, and, of course, the great Roy Orbison.

There were other musicians, too. The Gatlin Brothers and John Denver, for example, spent some formative years in Lubbock as students at Texas Tech, as did Natalie Maines. A new generation of area musicians of fame includes Butch Hancock, Joe Ely, the Maines Brothers, the Home Boys, Bruce Smith, the Flatlanders, Pat Green, Lee Ann Womac, Nancy Griffith, and Natalie Maines with her oh so powerful voice.

Reasons for the success are many, of course. But I like those offered by David Hackett Fischer. He would trace the Lubbock and South Plains music tradition eastward back through Texas and the Old South to Virginia, and ultimately to southern and western England of the 17th century. In his big book, *Albion's Seed*, on British folkways in America, Fischer impressively argues that many traditions in the United States came from one of four distinct and different sections of England. Many of those folkways relating to the South and to Texas came originally from southwestern England to Virginia and spread from there westward across the South. Over time, folkways changed and evolved, of course, but germs and seeds of the original spread to take root as people moved to and eventually settled in the West Texas region. These "germs," as Fischer calls them, included music traditions.[6]

Whatever the answer, the energetic, high voltage, drum-and-guitar-dominated rock and roll music of the kind represented by Chuck Berry, Ruth Brown, and Buddy Holly reminds me—*reminds me*, at least—of the joy and energy of Beethoven.

My mother, who once was a professional piano player, suggested that Mozart will sometimes help your digestion, but Beethoven will give you an ulcer. My mother and many people of her generation also got an ulcer from Big Joe Turner, Little Richard, Elvis Presley, and Buddy Holly. My mother's gone now, but I still listen, as I did when I was a young teenager in the late 1950s, to the lively music that now forty years later, like a Beethoven symphony, still grabs my attention, still stiffens my spine, still gives me goose bumps, and still fires my soul.

RAVE ON!

ENDNOTES

1. Holm, Bill. "Beethoven." *Minnesota Monthly* 31 (September 1998). 54.
2. Ibid.
3. Ibid.
4. Graves, Lawrence L. ed. "Lubbock From Town to City," *The Museum Journal* 23 (1986). Lubbock: West Texas Museum Association. 1986. v.
5. Ibid.
6. Fischer, David Hackett. *Albion's Seed: Four British Folkways in America*. New York: Oxford University Press, 1989. 4–10.

Carol Bolland fiddling around

WALTZ ACROSS TEXAS: AN EXPLORATION OF THE MUSIC IN THE GERMAN AND CZECH DANCE HALLS OF SOUTH CENTRAL TEXAS AND THE BANDS THAT PLAYED THE MUSIC

by Carol Bolland

"Waltz across Texas with you in my arms, waltz across Texas with you" goes the line from the Ernest Tubb country hit of 1965 that has become a standard at any dance hall in Texas.[1] Growing up a good Southern Baptist girl in Waco and Fort Worth in the 1940s and 1950s, dance halls (honky tonks) and country music were not a part of my experience. I began my musical career at age three with piano lessons and added violin lessons at age ten in the fifth grade. Lessons were during English class once a week and I couldn't imagine not wanting to take advantage of that. Besides, my mother had studied violin as a child and we still had her instrument. All of the music I learned was strictly classical, except that as a seven- or eight-year-old I learned what I thought was a great version of "Alexander's Ragtime Band," which I played one Sunday morning for the Sunday School class at North Waco Baptist Church, to the chagrin of my aunt who was in the high school class on the other side of the wall listening.

That all changed when I went to Baylor University as a music major and met one of fifty or so Lutherans (and a guitar-playing German country boy, at that) and subsequently married him. Country music quickly became a part of my experience, although, as a Missouri Synod Lutheran, he also didn't dance. My interest grew when, many years later, we retired and made our home in New Braunfels. Gruene Hall, the oldest continuously operating dance hall in Texas (or so they claim), became one of our hangouts.

Music has been a part of the heritage of Texas from the days of the Alamo (where Texas history begins, according to some). Davy Crockett is reputed to have been a fiddle player and to have played in the evenings during the battle to counter the effects of the Mexican bugler sounding "El Deguello," the Call for No Quarter.

What is of interest to me, however, is the regional dance bands that played at the small German and Czech dance halls. In particular:

- What was the makeup of the band in the '40s and '50s and how has it evolved?
- How has the set list, that is, the tunes they played, changed through the years?
- Was there a different set list according to the ethnic makeup of the hall?
- How many halls would a band play in a week?
- What was the geographic distance between halls?
- What would they have been paid?
- Were the halls considered honky tonks?

I attempt to answer some of these questions in this paper.

The middle years of the 19th century saw a large influx of settlers into Texas from the United States and Europe, especially from Czechoslovakia, Germany, and Poland. These groups tended to settle in communities of like background and maintain their language and culture. Geronimo Treviño, in his book *Dance Halls and Last Calls*,[2] notes that the dance hall/community center became a focal meeting place for their favorite pastimes of listening to singing groups and dancing. It provided the medicine (and respite) they needed from the rigors of farm work. This practice continued for at least a century and can still be seen on a limited scale today. Treviño's book documents over 100 of the old dance halls, about forty of which can be traced back to the Czech and German societies. Not all are still in existence today. Information from the Texas Dance Hall Preservation website notes that there were up to 1,000 dance halls. Although the number has diminished, a map on the website pinpointing current halls shows the majority of them being found in south central Texas, in the corridor between Waco and San Antonio and Fredericksburg and Houston.[3]

According to John and Marlys Rivard on their polka and Cajun dance website, the Czech influence is great along the I-10 corridor connecting Houston and Seguin, stretching north to Dallas and south to Victoria. The Czechs brought with them their love of music in general, and polka in particular. Soon they were gathering together, forming organizations such as Slovanská Podporující Jednota Statu Texas (SPJST) *PJST*, Sokol and Katolicá Jednota Texaská (KJT). These organizations helped to maintain their heritage while also providing socialization, insurance, and promotion of strong minds and bodies (Sokol). These organizations (and the halls that they built) became natural venues for dances. The Czech culture still dominates polka music in Texas, the authors conclude.[4]

Many sources note that the Texas sound differs from the other polka traditions that would develop in other parts of the U.S., particularly in the North and Midwest. The Texas Czech sound is considered "less Mickey Mouse," as Vrazel Polka Band leader Albert Vrazel has characterized it, than the bands up north according to Mark Rubin.[5] It is a harder sound, with more swing. In the liner notes for an album entitled *The Texas-Czech, Bohemian and Moravian Bands*, Chris Strachwitz notes that the Baca Band of Fayetteville is generally considered to be the first Czech orchestra in Texas.[6] The family arrived in 1860 from Moravia, and by 1882 Frank Baca had formed the first band with about eleven members, primarily playing brass instruments. When the band made its first recordings in 1929, the group included trumpets, drums, hammered dulcimer, violin, and clarinet. According to Mark Rubin in his review of the album, the trademark of the Baca band was the powerhouse hammered dulcimer.[7] The hammered dulcimer is a common folk instrument in almost all European cultures, but the tone Ray Baca produced on his dulcimer was a far cry from the wispy, ethereal sound of Celtic dulcimer music most folks associate with the instrument. This was a big, manly sound, bringing a whole new meaning to the term "hammered," according to Rubin. By the 1930s, Joe Patek and his Bohemian orchestra in San Antonio had added the accordion. In the 1950s, Adolph Hofner combined the oompah style with the Country-Western swing style that was so popular, and made extensive use of fiddles and guitars.[8]

Baca Band of Fayetteville (Courtesy Dolph Briscoe Center for American History)

German immigrants settled throughout Central Texas, establishing communities alongside the Czechs but also settling in Fredericksburg and New Braunfels, which remain centers for German heritage. Like their Czech neighbors, the Germans banded together for the common good. They formed *vereins* (associations) to promote their general welfare, including learning how to farm successfully and live in their New World. These *vereins* also became centers for the preservation of their music.[9] German artisans built a number of interesting dance halls around the state, including the unique eight- and twelve-sided halls constructed by Joachim Hintz in Austin County. Gerald E. McLeod, in a March 5, 2010, article in the *The Austin Chronicle*, notes the oldest and grandest of Hintz's halls, the Turnverein Pavilion, was built in Bellville.

The oldest and most elaborate of Joachim Hintz's buildings (used with permission from Geronimo Trevino's *Dance Halls and Last Calls*)

Designed around a center pole and first opened in 1897, the building has twelve sides. The windows let the breeze in and the heat escapes out the peak of the roof; and the tables swung up flat against the wall on hinges. "The band would set up around the pole," says Helen Armstrong, a member of the Austin County historical society. "Then everyone would dance around the band."[10]

Poles also came to Texas, bringing their particular style of polka music and dance to an area to the northwest of Houston, primarily Washington, Grimes, and Burleson counties. They also formed local organizations. Polish halls developed in some locations, but the music was preserved mainly within the families, playing a major role in events such as weddings and anniversaries, a tradition that continues today. The dance halls at Panna Maria and Cestohowa were built after 1900, and were not set up as social halls for the community, but rather as dance halls open to all.[11]

Brian Marshall, in an article entitled "Polish Music in Texas," featured in *Texas Polka News*, says that Polish music has been passed down orally from generation to generation, and this tradition continues today. The music of these peasant Poles typically consisted of a fiddle, a bowed bass, and an occasional clarinet. Because of the distance and separation of Texas from the northern states, the instrumentation and sound of Polish music in Texas did not progress as it did in Chicago and New York, where the bands might have wind and brass instruments. In fact, many Texas Poles shunned the idea of horns in Texas Polish bands because they felt that it "Czechanized" the music, according to Marshall.[12]

Rural communities in general and these single ethnic communities in particular, because of language and culture, were often a closed society. There was not much association with the outside world and things that were going on there. This seems to have changed to some extent after World War II, as the younger generation began to get out into the larger communities for work and school or to serve in the armed services.

I spoke with Jimmy Cuccia of New Braunfels, who played with the Texas Tune Wranglers during the 1950s. The Wranglers included guitar, steel guitar, mandolin, fiddle, and drums. According to Jimmy, after World War II both oompah bands and string bands might play at the various halls in the area bounded by San Antonio and Austin, extending east as far as Gonzales. He named about a dozen venues in Comal and Guadalupe counties alone where the Texas Tune Wranglers played regularly. They would be paid a percentage of the ticket sales, most often 70–75%, although Smithson Valley was a favorite location for them, according to Cuccia, because they received 80% of the gate there.[13]

In the small community halls, the bands that would play every Friday and Saturday night would probably be local, although Cuccia said the Czech bands might come to German halls and vice versa. The big bands, such as Bob Wills and Adolf Hofner, didn't come to the smaller halls because the old farmers weren't willing to pay the price required to attract them. According to Cuccia, the dances generally lasted four hours with a twenty-minute break for the band after two hours.

The music, at least early on, would be very similar, with all bands, oompah or string, local or Czech, playing primarily dance music, with a lot of waltzes and polkas. The Tune Wranglers generally opened their dance with "Out on the Texas Plains," a popular country/western song; "Over the Waves,"a German-style waltz; and the Polish classic "Julida Polka." From that point on it was strictly requests made by walking up to the band stand and asking for a tune. The band would have a repertoire of 100 or so tunes from which to draw, which would include the aforementioned German waltzes and polkas, modern country hits by singers such as Eddy Arnold and Ernest Tubb, and some Bob Wills swing tunes. Cuccia's theory is that, with the rise in popularity of radios in the homes and the return of soldiers after the war, there was greater interest in the more modern, country-western music, which featured string bands, particularly among the younger generation. It didn't seem to matter if they played in a German hall or a Czech hall; the music pretty much was the same.

One of the popular waltzes was the "Westphalia Waltz." Just east of Temple, off I-35, is a small community of Westphalia, founded by Germans from the Westphalian region of Germany. One story is that a returning soldier played a waltz he had learned in Germany and it became so popular in that hall that it was named the "Westphalia Waltz."[14] Another story, presented in a documentary "The Waltz to Westphalia" is that in the late 1930s and early 1940s Cotton Collins, a fiddler from Waco, heard the tune in nearby Bremond, then the largest Polish settlement in Texas. Collins, influenced by the Texas fiddle tradition, heard the Polish song and re-worked it into a Texas fiddle waltz. Collins performed with the Lone Star Playboys, a popular radio and touring band that frequently played nearby Westphalia, only thirty-five miles south of Waco. The locals suggested to Collins that he name the piece the "Westphalia Waltz."[15] Whatever the truth of the origin, it continues to be a popular waltz heard at most dances in the halls even today, and often features twin fiddles.

A highlight of the evening at most dances, according to Cuccia, was the Paul Jones, in which the men would form an outer circle with the women on the inside in a circle. A whistle would blow, the band would play, and the women would circle in one direction and the men the other. At the sound of the whistle everyone stopped and danced a waltz with the person they faced. At another whistle the rotation began again. At the next whistle it was a new partner and a polka. This apparently continued for some time.[16]

The Martinez Social Club near San Antonio, and probably others, still has a Stroll, which is similar in intent but the sexes simply line up on opposite sides of the hall, meet in the middle, dance the length of the hall, and join the line. In 2002 or so, we attended a dance at Anhalt Hall, which opens its doors a couple of times a year to the public. There was no Paul Jones or Stroll, as I recall, but the dancers were dancing in a large circle, rather than the scattered patterns you might see at other dances. It was fun to watch as they all bobbed up and down in unison.

At the height of the popularity of these dances, the 1920s–1940s, according to Cuccia, the entire family would come to the hall. The community might be primarily one extended family, and the Saturday night dance was the chance for everyone to get together and visit in a social setting. Typically, no alcohol was permitted inside the dance hall, distinguishing it from the saloons or honky tonks, which were not so family friendly and probably not to be found in these small outlying farming communities. Outside buildings were erected for the sale of alcohol and food. Cuccia said the hall at Geronimo served the best burger for 30 cents. Soft drinks were 8 cents and beer 18 cents.[17]

I recall in the mid-'60s attending such a dance in Fredericksburg with my new "Lutheran German, guitar playing" husband. There were folks of all ages from toddlers to senior citizens on the floor having a grand time. Try as I might I couldn't find any sinning going on. With more homes acquiring television in the '50s the outlying dance halls suffered. Transportation improved and people began to go into the larger cities. According to Cuccia, Charlie Walker, a deejay at KMSE radio station in San Antonio, was largely responsible for Gruene Hall in New Braunfels becoming a popular destination.[18]

Today, the dances are not held every week at most places, but may only occur several times a year. Anhalt Hall, between Bulverde and Boerne, hosts dances a few times a year, which generally have a German oompah band in the afternoon and a country string band in the evening, a practice which only began in the 1990s, according to a long-time member of the Verein. Fall "Octoberfest" celebrations, particularly Wurstfest in New Braunfels and Oktoberfest in Fredericksburg, bring an onslaught of old-time oompah sounds, polkas, and the Chicken Dance.

The rise of Rock and Roll in the 1950s created a chasm between generations in kinds of dances and music which was not always spanned. However, even today, at halls such as Anhalt and Gruene, one still sees tots dancing in the arms of dad, youngsters on the floor learning the two step, teenagers showing off their swing skills, and adults of all ages enjoying their own style of dancing to the same music from the band, whether it be a two-step, a polka or, of course, a waltz.

ENDNOTES

1. Tubb, Ernest. "Waltz Across Texas," rec. Decca Records. April 19, 1965.
2. Treviño III, Geronimo. *Dance Halls and Last Calls: A History of Texas Country Music*. Plano, Texas: Republic of Texas Press, 2002. 1.
3. "Historic Texas Dance Halls." map. *Texas Dance Hall Preservation, Inc*. website. http://www.texasdancehall.org.
4. Rivard, John & Marlys. "Polka in Texas." *John and Marlys Rivard*, website. http://www.angelfire.com/folk/polka/texas/html.
5. Rubin, Mark. "Review of Texas-Czech, Bohemian-Moravian Bands: Historic Recording, *1929–1959*." *Mark Rubin*, website. http://www.markrubin.com/published/texczech.html.
6. Strachwitz, Chris. CD liner notes. *Texas-Czech, Bohemian-Moravian Bands: Historic Recording, 1929–1959*. Arhoolie/Folklyric, Inc. 1993. 2.
7. Rubin.

8. Strachwitz.
9. Rivard.
10. McLeod, Gerald E. "Day Trips." *The Austin Chronicle*, E-Edition. March 5, 2010. http://www.austinchronicle.com/columns/2010-03-5/975324.
11. Rivard.
12. Rivard. "Polish Music in Texas."
13. Cuccia, Jimmy. Personal interview by the author. New Braunfels. May 26, 2011.
14. Coppedge, Clay. "Westphalia Waltz." *TexasEscapes.com.* On-line magazine.http://www.texasescapes.com/ClayCoppedge/Westphalia-Waltz.htm.
15. Weed, Joe. "A brief overview of "The Westphalia Waltz Story." *Joe Weed* website. http://www.joeweed.com/documentaries/westphalia_waltz/htm
16. Cuccia interview.
17. Ibid.
18. Ibid.

Carol and her husband Herb Bolland at a TFS Hoot

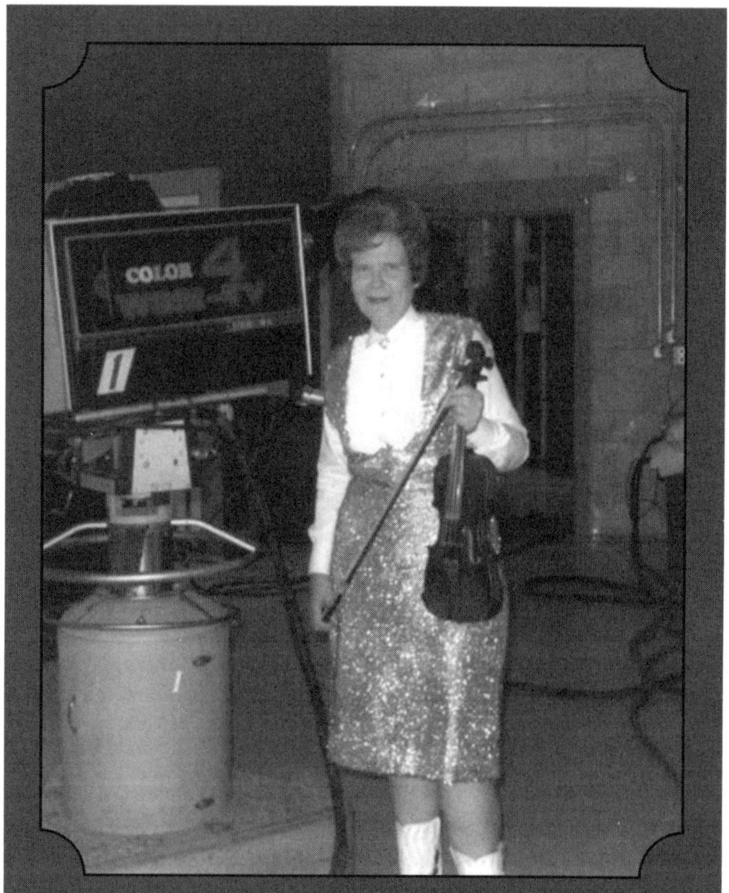

Ruby Allmond, 2005 (Photo courtesy of Audra Brock)

THE MUSIC OF RUBY ALLMOND

by Jerry B. Lincecum

Like all good stories, the one of Fannin County musician Ruby Allmond's career has three distinct parts. First was the struggle to gain recognition as a performer. Then came three decades as a songwriter, with several Nashville hits, including one top-ten single. Part three, defining a legacy, continues through an annual Ruby Allmond songwriting contest (with $600 in prize money) administered by Texas A&M University–Commerce, which also has an extensive archive of her life's work, with a biography planned.

Ruby Nell Allmond was born in 1923 on a farm in southeast Fannin County, near the Bailey community. Her parents were Arthur M. Allmond and Lou Cole Allmond. Arthur Allmond, who came from Missouri, grew cotton and corn on a blackland farm. Lou Cole came from Tennessee, and she had blue eyes and sparkling humor that Ruby inherited. Ruby was the youngest of four children, with a sister, Delia Mae, and two brothers, James Roy and Charlie Raymond. Many of her friends called her "Chub," which was a nickname given her by an older brother when she was a toddler. Ruby passed away on January 23, 2006, at the age of eighty-two.[1]

Ruby was born into a musical family, with members who played the fiddle, guitar, banjo, and mandolin. As a small child, she learned to play the guitar while sitting on the lap of her father, who also held the instrument for her. At the age of four she first performed on the guitar at a nearby school, and the enthusiastic response to this event spurred her on. Soon, she was learning to play her brother Raymond's fiddle. In an effort to keep his fiddle out of her reach, Raymond placed it high up on the wall, but she always managed to get it. One day as he and Roy were coming home from work in the field, they heard the fiddle being played by Ruby. Roy said, "Listen to that, Raymond, she can already play better than you can." So Ruby was then allowed to practice on the fiddle. As her playing in public drew more praise, Ruby became determined to disprove the common idea that "no woman could play the fiddle well." After high school she practiced as much as eight hours a day in order to master the instrument.

Ruby was highly intelligent and schoolwork was easy for her. In high school she excelled in essay writing, and was eligible to go to state-level competition one year. But these were hard times, and the basketball team was also eligible to go to state. The school district decided there was not enough money to go around, so Ruby stayed home. But her skill in composing songs was certainly foreshadowed by the verbal ability she demonstrated in school.

After completing high school, Ruby continued to live at home with her parents. She farmed in partnership with her dad and also worked on her fiddle playing and her stage personality, taking part in local performances in homes, schools, and community centers. She developed a style of play that involved making a rhythm with the fiddle bow as she played and also emphasized harmonies and double notes. She also began traveling as far as Abilene, Texas, and Durant, Oklahoma, to perform with other musicians and play in shows.

Two top-notch fiddle players who regularly performed with her for a trio fiddle show in the late 1940s were Georgia "Slim" Rutland and Howard "Howdy" Forrester. There was no telephone on the Allmond farm, and Rutland and Forrester had an interesting way to inform Ruby about where to meet them for the next show. They appeared regularly on the "Cornbread Matinee" show daily at noon on KRLD radio in Dallas, hosted by Hal Horton. During the course of the show they would announce where they would be performing that weekend. Ruby made sure she listened to the show, and her brothers Raymond and Roy, who played with her, would then pick her up and drive to the show. Harold Carder also played stand-up bass with them. Greenville Municipal Auditorium was their favorite venue, and there Ruby was billed as the National Champion Woman Fiddler.

Ruby then put together her own band, called "The Texas Jamboree," which was advertised as a "Top-notch Fiddle Band." In addition to her, it included Guy Bryant and his son and daughter, Gene and Joyce, on mandolin and acoustic guitars, plus Clay Har-

Texas Jamboree Band: Guy Bryant, Joyce Bryant, Ruby Allmond, Clay Harvey, and Gene Bryant (Photo courtesy of Audra Brock)

vey on stand-up bass. Congressman Sam Rayburn, Speaker of the U. S. House of Representatives, carried them with him on the campaign trail as he ran for re-election in 1950. An article that appeared in the *Ladonia News* in the fall of 1950 read as follows:

RAYBURN RALLY: CANDIDATE SPEAKING HERE

GOOD PROGRAM PREPARED; MUSIC BY RUBY NELL ALLMOND AND BAND OF BAILEY

> The program of the evening is scheduled to get underway at 7:45, with thirty minutes of music by Ruby Nell Allmond, famous woman fiddler and her string band, will precede Mr. Rayburn's address. After the talk there will be more music by the band and all candidates for Fannin County offices will be invited to speak.

Ruby thought very highly of Mr. Rayburn and was happy to support his campaign by having her band entertain at rallies where he spoke. She also gained valuable experience and public exposure from those shows.

In the early 1950s, interest in the local music shows died out as the public turned to TV and other forms of entertainment, and that is when Ruby began writing songs. Audra Brock recalls that when she returned to the Bailey community in 1953, after having been away for a while, it was evident to her that Ruby had gained skill in performing and also in composing. In order to preserve her songs as Ruby composed and performed them, Audra bought a good quality tape recorder, and Ruby allowed her to tape the songs as she sang and played them as part of her composition process. Making these tapes of her songs greatly encouraged her. For about the next thirty years, until 1982, she concentrated on writing songs and produced many good ones. As Ruby composed dozens of songs Audra continued to make audiotapes, and her extensive collection offers a rare documentation of the creative process in musical composition.

Ruby's composition technique was unusual. From 1956 to 1988, she worked full-time at Bonham State Bank (as did Audra), and during the day she would think about ideas for a new song and begin composing words and music in her mind. After working a full day at the bank, she would come home to her father and eat supper and visit with him. Then she would go to Audra's house, where they had a small studio. She would pick up her guitar and begin to play and sing the new song. She already had a version of the words, the tune, and the melody all worked out in her head, and she always insisted on playing and singing it through without stopping. She used a classical guitar so her voice could be heard clearly over the music. If the guitar needed to be tuned or have a string tightened, she did not want to stop until she had played and sung the new composition through and gotten it out of her head and on tape. Although she might have the words jotted down, she never wrote the notes out on the music staff. It was all worked out as a whole in her head. When she finished revising a song, it was layered with meaning, like a poem or other quality literature.

In 1968, Ruby and Audra decided they wanted to take some of her songs to Nashville to see if well-known performers would like to record them. Before making the trip, they visited Cindy Walker, a famous songwriter who lived in Mexia, Texas. Without even hearing Ruby's songs, Cindy was so impressed with her talent that she told them to go to Nashville and talk to Bob Jennings at RCA Music. She said she would call Bob and tell him about Ruby, and she felt sure he would introduce her to Chet Atkins, one of the most prominent musical performers in Nashville.

Taking a week of vacation from their jobs at Bonham State Bank, Ruby and Audra traveled to Nashville and met Bob Jennings. He later said that when he first listened to the tape of Ruby performing some of her songs, they were so good that "the hair stood up on the back of his neck." He took them to a studio for a demonstration recording session, using as a drummer D. J. Fontana, who had performed with Elvis Presley.

By the time they left Nashville, Jennings had agreed to contract six of Ruby's songs. She did not have to pay anything for the use of the studio or the musicians, and the contract she signed with Four Star Music gave them the right to publish her songs and place them with an artist, with her receiving royalties for all sales of recordings and play times on radio shows. Chet Atkins took two of her songs, and Dottie West made her song "Reno" a top-ten hit.

Other artists who recorded some of her songs were Stu Phillips, Ferlin Husky, Jimmy Ellis, and George Morgan. Beginning in 1968, Ruby received annual royalty payments for her songs. Whenever Audra hears some young composer say that he or she sold a song for $50, she thinks, "What a waste! If it was good enough to sell, you could have collected royalties on it for many years."

Ruby and Audra began using their vacation time from the bank to take trips to Nashville twice a year, because it was evident that making those visits enabled them to keep their contacts fresh and meet more artists. Whenever they went to Nashville, they were allowed to sit in on recording sessions. Audra recalls observing sessions with Jimmy Dean, Dottie West, and other stars of country music. From time to time, Ruby would receive calls from Bob Jennings or others in Nashville requesting songs of a certain type, especially love songs or songs for male artists.

These semiannual trips to Nashville continued for a number of years, until the illness of Ruby's father in 1974 interfered with her writing and also her desire to make the trips. But from about 1982 to 1988, she made guest appearances at country music shows in the local area. One of her reasons for doing this was to encourage young musicians and teach them how to perform on stage, as she had learned to do. Her personality and good humor made her a favorite, especially among young male performers.

In 1979, Ruby suffered a fall that broke her hip and wrist, and she had to undergo three surgeries to repair her hip. Afterwards,

Ruby (second from right, back row) and her band (Photo courtesy of Audra Brock)

she had to walk with a cane. She always left the cane backstage, using a male escort to bring her to the microphone. She would wave her fiddle to the audience and immediately win them over with her combination of a beautiful singing voice and skilled play. During this period she performed on numerous occasions with Joe Shelton's band at a school auditorium outside Sulphur Springs, Texas. She took part in two shows with June Carter, and sang with her in a spontaneous skit that was humorous. Audra remembers that the audience was filled with laughter by their comic duet.

Before Ruby passed away, she and Audra worked on producing a book and a set of compact discs that would preserve and

The book featuring lyrics to Ruby's songs

showcase her music. Ruby chose the title for the book: *Today I'll Think About the Rain*, which comes from one of her songs. The subtitle is *An Anthology*, and it prints the lyrics to forty-one of her songs. Part One, entitled "Sounds of Texas," includes lyrics to nine songs. The second part, "A Little About Life," has fourteen songs. Part Three, "A Lot About Love," presents eighteen more. The book comes with a pair of compact discs that feature Ruby performing the songs in each of the three sections. Prefatory notes in the book indicate that copyrights to 14 of the songs are owned by Sony/ATV Music Publishing in Nashville, while the remaining 27 are copyrighted by Ruby Allmond. This handsome hardbound book, with the two accompanying compact discs, provides easy access to the life work of an important artist and performer. For more information, visit the website: www.rubyallmond.com.

In a prefatory note about the recordings, Audra writes: "These are not meant to be slick, commercial-type recordings; they are historical, natural, real—to be enjoyed, appreciated now and carried into a future time to show the music of the period. They were made in Ruby's home when she was composing the songs. She used a classic guitar and usually there was a different type of accompaniment on each song."

Other Nashville writers and performers saw a high level of artistry in Allmond's work. For example, one of her fellow writers, who used the pen name Jean Chapel, had a #1 hit record on the Billboard chart one week in 1973, entitled "To Get to You." She and Ruby worked for the same publisher, and when Ruby complimented Jean on her hit, the writer said, in all sincerity, "Oh, Honey, I can't even carry your shoes." Chet Atkins, who was very careful about his comments on artists, told Ruby that he considered her "a great songwriter."

Fortunately, the Ruby Allmond Music Collection is now a part of the Special Collections of Texas A&M University–Commerce. This extensive archive of audiotapes, sheet music, photos, instruments, and other materials is being administered in a way that will insure the preservation of this Fannin County artist's life work.

Endnote

1. Rather than print sources, this essay is based almost entirely on a series of interviews with Audra M. Brock, the close friend and literary executor of Ruby Allmond. One source was an unpublished essay by Audra M. Brock, "Ruby Allmond: Sounds of Texas Music, 1923–2006." Many thanks to Joan Snider, who initially interviewed Brock for the Fannin County Oral History project, and to Joyce Bryant, who was generous in sharing scrapbooks put together by her mother, Mrs. Veola Bryant of Bonham. These included posters and newspaper clippings that proved invaluable as my own interviews were shaped first into a magazine piece (for *Texoma Living*, Spring 2008) and then a TFS presentation. A short version of the piece (with numerous photos provided by Audra Brock) appeared in the *Herald Democrat* newspaper (Sherman, Texas) January 22, 2013 (pp. B1, B3). The Ruby Allmond Music Collection at Texas A&M University–Commerce deserves careful scrutiny by historians and scholars.

A Dustbowl family

SONGS OF THE DEPRESSION

by Francis Edward Abernethy

"Beans, Bacon, and Gravy"

I was born long ago, in 1894,
And I've seen lots of hard times, that is true;
I've been hungry, I've been cold,
And now I'm growing old.
But the worst I've seen is 1932.

Refrain:
Oh, those beans, bacon, and gravy,
They almost drive me crazy,
I eat them till I see them in my dreams,
In my dreams,
When I wake up in the morning,
A Depression day is dawning,
And I know I'll have another mess of beans.

We have Hooverized our butter,
For blued our milk with water,
And I haven't eaten meat in any way;
As for pies, cakes, and jelly,
We substitute sow-belly,
For which we work the county roads each day.

There are several advantages to living a long time, one of which is that you become historical. You begin to find the commonplace times of your life in history books. The Depression was a distinct part of my life, and I talked to my father about these years and it was even more distinctly a part of his.

Every generation is the product of its parents. The Depression was the offspring of the Roaring Twenties. Will Rogers said of the Depression: "We're the first nation in the history of the world to go to the poor house in an automobile." So, you can better understand a child by knowing its parents.

And speaking of parents, traditional mothers in the *early* Twenties, before it was in full roar, still required their daughters to wear the restrictive foundation garment of the day, corsets that were equipped to hold up black hose. Traditional daughters hastened to restrooms and removed such impediments to the Charleston, Black Bottom, and the Shimmy. An illustrative classic of the Jazz Age was sung, "I wish I could shimmy like my sister Kate. / She could shimmy, she could shake it like jello on a plate." For those of you who are interested, the word "shimmy" comes from the French *chemise*, and the full name of the dance was the Shimmie Shewobble.

The Twenties were soon in full roar, and the culture shock suffered by that decade's elders must have been massive. Few times, standing so close together, has there been such a sharp line of distinction as that which existed between pre- and post-WWI. The world before WWI had been Jeffersonianly rural with all the conservative moral values of that way of life. The post-war Twenties were urban and in direct reaction against all relics of Victorian morality. The Twenties continued with a material prosperity such as ordinary Americans had not known before. With jobs to be had and good wages, the American people were able to buy cars, radios, phonographs, and a host of labor-saving electrical appliances. They paid to see professional sports. They went to college—and Europe. They borrowed money and they bought things on credit, and this is what will come back to haunt them. They lived better than any pre-WWI American society, and they tried to be everything their parents had not. As a parent during the Hippy Sixties and Seventies, I can sympathize with my own grandparents who had the rearing of their children in the Twenties.

By the mid-Twenties female style had achieved the asexual flat look, bustless and buttless, that announced that recreation, not procreation, was the purpose of sex. Ironically, the young Flappers who had earlier divested themselves of their corsets to free their bodies for the Shimmy and the Charleston, by 1926 were wearing tube-like foundation garments to flatten out their curves. The generation announced through its worldly ways that pleasure was the purpose of life.

And do you realize that the Roaring Twenties are the first years in recorded western civilization when women wore skirts that revealed their legs and cut their hair short or wore *flesh*-colored hose—and pants! This was the world of our now-sainted mothers and grandmothers, we must remember.

We came to the end of that roaring, fast changing time, in 1929, with Americans singing the theme song of that entire decade, Irving Berlin's "Blue Skies":

> Blue skies, shinin' on me
> Nothin but blue skies
> Do I see.
>
> Blue birds, singin' a song
> Nothin but blue birds
> All the day long.
>
> Never saw the sun shinin' so bright
> Never saw things lookin' so right.
> Oughta see the days hurryin' by
> When you're in love
> How time does fly.
>
> Blue days, all of them gone.
> Nothing but blue skies
> From now on.

The prosperity and boundless optimism of the Twenties *almost* made it through that decade; there would be "blue skies from now on." America had seen eight years of an expanding Stock Market and believed in its continuation. Proving the investor's optimism, the stocks went up in what was called the Great Sleigh Ride of the summer of '29 to an all-time high on September 3. After that there was no way to go but down.

On October 24, Black Thursday, the Market tumbled. A group of bankers rushed in and bought stock and restored some of the trust, but confidence faltered over the weekend, and investors came back Monday morning ready to sell. Tuesday, October 29, was The Day of the Crash. The financial world of the Twenties and everything that was a part of it turned upside down on that Black Tuesday. Savings and investments were lost, and the financial dominos began a tumble that soon would reach down to the least of persons in this bountiful land of ours. The Great Depression came to Texas, the U. S., and the world. It stayed until it was rescued by the World War II economy, and the effects were felt by everybody before it was over.

I move into an autobiographical mode, not to regale you with the details of my childhood, but to reveal how one family lived through the early years of the Depression.

In 1929, Dad had the Dodge agency in Shamrock, Texas, but lost it within a year of the Crash, and we moved back to Granddad's ranch in the Panhandle. Mother did not last long in the high lonesome of that place. The ranch was five miles from the mailbox and nearest neighbor, and seventeen miles from the nearest town. Mother was an East Texas girl, and the wind and the treeless space of the high plains depressed her considerably. A mockingbird in a bush outside her bedroom window afforded her some relief, some piece of beauty in that bare expanse. Then, one morning as she watched him sing, a cat sprang upon him and reduced him to feathers. That was the end. Mother had them drive her to Childress, where she caught the Fort Worth and Denver back to Dallas, where her parents lived. Dad and I stayed on the ranch.

Families lived together and held together during the Depression just to survive. Dad's three brothers, and Mother's two brothers and sister helped each other. When I started to school in '31, I was moved to my maternal grandparents' home in Dallas, where it took four people working to support six, my grandmother and I the only ones not working. Granddad Cherry, who had been the contractor for several major buildings in Dallas, and who owned his home, an apartment building, and a farm, had lost everything and was reduced to maintenance and repair work. My Uncle Francis, who was a mechanical genius, lost a car one year because he could not make a $7.50 payment. Mother worked in a ladies' ready-to-wear store in downtown Dallas selling dresses on commission. Dad worked on the ranch when the seasons required, and between crops and roundups sold shoes on commission or helped

Granddad Cherry and worked at anything he could find. Until he died he would still shake his head in wonder when he remembered how it was to have nothing and not have any idea where he was going to find work. When school was out, he and I would hitch-hike the 350 miles from Dallas back to the ranch.

Dad wandered all over Texas and Oklahoma looking for work—as did thousands of other men. He did not get a steady job until 1934. One of the folk songs circulating during the Hoover years described the drifting, hopeless situation of the wanderers of the Depression.

"Wanderin'"

I've been wanderin', early and late
From New York City to the Golden Gate.
Looks like I'm never gonna cease my wanderin'.

I've been wanderin' far and wide,
I go with the wind and ride with the tide.

Been workin' in the army, been workin' on the farm,
And all I've got to show for it is the muscle in my arm.

Ashes to ashes, dust to dust,
If the Republicans can't help us the Democrats must.

Granddad Abernethy's ranch (an original watercolor by James Snyder)

1930 was the year of the apple sellers. A bumper crop of northwestern apples for a short while provided the Depression's unemployed with an opportunity at capitalism. The ambitious jobless could buy a crate of seventy-two apples for $1.75, sell them at a nickel apiece, and make a profit of $1.85, which was a good day's pay. This lasted until the competition increased and wholesalers kicked the price up to $2.25 a box and higher. But as short-lived as it was, selling apples became a symbol of Depression entrepreneurialism. One of the enduring comic strips began in 1938 as "Apple Mary," about a Depression woman who was reduced to selling apples on the street corner to support herself and her crippled grandson. The strip evolved into our present "Mary Worth," with little or no resemblance to the Depression ancestor.

Calvin Coolidge, at the time an editorialist, had said, "When more and more people are thrown out of work, unemployment results." By 1931, over eight million people had been thrown out of work and there was nationwide unemployment. Every city had its bread lines and soup kitchens managed by individual charities. President Hoover was not yet convinced the nation was in a depression, or if it was, it was caused by the Europeans. Hoover also believed that federal relief would rob the people of their dignity. Thus, the national government did little for the welfare of the jobless and the homeless, and the result was a new generation of panhandlers, men who had once been self-supporting, who had fought for their country in WWI. Out of this common experience came the theme song of the Depression.

"Brother, Can You Spare a Dime?"

They used to tell me I was building a dream,
So I followed the mob—
When there was earth to plow or guns to bear,
I was always there—right on the job.

They use to tell me I was building a dream
With peace and glory ahead—
Why should I be standing in line
Just waiting for (a piece of) bread?

Once I built a railroad, made it run,
Made it race against time.
Once I built a railroad, now it's done.
Brother, can you spare a dime?

Once I built a tower to the sun,
Brick and mortar and lime.
Once I built a tower, now it's done.
Brother, can you spare a dime?

Once in khaki suits, Gee, we looked swell,
Full of that Yankee Doodle Dum.
Half a million boots marched into hell—
And I was the guy on the drum!

Hey, don't you remember me; they called me Al.
It was "Hey, Al" all of the time.
Don't you remember; I was your pal.
Hey, Brother, can you spare a dime?

Herbert Hoover was packing for a move in 1932, and his last year was not a happy one. Banks and businesses were failing, unemployment was rising, and a spirit of hopelessness was on the land. Americans blamed the president, and the dispossessed called their shanty towns "Hoovervilles." The poor ate "Hoover hogs" (armadillos) when they could catch them, and slept in the cold, sheltered by "Hoover blankets," or newspapers. Wanderers, hobos, and bums became a visible part of American life, and living off the land and handouts became a way of life for many. An amazing number of songs grew out of this new element of society.

"Hallelujah, I'm a Bum"

Oh, why don't you work
Like other men do?
How the hell can I work
When there's no work to do?

Hallelujah, I'm a bum,
Hallelujah, bum again,
Hallelujah, give us a handout,
To revive us again.

I went to a house
And I knocked on the door;
The lady came out, says,
"You been here before."

I went to a house,
And I asked for some bread;
The lady came out, says,
"The baker is dead."

When springtime does come,
O won't we have fun,
We'll throw up our jobs
And we'll go on the bum.

Visionary songs—some cynical, some resigned—appeared, including parodies.

"Sweet Bye and Bye" (a parody)

You will eat bye and bye,
In that glorious land in the sky.
Work and pray, live on hay,
You'll have pie in the sky when you die.

Definitely not a children's song, "The Big Rock Candy Mountain" was the hobos' classic fantasy song, describing a perfect world for the Knights of the Open Road.

"The Big Rock Candy Mountain"

In the Big Rock Candy Mountain
You never change your socks,
And little streams of alcohol
Come a-trickling down the rocks.
The box cars are all empty
And the railroad bulls are blind,
There's a lake of stew and whisky, too,
You can paddle around in a big canoe
In the Big Rock Candy Mountains.

Chorus:
O—the buzzing of the bees in the cigarette trees
And the soda-water fountains,
And the bluebird sings by the lemonade springs
In the Big Rock Candy Mountains.

In the Big Rock Candy Mountains,
There's a land that's fair and bright,
Where the hand-outs grow on bushes
And you sleep out every night,
Where the box cars are all empty
And the sun shines every day,
O I'm bound to go, where there ain't no snow,
Where the rain don't fall and the wind don't blow
In the Big Rock Candy Mountains

The most famous Hooverville sprang up in Washington, D.C., when the Bonus Expeditionary Force arrived that summer of '32 lobbying for early payment of their WWI bonus. They camped on the Potomac until July 28, when the President sent troops under General Douglas MacArthur (with Major Dwight D. Eisenhower in the ranks), who very unpolitically rousted them out with fire and sword. Veterans remembered the bonus marchers that November when Herbert Hoover met Franklin D. Roosevelt at the polls. There was no way that the glum, Depression-ridden Hoover could beat a man who smiled like sunshine and whose theme song was "Happy Days Are Here Again!"

Incidentally, several songs of optimism illustrated the hope that was—and is—always a part of life: "Let a Smile be Your Umbrella on a Rainy, Rainy Day," "Let's Have Another Cup of Coffee" ("Just around the corner, there's a rainbow in the sky, / So let's have another cup of coffee and let's have another piece of pie"), and "Life is Just a Bowl of Cherries" ("Don't make it serious; life's too mysterious / You work, you save, you worry so / But you can't take your dough when you go go go. / Life is just a bowl of cherries, so live and laugh at it all").

Back to "Happy Days": The nominating committee had planned to play "Anchors Aweigh" to welcome Roosevelt, who had been Assistant Secretary of the Navy, but the tune sounded so glum after the nominating speech that his campaign manager suggested "Happy Days," a pop song from the 1929 musical *Chasing Rainbows.* In the musical, the song was sung in the trenches when the soldiers heard about the Armistice.

> Happy Days are here again,
> The skies above are clear again
> Let's sing a song of cheer again,
> Happy Days are here again.
>
> All together, shout it now!
> There is no one who can doubt it now,
> So let's tell the world about it now,
> Happy days are here again.
>
> Your cares and trouble are gone.
> There'll be no more from now on—
>
> Happy days are here again,
> The skies above are clear again,
> Let us sing a song of cheer again,
> Happy days are here again.

Enough people were looking for a new way of life—a New Deal!—to overwhelmingly elect Franklin Delano Roosevelt as the President of the United States. He took office on Saturday, March 4, 1933, announced a bank holiday for Monday, March 6, and on March 9 began a Hundred Days of restructuring the socio-political system of the U.S.A. He told Americans that "the only thing we have to fear is fear itself—nameless, unreasoning, unjustified terror which paralyzes needed efforts to convert retreat into advance." In his first Hundred Days, between March 9 and June 16, Roosevelt fought that fear with action. He called for the legalization of beer and the abolition of the gold standard and created an Alphabet Soup of agencies—AAA, CCC, TVA, NRA, PWA, ad infinitum—designed to help Americans regain financial control of their lives. He started America on a course of government involvement in citizens' lives that the nation is still following. But mainly, Franklin D. Roosevelt was taking decisive action to help a struggling people, and most Americans thanked him for it.

In 1932 Will Rogers said, "Last year they said things couldn't go on like this. They were right: they didn't—they got worse." Particularly so for the farmers. Farm prices had not been good since WWI, and they fell even more after the Crash. Roosevelt established a Bureau of Farm Relief, which established a commission to study the plight of the farmer. Will Rogers said: "They won't take the farmer's word for it that he's poor. They hire men to find out how poor he is. If they took all the money they spend on finding out how poor he is and give it to the farmer, he wouldn't need any more relief." Cotton hit the bottom in '31 and '32 at 6¢ down to 5¢ a pound. It wasn't worth the picking.

"Seven Cent Cotton, Twenty Cent Meat"

Seven cent cotton, twenty cent meat
How in the world can a poor man eat?

Flour up high, cotton down low
How in the world can we raise the dough?

Our clothes worn out, shoes run down
Old slouch hat with a hole in the crown
Back nearly broken, fingers all wore
Cotton goin' down to rise no more.

Seven cent cotton, twenty cent meat
How in the world can a poor man eat?

Then, on top of the bottom dropping out of the cotton and grain market, the boll weevil hit in '33 and '34 and destroyed what little cotton the farmers could pray up out of the ground. The following is a black blues song. Blacks were worse off than whites.

"Boll Weevil Song"

De first time I seen de boll weevil,
He was a-settin' on de square.
De next time I seen de boll weevil, he had all of his family dere.
Jus' a-lookin' foh a home, jus' a-lookin' foh a home.

De farmer take de boll weevil,
An' he put him in de hot san'.
De weevil say: "Dis is mighty hot, but I'll stan' it
like a man,
Dis'll be my home, it'll be my home."

De farmer take de boll weevil,
An' he put him in a lump of ice;
De boll weevil say to de farmer: "Dis is mighty cool and nice,
It'll be my home, dis'll be my home."

De boll weevil say to de farmer:
"You better leave me alone;
I done eat all yo' cotton, now I'm goin' to start
on yo' corn,
I'll have a home, I'll have a home."

De merchant got half de cotton,
De boll weevil got de res'.

Didn't leave de farmer's wife but one old cotton dress,
An' it's full of holes, it's full of holes.

An' if anybody ever axes you
Who it was done writ dis song,
Jus' tell 'em was a poor old cullud man wid a paih
o' blue duckin's on
Ain' got no home, ain' got no home.

And then, on top of the Depression, a crashed market, and boll weevils, the Drouth hit, and the crops dried up and the land blew away. The farmers plowed again, all up and down the Great Plains, and the soil stayed dry and loose. The winds blew, as they always do on the Plains, and Kansas ended up in the Panhandle of Texas. And the Panhandle of Texas became the Dust Bowl.

Lubbock's C of C advertised that it was The Land of the Five-inch Rain—the drops were five inches apart. It was so dry in the Panhandle that cows gave evaporated milk, and chickens plucked themselves to escape the heat. The dusters came in so hard that one hen got caught with her tail pointed north and had to lay the same egg twelve times. The crops were so bad that the crows had to lie on their stomachs to steal corn—and ducks and frogs fell into buckets of water and drowned. It got so dry that the Baptists started sprinkling and the Methodists just used a damp cloth. And one Panhandle cowboy got struck by a drop of rain, and the shock was so great it took two buckets of sand to revive him. The Waggoner ranch needed water so bad that they offered to swap oil for water, barrel for barrel. That's supposed to be true. They drilled for water and got oil.

Woody Guthrie, who lived in and around Pampa town, was Texas' Dust Bowl troubadour. He wrote this song about dusters, particularly Black Easter (April 14, 1935) in Gray County in the Panhandle during the Depression.

"Dusty Old Dust"

I've sung this song, but I'll sing it again.
Of the place that I lived on the wild windy plains.

In the month called April, the county called Gray,
Here is what all of the people there say:

Chorus:
So long it's been good to know you,
So long it's been good to know you,
So long it's been good to know you,
This dusty old dust is getting my home
And I've got to be drifting along.

A dust storm hit, and it hit like thunder.
It dusted us over, and it covered us under.
Backed up the traffic and blocked out the sun.
Straight for home all the people did run – singin'

Chorus

The church it was jammed, and the church it was packed.
And that dusty old dust storm it came up so black
That the preacher could not read a word of his text,
So he folded his specs, and he took up collections—and said

Chorus

Dish towels in the windows, dust on the horse trough and in the milk house, food was always gritty.

Back in the cities many businesses and industries went under with the Crash, and those that were left struggled to survive. The way many industries survived was at the expense of the working man. They cut wages and stretched the hours, and there were plenty of people desperate enough to work that they would take any job for just about any wages—and work from can to can't for a meager day's pay. The industries that took advantage of the Depression to hire cheap and work long, found themselves in the mid-Thirties facing the rising power of the unions. Unions were never generally popular and were equated by many with the breakdown of traditional capitalism and the rising power of world Communism. Lenin had said, "Workers of the world arise! You have nothing to lose but your chains." They were now arising and singing their own songs.

"Union Train (Coming Around the Mountain)"

I see that Union Train a comin,
I see that Union Train a comin,
I see that Union Train a comin,
Git on board, git on board!

It will take us all to freedom—It has saved
many a thousand

Here is another, asking for just bare necessities:

"I Don't Want Your Millions, Mister"

I don't want your millions, mister,
I don't want your diamond ring.
All I want is a living mister;
Give me back my job again.

Think me dumb if you wish, mister,
Call me green, or blue, or red.
This one thing I sure know, mister:
My hungry babies must be fed.

We worked to build this country, mister,
While you lived a life of ease.
You've stolen all that we built, mister;
Now our children starve and freeze.

By the end of the Thirties Roosevelt had instituted some reforms and was trying to help people get by. Young men joined the CCC, made $30 a month, of which $20 had to be sent home to their folks. The WPA (We Piddle Around) put a lot of men to work building dams and paving roads. The Tennessee Valley Authority (TVA), brought about through the Public Works Administration, rescued a large part of seven states and created a public power system. And for the first time, the old folks who couldn't work anymore received an old age pension check.

"The Old Age Pension Check"

When our old age pension check comes to our door
We won't have to dread the poor house anymore
Though we're old and thin and gray
Good times will be here to stay
When our old age pension check comes to our door.

When her old age pension check comes to her door
Dear old grandma won't be lonesome any more
She'll be waiting at the gate
Every night she'll have a date
When her old age pension check comes to her door.

With a flowing long white beard and walking cane
Grandpa's in his second childhood, don't complain
His life began at sixty
And he's feelin' very frisky
And his old age pension check is what to blame.

The Depression wasn't over by the end of the Thirties, but the worst was, and the nation had survived. A lot had happened since the Crash: bread lines and hobos and *The Grapes of Wrath*—a change from a capitalistic to a socialistic government—Shirley Temple, *Gone With the Wind* and *Snow White and the Seven*

Ab working for six bits a day

Dwarfs—Huey Long—Big Band swing, Glenn Miller, and "Star Dust"—John Dillinger, Pretty Boy Floyd, Bonnie and Clyde. During the Depression you could get a hamburger and a cup of coffee for fifteen cents; milk was ten cents a quart (nobody bought gallons), bread five cents a loaf, eggs twenty cents a dozen. A package of cigarettes was fifteen cents, a gallon of gas the same. You could buy a Pontiac coupe for $585, a gas stove for $24. And a peanut pattie and a big orange were a nickel apiece.

The trouble was that not many people had the nickels. College teachers were making around $2500 a year; public school teachers half that—if the state had the money to pay. A doctor made about $3500, a lawyer maybe $500 more. Steelworkers and textile workers were making about $400 a year. I worked on a ranch as late as the summer of 1940 for 75 cents a day, room, and board. A generation that is raised around those kinds of prices has trouble paying a dollar for a candy bar or a coke.

During the Sixties, when *The Graduate* was filmed, this Depression generation was satirized as "materialistic" because of their consuming consciousness of income and outgo, and jobs and the general cost of things. They were still very conscious that dollar bills put food on the table, clothed the kids, and paid the rent. They were still trying to get over the Depression. Some never have.

John Igo

"JULY 4, 1976": A FOLKTALE FROM THE HELOTES SETTLEMENT

by John Igo

Instead of a sermon that day, Our Lady of Guadalupe Church in Helotes had an organ recital by Marie Conley. Without preamble, Father Louis Trawalter introduced her.

She was old, *old*—upper '80s, maybe '90s—but her fingers were agile. I can believe that she had introduced Khachaturian, Shostakovich, and Prokofiev to San Antonio with Max Reiter decades back, from her house/studio in the now long-gone Irish Flats. Her program was unannounced and there were no printed programs: "The National Emblem March," a Stephen Foster, a colonial tune, "Battle Hymn of the Republic," "Tenting on the Old Camp Ground," an unfamiliar 19th century hymn, a minstrel show tune, "Rock of Ages," a spiritual, a George M. Cohan song, "America the Beautiful," "I Love You Truly," and "Dixie." Every resource of that organ was called into use: whispering, humming, fluting, booming, with bugle effects, drum effects, crashing and roaring, and chiming. Her "Battle Hymn of the Republic" was enough to give hackles; it was a *martial* hymn, with drums and muskets in it. It was not a pious sentimentality but a triumphant war cry. Her Hallelujahs floated over drums.

Then she started into "Dixie." Marie Conley was old enough that her parents would have had personal experience of the Civil War—and it remained with her, probably from childhood family stories. Her "Dixie" started somewhere off there in a mist, almost like music drifting across water, as if memory-blurred. Then she saw it more clearly, and the vision sharpened and the notes came clearer. The distance faded.

Old emotions became new again; forgotten responses stirred and awoke. And those old fingers willed an urgency, a commitment, and an exultation that performances over the years have forgotten. The organ swelled and opened. A cause long-lost now, a way of life that has been prettified into romance, a cultural identity obscured by time and clichés came through—direct, strong, beautiful, and doomed. That organ spoke as it never had before, and never would again. Marie Conley in a tacky old-fashioned blue dress and white blouse, with a ten-foot red Isadora Duncan scarf, leaning over the keys to be sure of her skills, became the Pied Piper, a Sibyl, and Bard recounting the history of the tribe. "Dixie" crashed to a halt and hung there, not to be violated. The pause after she finished was an exquisite tribute.

Then the applause started and swelled, and went on and on—and on. She had reached more deeply into her listeners than they had realized. One young woman with a small child was crying openly.

After Mass, I spoke with Marie briefly. She was elated at the response. Then she said, "Dear, it wasn't right—it wasn't just *right*!"

"It was perfect," I replied.

"No, dear. I wanted to do a little 'Rhapsody in Blue'—it should be there—but I couldn't work it in."

"Your 'Battle Hymn' and 'Dixie' couldn't need help. You did everything but a cowboy song."

She looked at me. "That 19th century hymn wasn't a hymn—it was an . . . arrangement." She smiled a conspiratorial smile and said, to head off comment, "Would you see me to the car, now, dear?" Holding my arm, that fragile little old lady left the church door, regally, through a group of awed neighbors. Elizabeth Schwarzkopf, that most regal of all singers, would have stumbled with envy at the sight.

After she was gone, Father Trawalter said, "I didn't know what I was turning loose."

I said, "You should hear her 'Can-Can'!"

"You knew didn't you? But the 'Can-Can'—I'm glad she didn't work it in."

"Are you sure she didn't?" He looked at me. I went on, "She has a gift for . . . arrangements."

He just smiled.

[This is one of dozens of stories the author has compiled about the small community northwest of San Antonio where he grew up. He calls the collection "Folktales of the Helotes Settlement"—*Untiedt*]

LEGENDS IN THEIR TIME—

AND OURS STILL

Frances (left) and Mattie are looking at the new carpet and wallpaper during the first major remodel of the store in 1959

FRANCES LANE AND MATTIE FELKER: TWO LEGENDARY LADIES OF TEXAS

by Mike Felker and Liz Brandt

The rags-to-riches fable: Poor young person works hard, pulls himself up by his bootstraps, and becomes unbelievably successful. The stories wouldn't exist if, every once in a while, they didn't actually happen.

As young girls helping their mother design and sew their clothes in the small farming town of Haskell, Texas, Mattie and Frances Walling dreamed of owning their own fine dress shop. They worked at local department stores on Saturdays and after school, learning the business and winning saleswoman of the month multiple times. Their opportunity arose when sister-in-law Ida opened her beauty salon, and offered Mattie the front twenty-by-forty-feet. Frances left her job at the theatre. Mattie left Perkins Timberlake, where she earned $8.00 a week less social security—the manager kindly told her he would hold her job for her until she and Frances were forced to declare bankruptcy. Brother J. E. lent Mattie $400 and Frances's husband Shady borrowed from their insurance, and the Walling sisters followed their dream.

J. E. wouldn't dream of letting them go to Dallas alone to buy clothes, and, as he drove them, he was horrified to discover they had no name for their store yet. Because they felt it had a more sophisticated ring, they had decided on their last rather than their first names for "the shop" as they always called it. J. E. had them flip a coin, and the name became Lane-Felker, rather than Felker-Lane; there were never any arguments or disagreements about the way the coin toss turned out. Mattie and Frances planned a fine dress shop; at a time when Perkins was selling dresses for $4.95 to $20.00, they planned to stock dresses selling for $50.00 to $75.00.

The shop opened on March 1, 1940, stocked in Easter pastels, thirty-seven lovely floral dresses, pink, yellow, and blue suede purses, silk stockings, gloves and, of course, beautiful hats, all bought in Dallas with cash. The shop was as pretty as they could make it. They had had fixtures built for $200, and bought used display cases from a grocery store; they painted the concrete floor because they couldn't afford carpet. Mattie had turned 28 the day before, and Frances was pregnant and six months away from her 27th birthday. They had a good first day and good days after that. (In 2001, Frances could still remember the names of the customers from that day sixty years earlier.)

Frances chose her first daughter's name at the shop on July 4th, and gave birth to daughter Linda August 11 of that year,[1] continuing to work while pregnant to the dismay and anger of J. E., who thought no one would continue to shop with her under those circumstances. They did, even when she left and walked the three blocks home twice a day to nurse.

Frances holding daughter Suzanne, about 1943

With the war, the early 1940s were a period of slow growth. Neither Mattie nor Frances took home a salary, and it was the late 1940s before the store was truly in the black. Every penny of profit was poured into shop expenses and more merchandise, and the empty boxes were kept on shelves to make it look as if the shop had more stock than it did. One customer delighted in asking, loudly, why they had all those empty boxes, preferably when there were other customers in the shop to hear her. Frances had a second daughter, Suzanne in 1942, also named at the shop, but after a model in the Brewster hat ads.[2] Along with Jantzen Sportswear, Herman Marcus, Serbin, and Lady Bayard dresses—a moderate line which sold for $8.95 to $11.95—they started carrying Vanity Fair lingerie because Frances got tired of running down the street to Perkins whenever someone needed a girdle to go with a dress.[3] Yes, Lane-Felker was built on personal service.

By 1945, however, the two sisters needed help, and they hired a full-time alterations lady, Dovie Pate, who worked for them for the next forty-plus years. The following year, they hired a full-time salesclerk, Dovie's daughter Patsy Cobb. (When Mattie was in her 80s, Mattie's son Michael showed her a photo and asked if she had any idea when it was taken. Mattie recognized the Swansdown suit in the photo and remembered that they began to carry that line in 1946; they really knew their merchandise.) They bought both the beauty parlor and entire building in 1948; Ida was tired of having clothes all over her beauty parlor and customers using it as a fitting room.[4] The following year they hired a full-time bookkeeper; even though dresses sold for $2.49 at Jones Dry Goods, their higher fashion clothing shop was growing, and faster all the time. In the meantime, Mattie adopted a son, Michael, in 1947, and he spent a lot of his early years underfoot in the store. Michael celebrated his second birthday at the shop; Mrs. Pheney Howard ("Howardy"), his sitter, brought him down, and Mattie got a cake down the street at the Sweet Shop.[5] She gave birth to Walter Viars, Jr., in 1949. As Mattie later said, "We practically brought all of you children up in that shop."[6]

Mattie's son Michael at the store in 1949. In the mirror behind him, Mattie is visible at the left and Mrs. Howard, his sitter, at right.

In 1950, they closed the beauty shop (after first hiring a man to run it) and expanded into that space. They also began taking courses in business, conversation, memory, and grammar to supplement their on-the-job training. They soon hired another long-time salesperson, sister Hortense Lees. She later became their gift-wrap specialist; Lane-Felker packages were extraordinary. In 1952, they added another thirty feet at the rear of the building, and their husbands, Walter Viars Felker and R. A. "Shady" Lane, bought Felker's Café next door and turned it into Lane-Felker Men's Wear, the ladies having decided a shoe store in that space would require too extensive a stock.[7] Mattie and Frances added a gift wrap person in 1957, and the two stores, men's and women's, were featured in *American Fashions Magazine*. They bought out the men's store in 1958, did a major remodel, expansion, and had a grand re-opening in 1959. Frances pointed out that the shop was always kept fresh and beautiful; in the future they would redo the store about every ten years.[8] Viars Felker opened Dad 'n' Lad menswear across the square from the store, and ran it for the next twenty years; Shady Lane went back into farming and ranching.

Mattie and Frances went to market and made buying decisions together. Originally, market was held in Dallas hotels like the Adolphus, but they would eventually go to New York, Los Angeles, and other markets. During one market, while they were staying in Fort Worth and driving back and forth to Dallas, the weather became so bad they had to spend the night in a showroom. The salesman brought them toothbrushes the second night.[9] Once Frances had to attend an Atlanta market alone, and another time Mattie attended St. Louis and Chicago with Viars. At that market, she toted a hatbox on the train and threatened to throw the heavy box out the window; Viars dared her to, but she wasn't willing to waste the money. It was also at that market that a salesman tore up a dress order because it was too small.[10] Now, it's hard to believe such a thing could happen; by the 1970s, the Lane-Felker ladies were treated like royalty at the Dallas Apparel Mart. They took Frances's daughters, Michael, and their niece Hazel to market over the years, trying to teach them to be buyers, but Mattie and Frances bought for individuals, and that couldn't be taught.

On December 23, 1959, an armed gunman robbed the store, but Mattie and Frances convinced him the bookkeeper was the only one who could open the cash register. (He had walked past the safe which was closed but not locked.) Throwing the cash register on the floor, he smashed it open and, taking bills, checks, and coins, ran out the back, kidnapped a woman who worked at the pharmacy across the alley, and stole her boss's car. Fortunately, he released her unharmed and was captured soon after. Mattie's ten-year-old son, Walter, and his friend Riley were in the store when the robbery occurred, and Walter still remembers the gunman's name today.

The 1960s saw continued growth, as Mattie and Frances hired six college students to help high school seniors put together an "in wardrobe"; by this time, they sponsored modeling contests, held designer and trunk shows, held fashion shows, and cosponsored

At the Dallas market in the mid-1960s, Mattie and Frances were training their niece, Hazel Hodge (left), to buy for the store

Hey Days, Frontier Days, and Spring Frolics in Haskell and surrounding towns. They also cosponsored Miss Texas contestants and the South Plains Maid of Cotton winner in 1969. They ran ads in Haskell, Abilene, and other North Central Texas towns, especially around their 25th anniversary in 1965. They also worked tirelessly in civic affairs, like starting a youth center. But the store was taking more and more of their time, and late nights were the rule rather than the exception. Many were the nights when one husband or the other would call to ask, "When are you coming home?" At least at Mattie's home, Viars usually prepared dinner for himself and the boys, and Mattie ate leftovers at 9:00 p.m.

The year 1970 was a major milestone for the store and Mattie and Frances ran a year-long Pearl Anniversary celebration. They gave away almost 1,000 strands of pearls, and every customer got cake and coffee; inside the cake squares were gift certificates ranging from $5 to $100. A fashion show featuring clothing from three decades at the store was so well received that *The Fashion Showcase* ran an article about it in April of 1971. On a personal note, Mattie had a celebration of her own, as her older son married in 1973 and Mattie had a "daughter" to dress at last. When Mike and Liz would come home on Sunday, Mattie and Liz would head to the store after lunch; it now became Mike's turn to call and ask, "When are you coming home? We need to head back to Lubbock." By 1978, the store was featured in the *Abilene Reporter-News* with the headline "Sisters' Shop a Dream Come True;" the article called the store "a phenomenal success in this town of 3,000-plus."[11] For Mattie and Frances, their dream really had come true. Rags to riches, a sister act, a Cinderella story—the stuff of legends. When asked to relocate to the mall in the much larger town of Abilene, they refused. They wanted to continue working together and not divide their effort.[12]

In 1980, the store's sales hit $1,205,520; that initial $800 investment was now a million-dollar-a-year concern. (Sales would, in fact, reach almost a million-and-a-half by 1984 and '85, and then hold a little below that through 1995 when the store closed.) The store continued to garner attention as *Women's Wear Daily* in 1981 called it a "Retail oasis in [a] Texas hamlet." Mattie said, "We buy wide and deep because we believe in carrying a lot of merchandise, but we adhere to Stanley Marcus's philosophy, too—that is, to purchase the best quality item available in a given category and price range. Between Frances and I, we've raised four children while building this store. We gave up bridge and sacrificed our social lives, but we've never been short of customers and friends." The writer pointed out that those customers and friends were often the same. Sportswear (40% of the store's sales) ranged from a $40 skirt to a $300 jacket; the remainder was 20% dresses, 15% coats, 10% lingerie, 9% bridal and formals, and 6% accessories, including $190 Alexis Kirk snakeskin belts with 14-karat gold-plated pewter buckles that sold at six per week. Customers were predominantly 25 to 60 years old, above-average income, frequent travelers, and married to professionals, but high school and college students and working women were also well represented. The article concluded, "Lane-Felker is not a posh operation, but its understatedly elegant, Mediterranean inspired décor and its warm, knowledgeable but unpretentious service epitomize the best of Southern hospitality."[13] In 1985, *Eyes of Texas featuring Ron Stone* sent a camera crew to Haskell to film their story for KPRC-TV. Unfortunately, the 1980s also brought sorrow to Frances, who lost her husband "Shady" in 1982, and then to Mattie, who lost her husband Viars in 1986.

That same year, Mattie was able to write a $10,000 check to First Baptist Church in Haskell, and kept an average balance of $48,000 in her checking account; business was good. For perspective, a trip to Martha's Beauty Shop was $9.00. An *Abilene Reporter-News* article said Frances's specialty is weddings, while Mattie handles advertising and accounts receivable.[14] The store now employed nineteen people. The Haskell Chamber of Commerce chose Mattie and Frances as Citizens of the Year, and the next year they received the Golden Sun Award from the Dallas Apparel Mart, Southwest Apparel Manufacturers Association, and Dallas Apparel News in recognition of "their contributions to the industry and the communities they serve."[15] In 1987, Mattie married John English while dressed in a gown from, of course, Lane-Felker, which was by now renowned for its bridal department. Although a $100,000-a-year part of the store's business, Mattie told her "daughter-in-love" Liz that the department never operated in the black. The cost of keeping a large inventory of dresses, plus the hours spent putting together outfits for the entire bridal party, altering the gowns, and multiple fittings weren't cost effective. "We offered it as a service," she said.

1990 brought their Gold Rush 50th Anniversary, and the celebration was again huge; the store was advertising nationally by now, but Mattie was 78 and Frances 77. Fifty years of working six days a week, eight to twelve hours a day, plus traveling to market four to six times a year was taking its toll. Mattie also lost her second husband, John, and that put an extra emotional strain on her. None of

By the 1960s, wedding dresses were a big part of the store's business, and Frances always delighted in being the one to help the brides

the four grown children wanted to relocate to the small town of Haskell to take over the store, so the ladies began entertaining thoughts of selling the store and retiring. The store was still making over a million dollars a year in sales, but fashions were changing. Young women were going off to college in jeans from Wal-Mart, not dresses and pants suits from Lane-Felker. An aging clientele was retiring and no longer needed the fashionable, professional clothing they had been wearing. Even though Mattie's 1992 income tax showed $70,753 in wages, rent, and stock dividends, plus another

The store was remodeled in 1990, with an awning in front and a mini-park in the vacant lot next door. Mattie is standing at the door.

$60,104 in social security and her store annuity, those years in high heels had destroyed her back and she was in almost constant pain.

By 1995, the time had come to retire. The last two years had produced no buyer for the store; as had happened fifty-five years earlier, they were told, "It's impossible to make that kind of money in a town of 3,000 people." Although Stanley Marcus of Neiman Marcus had once called Lane-Felker their only competition in Texas, potential buyers didn't believe the sales could continue at their current rate. At Christmas, Lane-Felker closed after 55 1/2 years; Mattie was 83 and Frances 82. The store did sell and reopen the following year, but it was never as successful; fashions had changed, and customers were too used to being helped by Mrs. Lane or Mrs. Felker personally. In July of 2001, the new owners would take down the sign over the building and move to Burlington, Colorado, hoping to rebuild the business in a much larger city.

Mattie and Frances now devoted their energies to the city of Haskell; retirement did not mean not working. Both lived to celebrate their 90th birthdays, in 2002 and 2003 respectively, and to see an historical marker placed on the Lane-Felker building after its sale to the local Allstate representative. Mattie died on February 27, 2003; she would have been 91 the next day. Frances died on February 6, four years later, at the age of 93. Until Mattie's death, the two sisters had spent almost every day of their lives together, as children and then six days a week at the shop and Sundays at church, with the exception of one year when Mattie and Viars moved away from Haskell before the store opened. As Frances lay dying, her daughters gave her permission to let go by repeating what she had heard so many times while working late at the store: "Daddy wants to know when you are coming home. He says Mattie is already there." Frances let go and went to join them.

In late 1989 or early 1990, Diane Arthur of Abilene had come to Lane-Felker for the first time. As she left, she said, "You know, everything they said about Lane-Felker is true. It is really an experience. Coming to Lane-Felker is truly a rite of passage, second only to losing your virginity."[16] Through their personal connection

The store was always overflowing with clothes from which to choose

with their customers, and the importance of word of mouth advertising, the little store that began in 1940 had become a "rite of passage" for women in much of Texas. It had become legendary.

Endnotes

1. Lane, Frances. *Frances Walling Lane: A Love Story.* DVD. Jeanie Powell. The Powell Company. November 2006.
2. Felker English, Mattie, et al. "Lane-Felker: Notes for a Book." Two Audiotapes. 2001.
3. Lane.
4. Felker English.
5. Ibid.
6. Ibid.
7. Ibid.
8. Lane.
9. Felker English.
10. Ibid.
11. Jennings, Diane. "Sisters' Shop a Dream Come True." *Abilene Reporter-News.* April 22, 1978. I-B.
12. Ibid.
13. Kivestu, Pat. "Lane-Felker: Retail oasis in Texas hamlet." *Women's Wear Daily.* April 2, 1981. 15.
14. Zelisko, Larry. "Sisters' Haskell dress store is 'home'." *Abilene Reporter-News.* February 6, 1986. 1-B.
15. Jarnagin, DeAnna. "Siblings' Success Story Cited With Golden Sun: Sisters' Faith in Future Brings Retail Reward." *Dallas Apparel News.* March 1987. 22.
16. Felker English.

Additional Sources

"C-C salutes leaders at banquet." *The Haskell Free Press.* March 27, 1986. 1-A.

"Clothes-store owners named outstanding Haskell citizens." *Abilene Reporter-News.* March 26, 1986. 2-B.

Craig, Tom. "Sisterly success: Small-town store brings big-town customers to area." *Abilene Reporter-News.* September 19, 1993.

50th Annual Banquet Haskell Chamber of Commerce. Videotape. March 22, 1986.

Gibbs, Jason. “Lane Felker leaving for cooler climes.” *Abilene Reporter-News.* July 2, 2001. 1-A, 2-A.

“Industry Salutes Lane-Felker.” The Haskell Free Press. March 12, 1987. Reprinted from *Dallas Apparel News.* March 1987.

Jones, Joyce. “The end of a business era in Haskell, Lane-Felker closes.” *The Haskell Free Press.* December 28, 1995. 1-A.

Kaigler, Mary. “Final curtain falls on class act.” *The Haskell Free Press.* July 26, 2001. 1-A.

“Lane-Felker of Haskell, Texas.” *American Fashions Magazine.* May, 1957. 31–33.

“Lane-Felker’s Formal Opening Nov. 23–24: Lane-Felker’s of Today Had Modest Beginning As Small Concern in 1940.” *The Haskell Free Press.* November 19, 1959. 1-B.

Stone, Ron. “High Fashion Shop.” *Eyes of Texas* on KPRC-TV. October 19, 1985.

“30 years ago: Lane-Felker holdup recalled.” *The Haskell Free Press.* December 28, 1989. 1-A, 4-A.

“Three Decades of Fashion Change Presented at Show.” *The Fashion Showcase.* 6.11 (April 1971): 4.

“Top citizens named by Chamber.” *The Haskell Free Press.* March 27, 1986. 1-A.

W.D. Christopher, the author's grandfather

THE EVOLUTION OF A FAMILY EPIC

by Donna Ingham

Family folklore is frequently passed down from one generation to the next through the oral tradition, but each generation of tellers must interpret events and motives from their own frame of reference. Such is the evolution of a story I heard about my paternal grandfather from my father and my uncle. I didn't hear the story until I was grown, out of college, and working, for it was a story the men had kept alive. They told it while sitting around in my great-grandfather's hardware store or while driving somewhere to go hunting or fishing. They never told it among the women because my grandmother had said years ago that she didn't want to hear any more about the trouble. That's what she called it—the trouble—so that's what everyone else started calling it, too. I finally heard the story, or at least an anecdotal part of it, the day my grandmother was buried. I suppose my father then thought he had permission, in a way, to pass it on to his descendants, both of them daughters.

Then I got a fuller version of the tale from my father's younger brother, the real storyteller in our family. I taped his account and transcribed it, and then spent the next two years trying to make sense of the story so I could tell it to my son. My son, of course, will get both the transcription and my interpretation, so he'll have a double dose to draw on to form his own story. Here's the way I tell mine.

The Trouble

"Pop killed a man once." My father said this one winter afternoon following my grandmother's funeral. My grandfather had been dead a number of years, so it seemed an odd time to tell my sister and me that he'd killed a man. Although we were grown and out on our own working, we'd never heard a word about it until that day. Daddy said this—"Pop killed a man once"—said it conversationally, in the same tone of voice he'd been using to discuss the crop land and the Miami, Texas, landmarks he remembered from his growing up years. We were sitting in a downtown cafe in Miami looking at a collection of calendars on the wall and drinking one more cup of coffee before we drove back to Amarillo and, ultimately, home.

We took notes that day, my sister and I, and followed up later getting transcripts of our grandfather's trial from the county courthouse. Time passed, and our father died, but I finally got back to Amarillo with my cassette recorder and half a dozen tapes in hand to interview our uncle. I asked him to tell me specifically about what the family had come to call "the trouble," for it's as close to an epic as our family is ever likely to get. (I re-read *Beowulf* and saw a pattern.)

You've heard the tales of the olden days in Texas, how the pioneers did brave and sometimes reckless things. Well, the Christophers—my family on my daddy's side—were pioneers in far north Texas, way up in the Panhandle. They came out of Kentucky and filed on land and tamed it, and the men of the family formed a bond as protectors of that land and of their families and of their family's name. They were counted, the Christophers were, among the "good" families in Roberts County.

My grandfather, William David Christopher—most folks called him Bill or Billy—was the youngest son in the family, but it was he who would triumph in the time of "the trouble." Already considered to be an up-and-comer, young Bill had married the belle of Miami in 1905, and together they'd started their family and settled on their own spread not too far from town.

That's where the trouble started. Living neighbors to young Bill and his family were Rube Curtis and his family, not more than a half mile away. You see, the Curtises had dogs, and the Christophers had hogs, and one day a pack of the Curtis dogs might' near chewed the ears off of one of Bill's best shoats. And Bill let Rube know in no uncertain terms that he was very unhappy about the situation, yet he was not seeking to do battle with his neighbor.

Now the Curtises were not counted among the "good" families of Roberts County, and Rube was not considered to be an up-and-comer. He had a reputation, as a matter of fact, for being quite a fighter and something of a bully, and folks knew that he made home brew. It must be said, however, that he'd like to have been an up-and-comer, and he did have a sizable clan of his own followers. So he surveyed the situation and decided the best thing for him to do was to run for county sheriff.

For their part, the Christophers—all of them in the county—took it upon themselves to uphold the right and the good and to actively electioneer against the wild and uncivilized, pointing out Rube's failings and mentioning from time to time the incident with the dogs and the prize shoat and, of course, the home brew. Rube lost the election.

Stung by his defeat and feeling more the outcast than ever, Rube vowed to whip every one of the Christophers, and he started with Bill's brother Lassiter. He hunted him up on a downtown street one day and knocked him down and started beating on him with his fists until a group of men came along and pulled Rube off.

Bill's father-in-law owned the local hardware store, and it had become the gathering place for the Christopher men and their councils. The council met. What were they to do about Rube? Bill's dad was no match for him. Oh, he was plenty scrappy, all right. Word was that he would fight a circle saw and give it a half turn for start. But he was old, and the responsibility for fighting, if fighting there would be, must pass to the next generation.

So it was that Bill, this up-and-comer in the prime of his good life, began to go abroad in the streets of the town doing the family business and waiting for the inevitable encounter with his neighbor, Rube Curtis. At first Bill went unarmed, although it was quite common for men to carry pistols in that day.

One afternoon just before harvest season he was on an errand to the bank, and he walked along the railroad track on his way to town. He saw a bolt lying there next to the track, and he picked it up and put it in his pocket; it might come in handy to fix some of the farm equipment later. It was a big bolt: four inches long or better and three-quarters of an inch thick.

When he walked in the bank, his old friend Hod Baird was working the teller's window, and Bill pushed his deposit under the grilled front with his right hand. Hod put his hand over Bill's and held it down, for he saw what Bill could not: and that was Rube Curtis walking up behind him. Hod, knowing of the enmity between the two families, thought to prevent a fight right there in the bank by holding Bill's hand down. But there was no one holding Rube's hand down.

Bill sensed danger and reached into his left pocket for the only weapon he had: that big old bolt he'd found by the railroad tracks. He turned as far to the left as he could, what with Hod still holding his right arm pinned to the marble counter, and saw Rube's fist coming at his head. The blow glanced off his ear and down his shoulder as he dodged and brought his left hand with the bolt in it out of his pocket, and up and across Rube's nose.

The bolt cut a pretty good gash in his nose, and Rube began to bleed all over everything. And he began to holler, "Stop him! He's going to kill me!" But Bill hit him just the once, finished his business at the bank, and walked away. There was much rejoicing at the hardware store that afternoon, and young Bill was the hero of the day. Still, a certain sense of doom hung over the celebration, for Rube had shouted to Bill as he left the bank, "I'll get you for this, Christopher. I'll get you for this."

Now a man's epic, such as it is ever going to be, begins in just such a way sometimes. A set of circumstances brought about by the chance placement of two families at close proximity but forever at odds with one another. Conflict fueled by pride and passion and the pagan desire to be sung into immortality by the bards and minstrels of this generation and succeeding generations as if the promise of an eternal heaven is not sure—or not enough.

And so it was that Bill began carrying a gun. And later, in the winter—when dark comes early and the streets stay pretty much deserted—Bill was armed when he came home from a business trip to Amarillo and got off the train at the Hoover Station. When he walked into the depot, Bill saw a man named Pingle, one of Rube's cronies, straddling a chair and watching the door. Bill dropped his valise and wrapped his fingers in place around the .38 in his left coat pocket. Once again Rube came at him from behind—he must have been hiding behind the door—and this time Rube was wearing brass knuckles. The first blow to Bill's head cut through the double layers of the coyote cap Mrs. Cooper had made him, and the second and third blows nearly took him to his knees. But he turned enough to grab onto Rube, and he fired the pistol, still in his pocket. He heard a ping and knew he had missed Rube and hit a keg of nails. He raised the barrel and fired again and felt Rube sag against him and begin slowly to fold into himself until he fell to the floor. Then Bill turned and walked away.

He could hear his breathing and see his breath made visible in front of him as he walked out into the cold night. Some of his friends appeared and walked with him to the Carters' house nearby where Mrs. Carter tended to the wounds on his head where the brass knucks had cut through the coyote skin and made gashes in his scalp.

By the time he'd ridden out to the ranch, Bill had rehearsed the telling of it as if he were his own balladeer trying line and meter and refrain.

"I shot old Rube today," he told his wife.

"Is he dead?"

"I don't know."

"Will the sheriff come?"

"More'n likely."

"There'll be trouble."

"Maybe."

To his son he said, "Old Rube come at me today, and I shot him." He knew the beginning, but he didn't know the rest.

It was enough for the men in the family to know that their champion had won the day on two occasions, and there was celebration and feasting and boasting among the Christopher men that night.

Rube Curtis did die, but not before he said, in the presence of witnesses in the doctor's office, "Don't be too hard on Bill. It was my fault." As a result Bill was no-billed by the grand jury, and the affair was on its way into oblivion within a year or two. But Bill would not be cheated out of the rest of his ballad, his epic. He hired a lawyer who assured him that as a citizen he had a right to demand a trial by a jury of his peers. And so he did.

Bill moved his wife and family and welcomed his brothers and their families and his father and his father-in-law to the county seat where they set up tents on the courthouse lawn and rented a cook shack and hired two women to cook for them. It looked like an army encampment. "I shot old Rube, and he died, and now it's going to trial," he'd explain to the curious who wondered what the armed camp was doing on the courthouse lawn.

Oh, the other side was armed, too, of course. Rube's son had already vowed to avenge his father. Grown men paraded up to the witness stand carrying barely concealed weapons and eyeing each other with cold suspicion.

The case didn't take long to try. The jury decided it was clearly a case of self-defense and voted for acquittal, but the story played out in public spectacle and stayed in the minds of the observers. Moreover, they sensed the tension and the continuing threat of violence in the bearing and countenance of each man on either side.

Sidebars to the main story circulated, like the one about Bill's uncle Charlie Carter, who had a reputation for having a short fuse and a dead aim, walking into one of the rooms in the courthouse to retrieve a Navajo blanket after the trial was over. He was carrying his .351 automatic Winchester. When he stepped into the room, he saw that Rube's wife and some of the other Curtises were there, and Mrs. Curtis's littlest baby was playing on the Navajo blanket in front of the old pot-bellied stove. Well, he wasn't going to take that blanket out from under the baby, of course, but someone from the other side gave him some lip and made some threatening move. Uncle Charlie was quick to jump behind the stove for cover, raise his rifle, and say to the challenger, "Now, listen, there won't be anything left but just a little pile of you if you start anything with me."

The two men eyed each other, and, in between, was the baby. Uncle Charlie's gaze shifted from his antagonist to the baby. The baby looked at him and smiled an engaging baby smile. Uncle Charlie smiled back and lowered his rifle. "We have no quarrel with you, young 'un," he said. "And there's no hurry about that blanket. We'll fetch it later. Use it as long as you need to."

Well, in the years that followed, no one ever came after Bill, and, in time, he stopped carrying his pistol. Maybe the feud ended that very day in the courthouse. Oh, not in the court room, but in that room with the Navajo blanket when one of Bill's men smiled back at Rube's baby and said, "We have no quarrel with you, young 'un." And that is how the epic ends, for Bill died not a hero's death in battle but lived into his 80s to die of natural causes—from all reports at peace with himself and at peace with his neighbors.

In 2010, Lon Goldstein visited Locke Field located in Gainesville, Texas, where he once played ball (photo used by permission of *The Weekly News of Cooke County*)

LON GOLDSTEIN AND THE GAINESVILLE OWLS

by Kit Chase

The diamond is empty and the stands are vacant. Locke Field, located in Gainesville, Texas, is silent. However, there are those who still remember when the ballpark was filled with cheering fans and the sounds of long fly balls cracking off the ends of bats. Players put their heart and soul into baseball and lived and died with every pitch. They loved the game so much they prayed to be buried under home plate.

Locke Field was once home to the Gainesville Owls, a Class B circuit team that was part of the Big State League based in Texas. It was formed after World War II, getting started in 1947 and lasting until 1957. The League saw a lot of transitions and was known as an offense-oriented circuit that included the Gainesville Owls, Greenville Majors, Austin Pioneers, Waco Pirates, Sherman-Denison Twins, Wichita Falls Spudders, Texarkana Bears, and Paris Red Peppers.

Operating a lower-level minor league team during the 1940s was not limited to the rich, and teams thrived because ownership was easy. The Gainesville baseball club franchise was bought in 1947 from the Big State League by George Frizzell, Cecil Farr, Harvey Shanks and $30,000 in subscriptions from 300 Gainesville citizens. The night subscriptions were sold, the Gainesville Chamber of Commerce was jammed with eager would-be shareholders. Three local businessmen held top positions in the franchise's front office: Roy "Pete" Briscoe was named president, Fred Snuggs was vice-president, and Sol F. Zacharias was secretary-treasurer.[1] Their budget was tight, and although team members received uniforms, they furnished certain extras such as gloves and shoes on their own. Fans paid $1.00 admission and did not seem to mind, because it appeared to be a favorite pastime.

Locke Field was named for Dr. W. Herbert Locke and held ninety-nine box seats that sold for $48 each for the season—and the season had 152 games with more than seventy home games.[2] Pete Briscoe bought a box seat behind home plate and today his daughter, Kaye Briscoe King, remembers watching every game and recalled that she was able to name each player on the team.[3] It was common for the local children to call out players' names and their stats like memorized multiplication tables.

There was an intimate relationship that existed at small ballparks such as Locke Field. It was a relationship that fans could never have to the same degree with Major League players. Fans could call a player over to the fence and talk to him. Autographs were easy to get, and fans traded each other for players' old shirts, pants, and cleats to build a collection. It was simple to spot players on Gainesville streets, and kids were able to walk and talk with them, much to their delight.

Minor-league baseball teams kept close ties to their communities and drew as many as five to six thousand fans. Players were respected, and in Gainesville, people dressed in hats, heels, gloves, suits, ties, and fedoras to watch the games.[4] It was a social outing for the entire family. Loyalty was encouraged with customs like Ladies' Day. Picnics before games were like celebrations at the ballpark, and bands gave concerts afterward for more entertainment. Every so often a wedding was held before games. Recorded in a local newspaper was this account on September 19, 1947: "Not to be outdone by certain clubs in Texas, the Sherman-Denison Twins staged a baseball park marriage last night, Willie Reyes, popular young Mexican star, taking upon himself a bride just before the game with the Greenville Majors. These home plate marriages in the big State Loop are becoming quite a fad."[5] Local newspapers joined in the festivities by sponsoring contests and devoting column inches that told about the game and players. Back then it was possible for a ballplayer to sustain a long career, and forty-year-old-plus players were common in the minor leagues.

The Owls were revered by the people of Gainesville, especially those who had bought a piece of the action. Lon Goldstein was a favorite ballplayer for Gainesville fans. At age ninety-two, he is the last Owl baseball player still living. Leslie Elmer "Lon" Goldstein was born May 13, 1918, in Austin. He was 6' 2", 190 pounds and batted and threw left-handed. Today, he resides in McKinney and still has ties to Gainesville. "I was expecting Pop Wells to walk in the door when I was told a reporter from Gainesville was going to visit," Lon Goldstein said one day last summer to his visitors.[6] Goldstein was referring to A. W. "Pop" Wells, who wrote a Gainesville newspaper column called Uncle Ezra's Sports Sizzles that featured the Owls. Pop Wells was a high school math teacher by day and a sports writer at night. He wrote in his column about one of his favorite sluggers, "Fans should have received their money's worth last night if they enjoy seeing homers clouted. Lon Goldstein's drive over the right field fence was one of the longest hits here this season. In fact we doubt if there has been a longer ball hit in the local lot. He powered that one."[7]

It is fascinating to read about ballgames written in Wells' column because his words express a different culture and era. He was a snappy writer and devoted a huge amount of space to the town's minor league team. His words were more colorful and vivid than what is served today about modern ball games. Pop Wells peppered his column with game stats and colorful, vibrant descriptions that the public gobbled up.

Wells described how winning games paid extra for individual players, "And the local boys who hit 'em picked up quite a bit of lettuce too. We have several fans here who shell out greenbacks any time an Owl hits for the circuit. And last night they were diggin' deep and often, much to the delight of the Owl hitters."[8] Tips passed through the chainlink fence and were a welcomed addition to meager salaries.

Speaking in a voice that is still strong and carries across the room, Lon Goldstein recalled some of his days at bat. "First time I ever played for Gainesville we were on the bottom and I hit a home run. I circled those bases and everyone was hollering 'here,' 'here,' 'here.' I looked up and the fans were sticking dollar bills through the wire fence. It was a great season. The people up there had lots of money and no place to spend it," Goldstein said. "So they spent it on the ballplayers."[9]

In his first season of play with the Owls, Goldstein was not quite used to the kind of appreciation fans bestowed on their favorite players. According to an account about local Gainesville physician, the late Dr. Mead, Mead scolded Goldstein, saying, "You're going to have to go around those bases a little slower, because it takes me a long time to write a $5 check."[10]

Before playing for the Owls, Goldstein was a first baseman in the Major Leagues, playing for the Cincinnati Reds. He started in 1943, but his baseball career was interrupted by World War II when he joined the military. After the war, he played one more season for Cincinnati in 1946 before he left to teach in Dallas, Texas. However, baseball did not leave him, and he signed up with the Owls mid-season in 1947. And, boy, were they glad to see him. Goldstein taught school during the day, and his wife would drive him to Gainesville to play baseball in the evenings. Games started at 8:15 p.m.

Goldstein was a first-sacker, as first base was called back then. He was a handy defensive player. Fans say the ninety feet between home plate and first base is the closest man has ever come to perfection. Goldstein reportedly snatched that perfection away by catching baseballs and tagging many players out during his career. He was also a powerful hitter and could blast homers out of a ballpark and smack key hits as smooth as driving a 1947 Packard Sedan. Goldstein has a great sense of humor and tremendous modesty about his batting ability. "I had a few homeruns. I was lucky, though; the pitchers threw the ball and it hit my bat. I didn't really do much good."[11] In 1947 he appeared in eighty-five games, scored 44 runs and had 332 at bats, 133 hits, 33 homeruns, 19 doubles, 2 triples, and a batting average of .401.[12] Those numbers would be good enough for a call up to the Majors today.

Baseball fans have always loved numbers; they spill from their mouths like foam from a bottle of long neck beer. In the days of the Big State League, statistics were often argued about and their accuracy questioned. "Believe it or not, a scorekeeper in league baseball is just about as popular as an umpire," wrote Pop Wells. "You always find a small group of fans who seem to be more interested in how a batted ball is scored than in the outcome of the ball game. Some of these can argue intelligently. But we'd venture to say the majority of them know little about the rules of scoring and most of their baseball experiences have been confined to sandlot and cow pasture baseball."[13]

Just as statistics were argued, so were the calls made by umpires. Umpires have never been a much-loved feature of the game, unless close calls go for a favorite team. In his column, Pop Wells fondly labeled umpires as "Blind Toms" if he did not like their calls. "The umpiring has been a cause of general dissatisfaction," Wells wrote. "I'm told that the Big State League isn't the only league that has suffered in this respect, that competent umpires are scarce. The behind the plate umpiring in this league is largely a combination of guesswork and evening-up. Umpires are not meant to be loved, but most fans know the difference between competence and incompetence. Our only comment on the officiating is that in baseball, like in other vocations, you get just about what you pay for."[14]

With no local television station to cover games, Owls fans relied on the newspaper for game summaries. A summary of the '47 season stated, "This will wind up Gainesville's first season in professional baseball, which hasn't been as unsuccessful as you might think. We started with nothing at all, wound up sixth in the league, have had a heck of a lot of fun and amusement and are in pretty fair shape to get a better start next year."[15] The 1948 season opened to high hopes for the Gainesville Owls. By May 10, 1948, the Owls had won ten games and lost eight for an average of .556. The Owls ended the year in fifth place and might have squeezed into the playoffs but for a siege of injuries near mid-season that sent them skidding down the ladder. But, like they always say, there's always next year.

The April 1949 Owls' main objective was to land a spot in first place in the Big State Loop. During the previous year, fan attendance had packed Locke Field nearly every game, and a bond issue passed for funds to construct an expanded baseball park before the 1949 season started. Pop Wells describes the progress in his column on April 8, 1949:

> Dadblast the blankety, blank luck. We're disgusted. Latest fly in the ointment is the announcement of the Waco Company, who supposedly had the steel all ready for the stands. [No steel had been cut] . . . and wouldn't be until a signed contract had been received, and then, so the report goes, the steel wouldn't be ready for shipment until about time for the season to open. Of course a lot of our trouble has been caused from having to rush the project, there being too little time to plan things as they should have been planned. Guess maybe the bond issue was put to the voters 'bout a month too late. Since then everybody's been running round in circles trying to get something done but not knowing just which way to jump. That mistake, we betcha, won't occur on construction of the swimming pool. At least we hope.[16]

Locke Field successfully expanded after the bond issue and all the construction mishaps. Concrete was poured and the steel was finally laid for the new stands. The diamond was made to be as smooth as a rug. Dirt was brought in and used to fill the ruts and potholes. Finally, fans were admitted and the famous words were shouted. "Play Ball!"

During the 1949 season, Goldstein played in 147 games, had 535 at bats, 187 hits, thirty-eight doubles, three triples and fifteen homeruns. His batting average was .350. That year, he helped manage the team with Ray Taylor, and they finished seventh in League play. In the 1950 season, the Owls took second in the League, and in 1951 they finished first, but by then Goldstein had left the Owls and had taken up with the Temple Eagles. In 1952, the Gainesville Owls were sold to the Sooner State League and in

1955, they moved to Ponca City, Oklahoma, to become the Ponca City Cubs.

In all, Lon Goldstein played more than fourteen seasons of baseball. After all those years of playing baseball at night and teaching at Carter Riverside High School during the day, he retired from baseball for good. However, he continued his teaching career for many more years. Though his beloved Locke Field has fallen into disrepair, and you'd be hard-pressed to find anyone walking down the streets of Gainesville who knows the name Lon Goldstein, he is still remembered fondly by his students.

The following is from a February 21, 2008, journal entry from a Carter Riverside High School student's visit to Lon:

> Following our class get-together, Charlie, Nancy, Jo Ann, Paul and I went to McKinney to visit with Coach Lon Goldstein. It was like a trip back in time, with the five of us piling into a car, and pooling our money for tolls rather than gas. We finally arrived at the coach's complex. The coach was amazed that we found the place and he wanted to know, which of us was the honor student in charge of navigating? The Coach called it the National Ornery Society. The only honor society member was Nancy and she went to Paschal H.S. We all had a laugh over that. We presented Coach Goldstein with a framed copy of "Coach Lon Goldstein, Our Coach, Teacher and Friend" from the Class of '62. The coach started reading it out loud and his voice broke, so I stepped in and read the rest of the story. He was very appreciative and at 90 years young he's still very sharp and witty. I wouldn't have missed this opportunity to spend time with the coach. It was an enjoyable experience that I will remember the rest of my life. I'm sure Charlie, Nancy, JoAnn, and Paul, feel the same way.[17]

During a 2010 reception held for Lon Goldstein in Gainesville, a baseball from all those years ago showed up. It had been autographed by the team. The handwriting was tiny and scribbled in some instances, but Lon was able to pick out his own. He gazed at it and seemed lost in time and his memories as he recalled those summer days.

Lon Goldstein was inducted into the Texas Baseball Hall of Fame on October 31, 1995.

After the 1957 season, the Big State League teams disbanded or were absorbed by other Minor League organizations. Most of the small stadiums that the League teams played in have been torn down over the years. Today's youth in Gainesville are unaware that Lon Goldstein and the rest of the Gainesville Owls ever existed. But, Locke Field still remains, a little worse for wear, standing as a symbol of a time when men wore business suits to the ball game, team managers played alongside those they coached, and ballplayers loved the game so much they prayed to be buried under home plate.

ENDNOTES

1. *Gainesville Daily Register*. May 29, 1947. 4
2. Ibid.
3. King, Kay Briscoe. Personal interview by the author. Gainesville, Texas. June 2010.
4. *The Weekly News of Cooke County*. August 5, 2010. 2.
5. Pop Wells column. *Gainesville Daily Register*. September 19, 1947. 4.
6. Goldstein, Lon. Personal interview by the author. McKinney, Texas. June 12, 2010.
7. Pop Wells column. July 10, 1947. 4.
8. Ibid.
9. Goldstein.
10. Ibid.
11. Ibid.

12. "Lonnie Goldstein Minor League Statistics and History." *Baseball-Reference.com.* http://www.baseball-reference.com/minors/player.cgi?id=goldst001les.
13. Pop Wells column. August 5, 1947. 4.
14. Pop Wells column. April 6, 1949. 4.
15. Pop Wells column. September 19, 1947. 4.
16. Pop Wells column. April 8, 1949. 4.
17. "Carter High School 1962 Class Notes." http://carterclassof62.org/CarterClassNotes.htm. (scroll way down to bottom of page)

[The author wishes to thank Larry R. Williams; Keith King, owner of *The Weekly News of Cooke County*; Mary Lou Leftwich; Tanya and Travis Chase; and the Cooke County Library for assistance in gathering the material for this article. Useful background information was obtained from: Chadwick, Bruce. *Baseball's Hometown Teams: The Story of the Minor Leagues.* New York: Abbeville Press, 1994.]

"White migrant mother with children, Weslaco, Texas, 1939." (From the Russell Lee Collection, courtesy of the Wittliff Collections, Alkek Library, Texas State University-San Marcos, LC-DIG-fsa-8b37154 DLC)

RUSSELL LEE'S TEXAS PHOTOGRAPHS

by Carla Ellard

Russell Lee worked as a photographer for the Farm Security Administration (FSA) from 1936 through 1942, traveling all over America on assignment, and providing a visual history and survey of American life. He joined other photographers such as Dorothea Lange, Walker Evans, Arthur Rothstein, and Marion Post Wolcott documenting the nation during a time of crisis with the Great Depression. Lee took more pictures than any of his colleagues—approximately 19,000 of the over 60,000 FSA photographs catalogued and housed at the Library of Congress are by Lee.[1] Lee's work is characterized by a deep concern for his fellow man. He also was an innovator in the field of photography with the use of multiple flash, which allowed him to better photograph the living conditions of the migratory workers and farm-workers west of the Mississippi. He produced several memorable photographs of Texas during his tenure with the FSA. Lee's career with the FSA and his Texas images and the context in which they were produced made a lasting contribution to recording the culture of this state during an historic era.

Russell Lee was born in Ottawa, Illinois, in 1903. His childhood was marked with tragedy when he witnessed his mother being hit by a car which resulted in her death. Coming from a well-to-do family, he was cared for by his grandparents and legal guardians. Lee attended Culver Military Academy in Indiana and obtained a degree in Chemical Engineering from Lehigh University. In 1927, he married Doris Emrick, a painter from Ottawa. Lee worked as a chemical engineer and plant manager but resigned after growing bored with the job. He and Doris moved to San Francisco, where Lee began to pursue painting, and two years later they moved to an artists' colony in Woodstock, New York.

Lee struggled as a painter, since he was not adept at drawing, and produced many portraits with "deadpan expressions."[2] He abandoned painting quickly after a friend introduced him to the camera in 1935. His first camera was a 35mm Contax. Lee photographed his surroundings in Woodstock and also documented the effects of the Depression in New York. With his chemical engineering background, he enjoyed the technical aspects of photography involved in developing and printing his own images.

Lee learned about the Resettlement Agency (RA) from a friend in New York in 1936. The RA was organized under the Department of Agriculture and was created in 1935 for resettling farm families living on overworked farmlands. Roy Stryker was the head of the Historical Section of the Division of Information and coordinated the efforts of photographers working for him at the time, such as Walker Evans, Carl Mydans and Dorothea Lange. The photographers' role was to record the plight of the farm worker to produce "visual evidence of the need for government loans to rural areas of the country."[3] Stryker met with Lee and reviewed his portfolio but did not offer him a job immediately. Weeks later, when Carl Mydans quit the RA to work with *Life* magazine, Lee was commissioned. In 1937, the RA reorganized and became the Farm Security Administration (FSA).

Stryker would send all the photographers shooting scripts via U.S. mail, as long-distance phone calls were costly and rare at that time. These scripts would describe or list the types of images that should be taken. In time, Lee was given more freedom with his shooting scripts as Stryker saw the results of his work. A man of independent means, Lee would be out in the field for extended periods of time in the Midwest. It was evident that Lee had great rapport with people and had the "uncanny ability to move into an area quietly and emerge a few days later with pictures that showed he had been completely accepted as a member of the community."[4] Lee would photograph every feature of a home or farm, documenting it in detail. Stryker described Lee's photographic style as an "engineer who wants to take it all apart and lay it on the table and say, 'There, sir, there you are in all its parts.'"[5]

Under Stryker's direction, the goals of photographing for the FSA had changed from documenting the plight of the farm worker to a mission of composing a historical record and introducing "America to Americans."[6] Stryker asked for broader themes in his shooting scripts so that all aspects of life were documented, including meals, weather, movies, local baseball game, signs, and other ordinary events. Lee stated that his "assignment was to photograph those people whom President Roosevelt had called 'the one third of the nation which are ill-clothed, ill-housed and ill-fed.'"[7] He photographed the "results of the drought, depression and farm-mechanization on the people, the land, the economy of the small town."[8]

During the first few years on the road, he processed his own film by converting a hotel bathroom into a darkroom. Lee captioned the negatives and sent them to Stryker in Washington. By 1938, he (like all other photographers) had to send his undeveloped film to Washington D.C., and contact sheets were sent via return mail, which Lee then captioned.

By this time, Lee's marriage had been strained with all of his traveling and he and Doris divorced. In 1938, Russell met Jean Martin while on assignment in Louisiana. She was a journalist who proved to be invaluable to his FSA work by interviewing the subjects in Lee's photographs and writing the captions, which gave Lee more time to photograph. They married in 1939.[9]

"In 1939, Stryker gave Lee a roving assignment to photograph agricultural technology in the South," which brought Lee to Texas for the first time. Between "February and October, Lee photographed the mechanization of agriculture throughout the state, covering every aspect from retail, through maintenance and repair, to operation in the fields."[10] Lee photographed small cities in the Rio Grande Valley in February and documented the grapefruit, orange, carrot, broccoli, and cabbage industries from the fields to packing the trucks. He also captured images of migrant workers and their living conditions.

In March of 1939, Lee drove north and photographed the spinach industry in Crystal City, making stops in Quemado, Eagle Pass and La Pryor and eventually San Antonio. In April, Lee was in East Texas and took a series of images of the oil-field workers in Kilgore. Several of the pictures of pecan-shellers and interiors of homes in San Antonio and the oil industry in Kilgore were published in *Texas: A Guide to the Lone Star State*, which was a Federal Writer's Project initiative (another New Deal program).

The photographs that Lee took in San Augustine, Texas, in April 1939 were taken in a span of three to four days, and many were used in the book *Home Town* by Sherwood Anderson, pub-

"Activity in front of the courthouse, San Augustine, Texas, April 1939." (From the Russell Lee Collection, courtesy of the Wittliff Collections, Alkek Library, Texas State University-San Marcos, LC-USF34-033044-D DLC)

lished in 1940. Lee's images of one of the oldest communities in East Texas show all aspects of life, including children at school and play, and the activities of a community on a Saturday. Lee found that photographing on a Saturday was important because that was when people would to go into town. Being a government man, he was met with suspicion and was not able to take any interior images of homes in the community. His aerial picture of the downtown square is one of his most notable in this series. In addition to the people that represent different levels of society, the image also depicts the impact that modern transportation had in a small rural town, with the numerous cars seen parked on the street.[11] His photograph of the courthouse town hall meeting is an example of his "praise of civic responsibility and small-town democracy."[12] By choosing to photograph with a wide-angle lens, Lee shows the size of the crowd that "implies a high degree of citizen participation in local government."[13]

Of all of the FSA photographers, Lee and fellow photographer Arthur Rothstein were the most interested in the technical aspects of photography. They worked together to create a better lighting method to document interiors of homes with the use of multiple flash. "Film speed was slow and made natural lighting for indoor shots impossible," and Lee experimented with "open flash, flash off-the-camera and multiple flash" to get the results he was looking for.[14] Sometimes this produced harsh shadows, but "Lee felt that if he could get inside someone's home it was possible to gain a truer picture of that person's life than by simply observing them on the front porch. He had a warm and winning way that easily won his subject's confidence and, as often as not, an invitation inside."[15] Lee believed that all these "details became very important because . . . Congress could release more funds to the rural areas."[16] In an interview, Lee would explain, "I became concerned with details [in a place]. The things people kept around them could tell you an awful lot about the antecedents of these people."[17]

In Texas, Lee took hundreds of these interior shots. In Weslaco, he captured a migrant family seated on the dirt floor. Critics have stated, "Lee made no attempt to romanticize" the people and "sought to convey the conditions which he encountered," as there are many examples of the squalor of temporary homes of the itinerant laborer.[18] Many of his images include children in the interior of homes because "they are viewed as blameless victims of social circumstances."[19]

One of Lee's most recognized images is an interior shot captioned "Tenant Purchase Clients at Home, Hidalgo County, Texas 1939." The picture is of a man and woman, FSA clients after rehabilitation, seated in the clean living room of their new home purchased through an FSA loan. There is an obvious contrast between the new furniture and the couple in worn clothing. Another notable image is "Kitchen of tenant purchase client, Hidalgo, Texas." The image of the soda jerker taken in Corpus Christi,

"Tenant purchase clients at home. Hidalgo County, Texas, February 1939." (From the Russell Lee Collection, courtesy of the Wittliff Collections, Alkek Library, Texas State University–San Marcos, LC-USF34-T01-032010-D DLC)

Texas, in 1939 depicts the cheery side of life. It is another example of an interior shot with the use of flash.

Lee returned to Texas in March of 1940 and took over 600 images that included migratory workers in Robstown and Sinton, the wool and mohair plant in San Marcos, goat farming in Kimble County, and road construction in Menard County. A well-known image of the used tire shop in San Marcos has been published several times. However, the bulk of the images were taken of San Angelo, specifically the San Angelo Fat Stock Show. Lee took pictures that document all aspects of this event, and the most famous image from this series is "Cattlemen at auction of prize beef steers and breeding stock at San Angelo Fat Stock Show."

In December of 1940, Lee returned to Texas for the last time on assignment and photographed Corpus Christi. Several images depict the rehabilitation of clients into new homes, laborers and their families, and signage announcing new businesses opening. The pictures of the construction of a naval base in Corpus Christi hint at America's preparation for war. By this time, America had mostly "pulled itself out of the Depression."[20]

Lee's work in the FSA continued but his images focused now on war mobilization.[21] In 1942, the FSA was absorbed by the Office of War Information, and Lee photographed for the U.S. Army Air Transport Command Overseas Technical Unit. After the war, he documented coal miners, and much of his work was used for an official report, *A Medical Survey of the Bituminous Coal Industry*, for the Coal Mines Administration. He had success working for magazines such as *The Lamp* and *Fortune*, and later worked for Standard Oil documenting the oil industry. For five years, from 1950 to 1955, Russell and Jean co-directed the Missouri Photography Workshop. In 1960, he traveled to Italy to produce photographs for the *Texas Quarterly*. Russell and Jean moved to Austin, Texas, in 1947, and in 1965, he was hired as the first photography professor at UT-Austin, working there until 1973. Lee photographed for the 1954 Ralph Yarborough Campaign and for the *Texas Observer* for several years. Russell Lee died in 1986 at the age of eighty-three.

The Wittliff Collections at Texas State University-San Marcos house the Russell Lee Collection, which was established in 1986 by generous donations from Jean Lee, Bill Wittliff, Dow Chapman, and Wally Ellinger. Highlights of the collection include over 300 vintage and modern FSA prints with captions. Artifacts include Lee's first Contax camera, several paintings (including one that he abandoned after he purchased his first camera), three FSA-era notebooks with entries by Lee, and a caricature signed by all FSA staff describing Lee as "The Man who took America's Portrait."

In 1999, the Texas State Library and Archives Commission provided a grant to digitize the Wittliff photographs and make them available through an online image database, currently available from the Wittliff Collections website. In 2003, the Wittliff Collections featured a centenary exhibition of Russell Lee's images. The Russell Lee Collection is available for research use at the Wittliff Collections.

[Note: All digitized images from FSA photographers are available from the Library of Congress *American Memory* website.]

ENDNOTES

1. Appel, Mary Jane. *Russell Lee: A Centenary Exhibition.* San Marcos: Texas State University, 2003. 4.
2. Hurley, Jack. *Russell Lee, Photographer.* New York: Morgan and Morgan, 1978. 13.
3. Berland, Dinah. "Russell Lee, in the Service of History" *Los Angeles Times.* May 1, 1993.
4. Hurley, Jack. *Portrait of a Decade: Roy Stryker and the Development of Documentary Photography in the Thirties.* Baton Rouge: Louisiana University State Press, 1972. 80.
5. Mora, Gilles and Beverly W. Brannan. *FSA: The American Vision.* New York: Abrams, 2006. 17.
6. Ibid. 259.

7. *Russell Lee: Retrospective Exhibition.* University Art Museum, Austin: University of Texas, 1965. IV.
8. Ibid.
9. Appel. 20.
10. Kidd, Stuart S. *Farm Security Administration Photography, The Rural South, and the Dynamics of Image-Making, 1934–1943.* Lewiston: Edwin Mellen Press, 2004. 207.
11. Curtis, James. *Mind's Eye, Mind's Truth: FSA Photography Reconsidered.* Philadelphia: Temple University Press, 1989.108.
12. Curtis. 109.
13. Ibid.
14. *Russell Lee.* IV.
15. O'Neal, Hank. *A Vision Shared: A Classic Portrait of America and Its People, 1935–1943.* New York: St Martin's Press, 1976. 138.
16. Berland.
17. Hurley, Jack. "Russell Lee." *Image: Journal of Photography and Motion Pictures of the International Museum of Photography at George Eastman House.* 16. September 1973, 4.
18. Kidd. 218.
19. Appel. 18.
20. Appel. 27.
21. Ibid.

Professor Emeritus Américo Paredes in front of Parlin Hall during the 1990s. (Photo from the family archives of Alan Paredes)

AMÉRICO PAREDES, BORDER ANTHROPOLOGIST

by Manuel F. Medrano

His first name was Américo, like the explorer for which America was named. His last name was Paredes, which comes from the Latin word *parietis*, meaning walls. His life spanned over eight decades which included events that changed the world forever. Américo lived during some of the most dramatic events in U.S. history—World War I, the Great Depression, World War II, and the turbulent Cold War. Although he often wrote about life between two worlds, he lived in three worlds—first, his world during the early years on the border; second, his world during and after the second World War in the Far East; and third, his world of academia at the University of Texas at Austin. In many ways his early research of the late 1950s and early 1960s laid the foundation for his reputation as a scholar for the next four decades.

Paredes received his Ph.D. in English at the University of Texas at Austin in 1956, and then taught for a year in the English Department at Texas School of Mines (later the University of Texas at El Paso). In the fall of 1958, Paredes returned to UT Austin as an Assistant Professor of English and, in 1961, he was promoted to Associate Professor. In 1965, he was promoted to Professor of English, and one year later to Professor of Anthropology, as well. The publication of his dissertation and his groundbreaking research soon gained him a regional and national reputation as one of the leading experts on the *corrido*, or folk ballad. In 1962, Paredes was awarded a Guggenheim Fellowship, which provided a $10,000 stipend to fund his efforts to collect border folklore. Three years later he became a fellow in the American Folklore Society.

As part of his Guggenheim study, in September 1962, Paredes travelled to Brownsville and northern Mexico to collect *corridos* and *cuentos* (short stories) for his research. Several times while he was in Mexico, *bandidos* (bandits) attempted to rob him. Once they placed logs across the road and came down the mountain with guns. Américo had to drive in reverse back down the winding mountain road in his automobile until he could find a turnaround to escape. He then proceeded to the small town with his tape recorder and continued to record the ballads and folktales that would eventually appear in his journal articles and books.[1]

On one of his research trips to Brownsville, Paredes stayed with one of his brothers, Amador. Américo commented that he had been there for over two days and not been able to use the tape recorder at all. However, on September 6, Paredes' luck had changed at least minimally. He wrote:

> Morning was more or less a blank, except for a few side dividends. Eliseo [his oldest brother] told me a couple of comic anecdotes (which I already had forgotten and must write down) and also got some

Paredes (right) in the field on a northern Mexico rancho in 1963. (Photo from the family archives of Alan Paredes)

> decimas from him. Also met my padrino de confirmacion [godfather of confirmation] whom I had not seen for about 40 years. The afternoon was luckier. Stopped to talk with Martin Ruteledge, "El Lonche" [the lunch], met an old schoolmate of mine, Justin McCarty, who turned out to be a rancho owner now.[2]

One day later, he collected more information and described his activities to Nena, his wife:

> This morning went with Amador and met Dr. Magnifico, who turns out to be an Argentino from Cordoba! How do you like that . . . Talked to a number of people there and in the courthouse, where I was told a handful of anecdotes, including a dirty one by the federal judge, H. A. Garcia, an old friend. But really good for my purposes, really shows the Mexican psychology. . . .[3]

On Monday, September 10, Paredes answered a letter that his wife had sent three days earlier. He first responded to her rather cold phone conversations and then described his research of the previous days:

> At all events, I hope that this finds you well, and in a kinder and more Christian mood than you were last Thursday, when I called you on the telephone. I am slowly getting underway here, with the usual frustrations, delay and outpouring of "okane" la "biru" here and there, which I have not been drinking myself. . . . After some false starts, I started recording on Friday night, when Manfred [his nephew] got a few tale-tellers together. Cost me $4 in beer and did get one tape, mostly small talk, and a few good (good and dirty) anecdotes

> about Mexican and Americans. The morning of Saturday the 8th I woke up with a terrible stomach ache and a case of the "turistas" [diarrhea]. . . . Went around talking to people with Amador all day Saturday, and buying them beer now and then, feeling terrible. . . . To make matters worse, I found I could not handle the little battery recorder, tape, microphone, extra batteries, etc. easily enough to whip them out any old place once somebody got talking. So Saturday was a pretty bad—and—profitless day. That night I was able to down a bowl of soup and feel better.[4]

The next day was better because the day before, Paredes had purchased a $3 knapsack at Bernie Whitman's Army Surplus Store to carry his equipment. He visited two homes, a filling station and a bar, and was able to record those who were in the mood to tell jokes. Sunday had been the most productive day of the trip. In the evening, his brother Amador and his wife Ofelia hosted a dinner attended by friends and family. His eldest brother, Eliseo, recorded three anecdotes, two which were off-color, and told one himself at the gathering.

Although the separations were difficult at the time, the letters Paredes wrote to Nena are a rich source of information about his fieldwork. He said that the afternoons and nights were his busiest times because most of his interviewees worked in the morning. The process, however, was much more difficult in 1962 than it was in 1954. Paredes lamented:

> For one thing, many of the old folk have died. For another (perhaps because of the Memories of the old recording companies and the desire to become "famous") more people are willing to sing into a

> mike than to talk into one. Again, people are more likely to sing songs at the spur of the moment, or on demand, than they are likely to tell stories or jokes. Especially for jokes, they have to be in the right mood. Going up to somebody and saying, "Tell me a joke" is like asking somebody, "Say something in English—or Spanish." Again since most of the humor is off-color, there are times when I get the right informant in the right mood, but he can't perform because some woman or child joins the group.
>
> This job is like that of a salesman. There are days when things just fall in your lap; there are days when you spend all day seeing people with no results. I am averaging 50 miles a days on my Volks and have not been out of the Brownsville area except for two trips to San Benito, one to Los Laureles (near Los Fresnos) and one to Las Comas. . . . I taped an interview with Nicanor Torres yesterday; he's passed the 100 yr. mark already. But his age really is telling now. He didn't do much in an hour; his mind wandered, and his voice was weak. . . .[5]

Américo's humor repeatedly surfaced as he collected jokes and stories in nearby Matamoros. He wrote, "in spite of the heat and the 'turistas,' [diarrhea] . . . which the last had been a blow to my pride, getting it in my own home town . . . things were not so bad as this morning, when I went to get my tourist card."[6]

Paredes was considerably frustrated by the Mexican "system" of customs. On one trip he cleared his camera and recorder through American customs with some delay but not too much difficulty. At Mexican customs, however, he faced several obstacles. He had to "tip" the girl one dollar for filling out his car permit.

She told Paredes that his recording equipment was not included in the permit because it was not necessary. He then drove to the office next to hers and the inspector took the permit from Paredes, pointed to the camera and recorder and asked what they were. When Américo related what the girl had said, the inspector unpleasantly answered "no" and asked him to see the chief. Paredes refused and walked to the girl's office who seemed surprised.

Paredes kept his eye on his Volkswagen while someone was placing tourist stickers on it. The inspector came out and "thrust" the car permit into Paredes' hand and said, "Tengal Lleveselo asi" (Here! Take it as it is). Paredes later wrote:

> So the whole thing was clear. It meant that every time I crossed the river I would be stopped and badgered until I gave out with some sizeable *mordida* [bribe]. I wouldn't be surprised if they didn't phone immediately to the "garita" [guard house], to be on the wait for me. I drove to Eliseo's, feeling mad enough to turn around and go back home to Austin. But he called General Gonzalez Trevino, the customs chief, and we went to the main customs office where the good general had one of his sub chiefs add the camera and recorders to my car permit. According to him they belonged there; that is to say the inspector was right. I just wonder what happens to people who do not have the right brother and the right connections.[7]

Américo Paredes' professorial career was by many accounts no less than brilliant. His abilities in the classroom brought out the best in his students. His expertise as a scholar garnered him national and international accolades. Paredes not only wrote well, but could defend his writing with knowledge and honor. Although he retired from full-time teaching in 1984, he continued to teach part-time and continued his research until his failing health over-

Américo as a young professor at the University of Texas during the 1960s. (Photo from the family archives of Alan Paredes)

came him. Américo Paredes died in 1999, and left a legacy of scholarship and teaching that led the way to serious research in an area that had long been overlooked. And although he lived in the Valley only one third of his life, the border community was important to him all of his life, and for that, the academic community is a better place.

Sometimes in our lives we encounter a person who, without ever knowing us, has done something to make our lives better and when we actually meet and know that person, we immediately understand why. The more I knew Américo, the more I understood why.

Endnotes

1. Interview of Alan Paredes by Manuel F. Medrano on December 9, 2001.
2. Amelia Paredes, Letter to Américo Paredes, Américo Paredes Papers, Benson Latin American Collection, General Libraries University of Texas at Austin, September 16, 1962.
3. Américo Paredes, Letter to Nena Paredes, Américo Paredes Papers, Benson Latin American Collection, General Libraries University of Texas at Austin, September 7, 1962.
4. Américo Paredes, Letter to Nena Paredes, Américo Paredes Papers, Benson Latin American Collection, General Libraries University of Texas at Austin, September 10, 1962.
5. Américo Paredes, Letter to Nena Paredes, Américo Paredes Papers, Benson Latin American Collection, General Libraries University of Texas at Austin, September 19, 1962.
6. Américo Paredes, Letter to Nena Paredes, September 10, 1962.
7. Ibid.

[Portions of this article were previously published in the book by the author: *Américo Paredes: In His Own Words, An Authorized Biography*. Denton: University of North Texas Press, 2010.]

Américo and colleague doing field research in northern Mexico
(Photo from the family archives of Alan Paredes)

James Ward Lee

SAGES, PUNDITS, AND SPINNERS

by James Ward Lee

O sages standing in God's holy fire

As in the gold mosaic of a wall,

Come from the holy fire, perne in a gyre

And be the singing masters of my soul.

That quotation from Yeats's "Sailing to Byzantium" has nothing to do with what follows. I only preface my remarks with it to show that I went to college. My students never believed that I did.

Now to the business at hand: Sages, Pundits, and Spinners. Kent Biffle once called my old partner A. C. Greene the "Sage of Salado." A. C. was no sage, had no pretentions to sagacity, never uttered but one maxim in his life. He said, "Everybody loves a hit parade." And one sagacity does not a sage make. A. C. was a pundit and a spinner, and I will surely come back to A. C. later. Somebody once said that John Graves was the sage of Glen Rose, but Graves is no sage. Sages make up maxims that fit on bumper stickers or refrigerator magnets. What Graves does is to try to make you see how wonderful it is to buy a patch of sorry land and have a goated community. His books made me move from Denton to Fort Worth to get as far away from hardscrabble land as possible. I grew up on land so poor it took two men to raise an umbrella on it. In my home county, land was so bad it took ten years to rust a nail. So I was not spun in by Graves. After all, "My bones denounce the buckboard bounce and the cactus hurts my toes." There is another quotation that has no bearing on what follows. I don't think it is from Yeats, but it may be.

Sages are omphaloskeptics. They spend a lot of time contemplating their navels and finding them good. That would be all right, but then they have to tell everybody about it. And most of them tell it in words we can't understand. Byron got it right about that famous doper Coleridge. He said, "And there is Coleridge proclaiming metaphysics to the nation / I wish he would explain his explanation." Samuel Taylor was the puzzling, Delphic sort of sage, but not all are. Take Dr. Phil, for instance, the guy who is always threatening to open up a big old can of Whoopass. He is another reason I left Denton. I found out that my school had awarded him a degree. Now all they need to do is award an honorary degree to Dr. Joyce Brothers and a doctorate in law to Judge Judy. So, I moved to Fort Worth where the divinity school is just about to honor the preacher who says "God damn America" is in the Bible. I have started looking for it, but I can't find it. Of course, I am only up to Deuteronomy, and he may be referring to the book of Jeremiah. Am I digressing here? I will get back to sages in a minute. Have you figured out that organization is not my strong point?

Here is the dictionary definition of pundits: Pundits are know-it-alls. You could look it up. Turn on your TV. That medium is eaten up with pundits. There is Lou Dobbs, who is from Quanah or Chillicothe or Clarendon or somewhere up on the Red River, and he has driven himself mad worrying about building a fence along the Mexican border. People from Chillicothe or Quanah or Clarendon often become pundits; people from Matador or Roscoe or Jacksboro almost never do. And thank God for that. Pundit is a Sanskrit word that means know-it-all, and if you go into an Indian railway station there is always a pundit there who will tell you when the next train to Bombay or Mumbai or the Malabar Coast leaves. At least *they* tell you something that will do you some good. I am telling the truth about these railway pundits. I read it in a novel about India, so I am an expert. A pundit more or less. India produces lots of sages and pundits and very few spinners. The most famous pundit from India is Dr. Sanje Gupta, who knows every medical term ever invented, from hemorrhoids to hemophilia, from restless leg syndrome to rectal dislocation. But you must know by now that there is no such person as Dr. Sanje Gupta. That guy is a Bollywood actor.

Now then, spinners are people who put a spin on things. You may think the word comes from billiards. Or tennis. Or bowling. Wrong. It comes from an old song, which I will not sing. "There's an old spinning wheel in the corner / Spinning dreams of a long time ago." See, I am right on top of this research and quotation business. I may get to spinners before this is all over, but first I have to get back to sages. So be patient.

I pretty much hate sages—let me get that said right up front here. I learned to hate them many, many years ago when I was perning in a gyre like those sages in the Yeats poem. I may have been in the third grade or so, when I first took against sagacity, and my detestation grew and grew. I don't like Thoreau and Emerson, and I don't like anybody who does. Thoreau was a sage who said some stuff that gets crammed down school children's throats from very early ages. Dumb stuff. Old Henry wanted to back life up in a corner and strip away all that was not life and if it was mean to pronounce it mean. But, hell, I knew back in the fifth grade that he was not going to pronounce it mean. He was going to go on and on about how glorious it was to live beside a stock tank about a hundred yards from his pal Ralph Waldo Emerson. And he didn't even have goats. He said, "The mass of men live lives of quiet desperation." But there he was eating hot pies that Mrs. Emerson kept him supplied with. She cooked up rhubarb pies and mincemeat pies and Dutch apple pies and even huckleberry pies in season.

Let me pause here and quote a famous Texas folklorist—"I God, I love a pie." And that sentiment has no bearing on what follows, either. Anyway, back to Henry and his ilk. The only person who outdid Henry was his buddy Waldo, who spent his life saying dumb stuff like "a foolish consistency is the hobgoblin of little minds," whatever that means. Try a little inconsistency if you are running for office and see what you get. "Hello, President Guiliani." Hello. Governor Spitzer. Makes you wonder what *is* is, don't it?

I had enough Emerson and Thoreau crammed down my throat in the Leeds, Alabama, public schools to last me till the year 2032, when the pundits say my Social Security and Medicare will run out. Then I can dress like that Indian sage Ghandi and sleep outside the

Union Gospel Mission down on East Lancaster. Just don't get me started on the year 2032.

I am just getting warmed up here. When I was in the sixth grade, Miss Pate, the one we all thought was a devil worshipper, made us read the dumbest and most ignorant scribbling ever conceived by the mind of man. And this drivel was circulated to over 50 million people—most of them in grammar school probably. I didn't say "sold." I said, "circulated." I don't know who did this distributing, but whoever it was has a lot to answer for in my book. The dumb story was written by a man known far and wide as "the Sage of East Aurora." His name, as everybody who ever went to grammar school knows, was Elbert Hubbard. And the propaganda he saddled us with was called "The Message to Garcia."

Now, here is the story: during the Spanish American War, our first attempt at Imperialism and nation building, President McKinley needed a message taken to a guy out in the jungles or forests or wastes or swamps or mountains of Cuba. The guy was named Garcia, and he was a late nineteenth-century version of Fidel Castro or Che Guevara. Well Garsha, whose name is spelled G-a-r-c-i-a, and whose name is widely mispronounced by Spaniards and Mexicans and Cubans, and South and Central Americans—and possibly Filipinos, for all I know—was out there in the Oriente Province or somewhere messageless.

Here is a footnote and a digression. My friend Rolando Hinojosa had "The Message to Garcia" inflicted on him in the Mercedes, Texas, grammar schools back in the 1930s, and he tells me that his teacher also called him "Garsha." If I had a case here, I would surely rest it.

Okay. Back to the sordid story of the famous message. Naturally, they called in an Alabama boy to slog through the slough of despond that was nineteenth-century Cuba and find the terrorist or whatever Garcia was. The soldier in question was named Andrew Summers Rowan. They told him to take this message to Garcia. Rowan, possibly a distant relative of Walter Rowan, who was married to my daddy's first cousin Lizzie, asks no questions.

No, not a one. Here let me quote Elbert Hubbard, "the sage of East Aurora, New York":

> Rowan took the letter and did not ask, "Where is he at?" By the Eternal! There is a man whose form should be cast in deathless bronze and the statue placed in every college in the land. It is not book learning young men need, nor instruction about this and that, but a stiffening of the vertebrae which will cause them to be loyal to a trust, to act promptly, concentrate their energies: do the thing—"Carry a message to Garcia."

So the lad sets off, braving water moccasins and lizards and wildebeasts, or whatever they have in Cuba. And he found Garcia, by God. Though he should have died in the jungle or swamp or whatever. By rights, he should have got lost and starved to death. He should have been shot by Garcia's men when he broke the foliage around the Cuban camp. Fidel would have gunned him down like a dog. You can take that to el banco. But No. He made it through and we defeated Spain and took over Cuba and American Samoa and the Philippines, though we got the crap kicked out of us by the Huks before we settled the hash of the Filipinos.

I wish I had brought my copies of *The Notebook of Elbert Hubbard* and two volumes of *Little Journeys to the Homes of the Great Philosophers*. Those very titles should tell you something about the life of that purple sage. Fortunately, old Elbert and his long-suffering wife went down with the *Lusitania* in 1915, or no telling what he could have tortured school children with if he had lived. Miss Pate would have had us memorize more of his aphorisms than she did. Things like:

> Enthusiasm is a great hill climber.
> Don't sit down in the meadow and wait for the cow to back up and be milked—go after the cow.
> Love only responds to love.

> Women under thirty seldom know much unless
> Fate has been kind and cuffed them thoroughly.

If that was what Elbert really thought about the fair sex, Mrs. Hubbard probably welcomed her watery grave and went down singing "Nearer, My God, to Thee." Or was that the *Titanic*'s theme song? I really don't know what they sang as the *Lusitania* sank beneath the waves. I just know that lots of old ladies embroidered Elbert's maxims on cup towels. And that is where they belong.

Okay, I am now about to get to the meat of this paper. Old J. Frank Dobie had carved up over his mantlepiece this little maxim: "Fire is the great philosopher." Or words to the same defect. I don't know what he was getting at, but he may have meant that staring into the fire caused you to have deep thoughts. Well, maybe, but my Granny Lee said that sitting too close and staring into the fireplace before bedtime would cause you to wet the bed. I don't know about J. Frank's nocturnal emissions, but I am sure he thought a lot of deep stuff. But I don't think J. Frank, famous nowadays mostly for parting his name on the side, was a sage. He was a spinner. His main role in life was to spin Texas to the world. He wanted other Americans to see Texas as a land of sagebrush and longhorns and mustangs and rattlesnakes and trail drives and lost mines. He did not want them to view the Lone Star State as a part of the Old Confederacy where cotton was king and where slaves sang folksongs along the Brazos River and told tales about Aunt Dicy. But I had better get off that subject since James Frank is a saint of the Texas Folklore Society—as he should be. Besides, he and his two half-naked buddies are immortalized in bronze just down from the ticket booth to Barton Springs Swimming Pool. That is fame that even Andrew Summers Rowan of Garcia fame did not achieve despite Elbert Hubbard's great desire.

I have a friend who is a sage, and he drives me crazy. He wakes up every morning and sets out to solve the problems that have puzzled philosophers and theologians and other assorted sages down through the ages. If he wants to stir up deep thoughts, that is his business, but he always wants to tell me what he has thought up. And I am a person who thinks if you can't eat it or wear it or sit on it or drive it, I have no interest in it. But I hate to tell him that. He has a little notebook that he copies down his pensees in. That's right. That is what he calls them—pensees. If the French choose to mispronounce the word that is their business. Anyway, my friend has filled hundreds and hundreds of these little notebooks, and he doesn't exactly read them to me, but I know he wants me to ask him to see what came to him in the night—another kind of nocturnal emission, I suppose.

He is not my only sage friend. My late colleague from Denton who went out in his back yard and blew his brains out with a 30.06 rifle was overrun with wisdom, too. He also interpreted dreams and read tea leaves and smoked dope. He once talked me into telling him about my recurring dreams. In one, I was called back into the Navy and was a 60-year-old sailor emeritus on a ship manned by teenagers. In another one, I was always caught out naked. He posited that I had had some serious childhood traumas and prescribed some mantras and whatnot for me to mumble just before I went to bed at night. I hate to admit this, but his prescription worked. I quit dreaming that I was naked. I started dreaming about Renee Zellwegger. And danged if she wasn't naked. But we were both in the Navy. Me fully clothed in "bell bottomed trousers and coats of navy blue," as the song used to say. And she was standing in the wheelhouse naked as the day she was born. That cured me of making fun of dream interpreters, and nearly cured me of scorning sages. But not quite. As you can see.

Okay, I am ready to get back to my old pal A. C. Greene. Next to Socrates, he was the greatest spinner I ever heard of. You all know the Socrates story. He corrupted the youth of Athens City by making the best case appear the worser case or vice versa. I can't remember which, but the City Council sent him a twelve-ounce can of Hemlock to drink. That is what Dr. Phil would call a big old can of Whoopass.

Okay. Back to A. C. I told you that organization was not my long suit. A. C. spent his life spinning. He could make Abilene, Texas, seem like Palm Springs, California. He could make Dallas seem like a place you might want to move to. But mostly he spun A. C. He even managed to do it from beyond the grave. After he died, he wrote a book called *Chance Encounters*. That might be hard for you and me, but A. C. was a man of parts. In this posthumous book, he told about all the famous people he knew—most of whom adored him. I did, but I only get one line in the book. One encounter concerned Hermes Nye, late of TFS fame. A. C. was taking Joan Didion through the Baker Hotel, and he chanced to encounter Hermes Nye. Only it wasn't Hermes. Nevertheless, he puts Hermes's picture in the book. That was only right. Hermes deserves lots of credit as spinner, pundit, sage, and reciter. I loved that old reprobate, and I am always moved when I think of his reciting LASCA, especially the part that goes:

> But once, when I made her jealous for fun,
> At something I'd whispered, or looked, or done,
> One Sunday in San Antonio,
> To a glorious girl on the Alamo.
> She drew from her garter a dear little dagger,
> And—sting of a wasp! It made me stagger!
> An inch to the left, or an inch to the right.
> And I shouldn't be maundering here to-night,
> But she sobbed, and sobbing, so swiftly bound
> Her torn rebosa about the wound,
> That I quite forgave her. Scratches don't count
> In Texas, down by the Rio Grande.

Hermes Nye

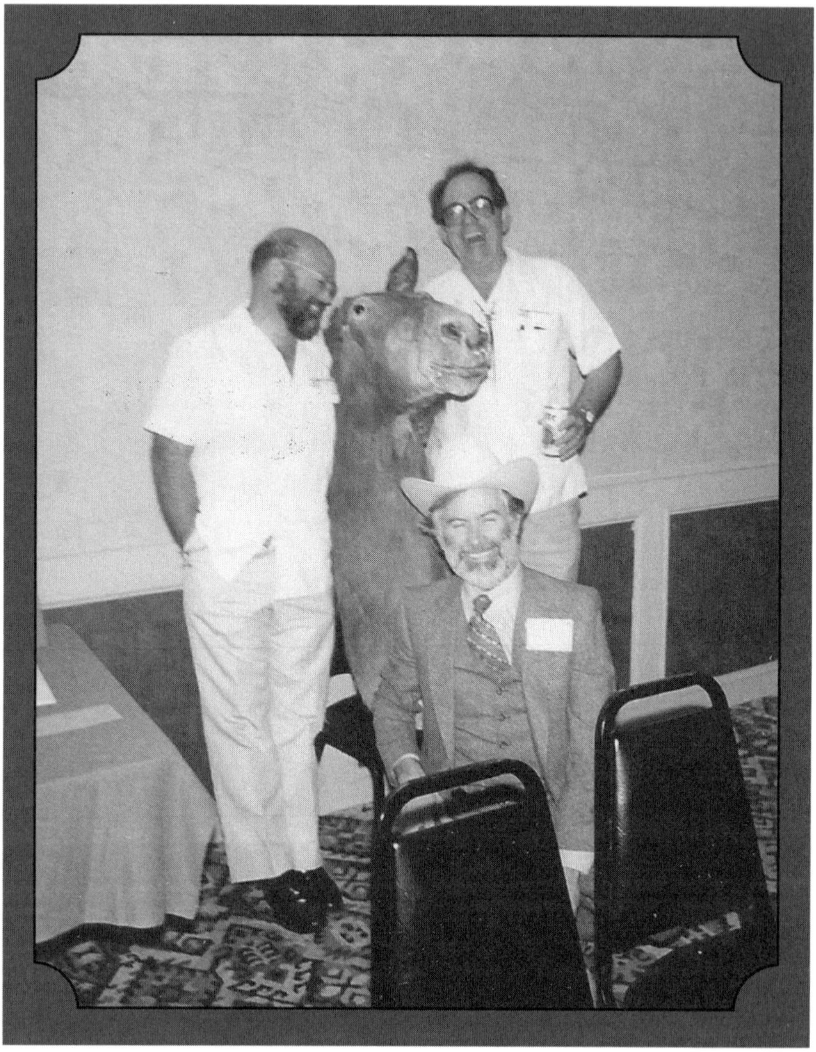

The author (front) with James Day and John O. West (in back, left and right) at a TFS meeting in Denton, 1981, where they first discussed bringing the NTSU published magazine, Southwestern American Literature, out west

JAMES AND JOHN: WILD AND CRAZY APOSTLES OF THE TFS WEST

by Jim Harris

For some readers of this informal remembrance of the Texas Folklore Society's deceased members James M. Day and John O. West, the names James and John of the title will bring images of the apostles of Christianity and Jesus' right-hand-men. Well, actually, they'd better imagine again. James M. and John O. were about as far from the Christian saints as Texarkana is from El Paso.

The scriptures tell us that Jesus rebuked his James and John for seeking their own glory. To be truthful, James M. and John O. did do a fair amount of glory seeking in their time—both were Texas Folklore Society (TFS) Presidents, and John even told me once that they wanted the Society's offices to go to El Paso when the TFS moved to Nacogdoches—but the times I was around James and John in the thirty-five years I knew them, they were more likely to be seeking the glory found in a Nebraska-raised T-bone steak and in a bottle of aged Mexican tequila, say a Jose Cuervo Especial.

The Bible James and John were brothers, their father Zebedee and their mother Salome. Before they ran with the disciples, they were fishermen, an occupation with which I strongly identify, although I never thought much about apostlehood. I do think of James M. and John O. as brothers of a certain kind, John having taken James under his wing in helping him obtain a job out west at UT-El Paso when things in the center of Texas looked bleak for James, the job market being tight for recent Ph.D.s and his first marriage in ruins. The two were brothers in arms in that John also had experienced a failed marriage.

To tell the truth, James M. and John O. acted just like blood brothers, often arguing then making up, or going for periods of time when they wouldn't speak to each other, then becoming the best of buddies again. It is said that Jesus referred to his James and John as "Boanerges," which sounds to me like residents of a backward country somewhere in the Middle East, but which translated means "sons of thunder." Sons of thunder. I'm not sure about the "thunder" part, but I did hear one bartender refer to our James and John as "sons of bitches." Actually, "thunder" might not be a bad word to use in reference to James M. and John O., since some of my memories of them are pictures of the two thundering down life's highways, one of their highway incidents soon to be related to the reader.

Another good parallel between the Bible guys and the Texas Folklore Society amigos was that the apostle John was referred to

James giving a paper at the 1983 meeting in College Station

as John the Beloved Disciple, that one of the twelve Jesus loved the most. Well, John O. was a beloved man in the TFS, his songs at the annual hootenannies and his presentations endearing him to more than one generation of the TFS membership.

Unfortunately, no one loved James M. that much. Or perhaps I should say, James M. was harder to love and usually rode the range with a burr under his saddle, with the bit between his teeth, and with his drawers in a wad. With several physical disabilities, James literally and figuratively had his bowels in an uproar quite regularly. I knew James to be a funny man who could be as good a company as you would want to have, but in large groups and more expansive social circles he seemed stuffy and contrary, a curmudgeon before his time. In one prolonged rage, he actually transferred from the University of Texas to Baylor to take his doctorate, something unimaginable in the parklands of Austin.

Now it should be obvious to most readers that the names James M. and John O. are a bit cumbersome and flow irritatingly slow to the ear. So, for the remainder of this essay the two men will be collectively referred to as "JJ," and individually referred to as "JM" and "JO."

No, maybe that's not such a good idea. Since there will be no other references from hereon to the Biblical characters, any future reference to James will be understood to mean James M. Day. The word John will refer to the contemporary beloved apostle who was the president of the TFS in 1969–1970, John O. West.

My memories of James and John are many, and they are all positive, save for the last one or two times I saw them in the final months and years of their lives—James in a wheelchair at the Paso del Norte Hotel, John looking through the screen in the doorway of his home watching the world continue to turn and lives move on.

Most of those fine and fun memories involve eating, drinking, and laughing in a variety of settings, including Texas Folklore Society gathering sites all over the state from El Paso to Jefferson and from Lubbock to Laredo. This informal recollection is all about two wild and crazy guys in the latter years of their wildness and craziness. In addition to the TFS annual meetings, the three of us were also together in a few other cities, such as Hobbs and Alamogordo, New Mexico, and Ciudad Juarez, Mexico.

Juarez was the one place in which we celebrated life's goodness more than any other; those times were, of course, before the city became the murder capital of the world. For James, John and me, Juarez was the Kentucky Club, the Cadillac, Martiniano's, the Cave, Casa del Sol, Julio's, and a few other places that would be referred to as joints or dives if they were north of the river. If certain of those places sound like bars, it's because they were, some of the finest historic and folkloric saloons in North America, where our talk always centered around motif types and folklore genres.

Yeah! If you believe that, I've got some Big Bend property for you that overlooks the Gulf of Mexico.

Fact is, I was never around James and John that we were not drinking, and our talk was more likely to be filled with tales other than the folk types. I'm sure the booze colored our relationship, but both James and John were good drunks, or good tipsy men, shall I say, at least in the times I was with them. Yes, there was a time in Texas history when a drunk could be a good guy, when a Texan had an inalienable right to drive his pickup with a six pack in the seat beside him and an open container in a hand.

With John taking the lead, jokes and laughter were always a part of our get-togethers, and there was just one time with them when my laughter momentarily stopped; even though the action in which we were involved was highly comic, at the same time it was a bit dangerous. We had started with "up" margaritas at the beautiful, historic 1920s Kentucky Club on a weekday. After several rounds, we moved to Julio's, my favorite cafe in all of Mexico. We drank more margaritas at Julio's while waiting for our steaks tampicano, then washed the side orders of enchiladas and beans down with Tecate and Corona.

When we were fat with lunch, around 3:00 p.m., James sobered up long enough to realize what time it was and to remember that he had a faculty senate meeting to attend in just a few minutes. He was president of the UT-El Paso faculty senate, and from the look on his face I knew it would not do for him to miss the meeting. This was classic, drawers-in-a-wad James.

So we ran out of Julio's, John pausing long enough to give all the female employees a hug and to shake the hand of the bartender, then James driving his boat-like Buick at breakneck speeds, aiming for the Juarez Avenue bridge. I was hunkering down in the couch-sized back seat, beginning my afternoon prayers early because the unfolding images all around the car looked to me like a sequence out of Gene Hackman's *The French Connection*, a film which featured one of the wildest chase scenes in cinema history. However, a better film comparison to this south-of-the-border ride might be several of the silent Keystone Cops movies.

The Buick engine's rpms were so high it sounded as if James had the transmission stuck in gear one or two. In addition, we were continually turning onto another street, James taking one of his back-road routes to the river. Along the larger streets, people were jumping back onto the sidewalks to get out of the way of the speeding car. A couple of times I dared to look out the back window to see if the police were following us or if one of the pedestrians did not reach the safety of the curb.

All the time this was happening, John was laughing his head off, one of his hands on the back of the seat and the other on the dashboard, bracing himself for whatever was to come. I mean John was roaring—never stopped talking, saying things like, "You almost got that sonovabitch!" Behind the wheel of the Buick, James was intent and focused, his face and bald head red and sweaty, hands at ten and two on the wheel. He looked like he was physically jerking the car right and left with his arm strength and his weight, which was considerable.

When we got within a few blocks of the Avenida Juarez Bridge, he started cursing. The "goddamned traffic" was backed up a block south of the bridge. At that point he turned off Juarez Avenue onto an especially narrow street with cars parked at both curbs, only one thin lane in the middle. James floored it. I didn't think big James could have walked through the middle of the street, much less drive the Buick, but he kept his foot on the pedal. With our speed increasing, John started singing, although I cannot remember if the song was "The Eyes of Texas," one of the Irish/Scottish ballads he knew by heart, or his temperance union song. By this time I was intermittently closing my eyes, opening them only when the tires screeched too long or someone on the sidewalk screamed.

Miraculously, James made it to the road that ran parallel to the river, but it looked to me like our luck was about to run out. Headed right for the banks of the Rio Grande, the four-ton auto slipped into a squealing, four-wheel drift that I thought would never end. John, who had stopped singing, whooped like a cowboy on a wild bronc. If he had been wearing a cowboy hat, he would have slapped it outside against the car's side.

When the Buick stopped moving sideways and with James driving like Sterling Moss, he gave it more gas and we were racing east along the river road, moving to the new International bridge which had several traffic lanes for crossing into the United States.

Still driving at what seemed like 80 mph, James was honking and weaving past slower cars, momentarily traveling in the wrong direction on the left side of the river road. This was about the time that I realized I needed to go to the bathroom. I was still praying, but now I was asking God that I would not have to excuse myself while the border patrol agents examined the Buick.

When we reached the bridge, James started cursing again, shouting to drivers and pedestrians, but luckily he found a lane with only one car. He sped across several lanes to get behind the one vehicle, and when we pulled up to the agent, James and John both knew the man in uniform. It was amazing, and I couldn't believe we weren't told to get out of the car, put our hands on the roof, and spread our legs. I never did understand if they knew the border patrol agent because they travelled into Mexico so much or if the federal worker had been one of their students. We were through the checkpoint with a laugh and with James laying down another track of sizzling hot and screeching rubber, this time on the new bridge's pavement.

I reminded James that we had three bottles of Jose Cuervo and Bacardi Anejo we were supposed to stop and pay tax on at the Texas kiosk. That brought more laugher from both men in the front seat. They didn't do no damn stopping for no damn Texas taxes. James never lowered the engine's rpms until we reached the UT-El Paso campus.

He pulled up to one building, jumped out of the car, leaving the door open and the engine running. He never said a word to us, as if he and John might have practiced this on an earlier occasion. John scooted behind the wheel, as I debated whether or not I should stay in the back seat or move up to the front. I still needed a restroom.

I didn't see James again on that trip to El Paso, but at the next TFS meeting, when I asked how he made out at the faculty senate meeting he simply said, "It went just fine." I tried to imagine him presiding while he was red-faced, sweaty, disheveled, and smashed, although riding in the speeding car might have sobered him up, as it did me.

James, John, and I were in Juarez several other times, but one other of the short trips into Mexico was especially memorable. It occurred in 1977, when the two El Paso amigos hosted the 61st annual Texas Folklore Society meeting at the Paso del Norte Hotel just a few blocks from the Juarez Avenue bridge.

James, John, and I had another lengthy meal at Julio's, but at this one the raunchy jokes weren't told and no one got wasted because we had some special guests. At this meal were my son Hawk, wife Mary, Jim Byrd, and Miss Martha Emmons, the grand lady of the Texas Folklore Society who had been a member since 1924. Miss Martha, as James liked to call her, had served twice as president of the TFS and had been active all that time except for a decade or so in the 1940s and 1950s. In his history of the TFS, Ab Abernethy has written that "Martha taught in Baylor's English department and stood guard over the Society's virtue with Baptist fortitude for sixty-five years."[1]

Always the guys wanting to shake things up, push the virtue boundaries, and have a good time, James and John conspired with Jim Byrd at the El Paso meeting to get Miss Martha across the river and into a Juarez bar. Julio's, with a bar attached to the dining room, was the best they could do.

Mary and I can't remember if it was James, John, or Byrd who put the margarita in her hands. When Miss Martha took a sip, several cameras flashed. Mary and I had a photograph of the occasion, but it must have been lost in the fire that took our home in 2008 because we have not been able to locate it among the pictures we salvaged. I will wager a six-pack of Dos Equis that among Byrd's belongings, those in his home following his death, there was an image of Martha abused by alcohol just across the Rio Grande in uncivilized and anti-Baptist Mexico. That's when Waco conservatism met Juarez radicalism, Baylor virtue introduced to UT-El Paso sinfulness.

As I mentioned, one of the traditions left out of the Martha Emmons foray into Juarez was the telling of dirty jokes. John always took the lead with the joke-telling. Anyone who was with him at a TFS Thursday night hoot would not be surprised to hear that John was not bashful in telling stories and that he always carried with him a wagonload of humorous anecdotes. He unloaded just a few of them in his book *Cowboy Folk Humor*, but he could go on all night and all day and never tell the same story twice. In that book, he wrote of humorous cowboy language, tall tales, pranks, the cowboy cook, and the ladies in cowboy culture. Many of these anecdotes and jokes had traveled around the state for several decades before John gave them his own twists and variations.

Although John did not relate this one in his book, the following story is short and in the spirit of the ones he liked, and could have been in the chapter he titled "The Ladies, God Bless 'em":

> A drunk cowboy entered a train and announced to the passengers he was going to rob every man and kiss every girl. A rancher stood up and said the thief could rob the men but he'd be damned if he was going to allow him to kiss the women. An old maid in the back of the train car told the rancher to sit down and shut up since he wasn't the man doing the robbing.

John O. giving a rather relaxed talk at the 1985 meeting in Abilene

In addition to being a good singer, John was a master teller of short anecdotes, tall tales, and limericks. I sure have missed his humor at this time when our nation is so ripe for a humorist's take on America's state of affairs. I can imagine how he would skewer the Tea Party hooligans in Washington or the Rick Perry prayer campaign in Austin.

Although they were both politically liberal, James was the perfect foil for John. Although he could be a very funny man, and often was, James tended to be reserved and serious in public. John was tall and boisterous, while James was short and reserved. James was more like Elmer Kelton's Hewey Calloway than John Ford's John Wayne characters. John O. gave presentations that made audiences laugh. James M. gave academic talks that made people think seriously about the folkloric implications of historic individuals and events.

The first TFS publication in which John's name appeared was *The Sunny Slopes of Long Ago*, edited by Wilson M. Hudson and Allen Maxwell, in 1966. John's article was on Billy the Kid. The first TFS book in which James's writings appeared was the book *Tire Shrinker to Dragster*, which was the 1967 TFS volume edited by Wilson Hudson. He wrote of "Silver Ingots in East Texas," which was about a legend of treasures buried in Hendricks Lake. I'm sure it was a real knee-slapper when James read it.

A few of the other writers with essays in the 1966 book, include J. Frank Dobie, John A. Lomax, Eugene Manlove Rhodes, Andy Adams, Paul Patterson, Mody C. Boatright, Everett A. Gillis, William D. Wittliff, Jan H. Brunvand, James T. Bratcher, John Q. Anderson, James W. Byrd, Francis E. Abernethy, James Ward Lee, and Wilson M. Hudson. Wow! What a collection of TFS royalty! And two of those guys are still energetic and active TFS members, forty-five years later, Ab Abernethy and Jim Lee, who look much younger than they really are.

For a little of the context in which James and John became my friends, the year of the 32nd PTFS, 1966, was seven years before Mary and I attended our first TFS meeting, held in 1973 at a hotel overlooking the Rio Grande in Laredo. We went to the meeting at the urging of Jim Byrd and Mason Brewer, whom I met at East Texas State University the year before.

The only person other than Byrd that I knew in that 1966 publication was Ab Abernethy, who taught in the English Department at Stephen F. Austin State University, where I received my bachelors and masters degrees. Ab was my professor one semester (1967) in a class called "Comedy and Satire," a class in which Fran Vick was also a student. The man who hired me to work in the English office when I was an undergraduate there was Ed Gaston, who served as the TFS treasurer for many years.

Accompanied by our half-crazed, Louisiana-born, mixed-breed dog we called Wolf (after Rip Van Winkle's dog) Mary and I drove from Cedar Creek Lake to the Laredo meeting in a Volkswagen, an un-air-conditioned sardine can that topped-out at 60 mph traveling down a hill. I don't remember much of the journey to Laredo;

quite possibly I have suppressed memories of the drive to keep me from having nightmares about traveling to our first TFS meeting.

I do remember some of the men and women we met at the meeting, folks who became *friends* of the Harris family. There were Paul Patterson, Joyce Roach, Jim Lee, Lou and Charles Rodenberger, Charles Linck and Ernestine Sewell, Sylvia Grider, Ernest Speck, Jack and Elizabeth Duncan, Sylvia Mahoney, Lawrence and Sonia Clayton, Kenneth Davis, Elmer Kelton, and Jim Byrd, for instance, all of whom came in later years to visit us in our home in Hobbs, New Mexico, the town to which we moved in the fall of 1974.

Jim Lee's visit was especially memorable, not because of the excellent presentation he gave at a Southwest writers conference, but because he almost beheaded himself when he ran into a double-two-by-six beam on our back porch. The accident had nothing to do with the Jack Daniels with Corona chasers we had been drinking; it had more to do with the fact I had built the porch awning to accommodate my height, and he is several inches taller than I am. After Jim picked himself up off my porch, he was not quite the same person for the remainder of the writers conference, and Mary thinks he has really not been the same for all the years since then.

I have strayed some from the subject of remembering James and John, but part of the reason for that straying has to do with the fact that it is hard for me to separate the two El Paso men from certain other TFS members. Jim W. Byrd was the man who connected me with the Society. Jim W. Lee was an English professor at nearby North Texas State University, which was a few miles to the west of Commerce.

In fact, for several years, a considerable portion of the TFS membership kept getting these two Jims confused, both being Alabama boys who got Texafied quickly when they moved to the Lone Star State. For years at TFS meetings, you could encounter elderly members examining the programs and asking, "Which one of those Alabama boys is this?" In their prime, both Byrd and Lee were hearty drinkers and eaters, Byrd preferring expensive scotch and "poke sallet" and Lee favoring anything with alcohol to wash down his chicken-fried steak and "mom an' 'em's" homemade pies.

Before I get too far from the subject of *The Sunny Slopes of Long Ago*, think about the context in which James Day and John West found themselves in 1966–1967. Along with several other members of that TFS generation, they were the young Turks, the men just getting their feet wet in the waters of the society founded on the banks of Austin's creeks and rivers. Since they were already members of an uppity academic world when I first met them, it's hard for me to think of either James or John as "young men," but the photographs of them at meetings in the 1960s and early 1970s show them to be among the youngest of the TFS presenters and activists. Forty years ago the Society was already old in the ages of its core membership, and Abernethy, Byrd, Lee, Roach, Day, West, and a few others were the youth needed if the organization were going to survive and prosper.

It looks to me like John rose quickly in the Society's ranks, becoming president in 1969, just three years after his first TFS publication. In the preface to *The Sunny Slopes of Long Ago*, Wilson Hudson mentioned Dobie, Lomax, Andy Adams, W. H. Hutchinson, Patterson, Boatright, Everett Gillis, and John, along with John's article on the legend of Billy the Kid. Hudson referred to Ab, Byrd, Lee, and others as "the rest of the contributors," although Lee had already been president and in just two more years Ab would become the secretary-editor.

The two other individuals Mary and I met in Laredo who became our longtime friends were, of course, James and John—who lived out West on the edge of the state, just as we did. Mary and I still live just across the state line in what is called "Little Texas." Living in El Paso, James and John had homes in a place which some New Mexico residents call "Little New Mexico," since it was "el Paso del Norte," along "el Camino Real," the road into the heart of the Land of Enchantment. New Mexicans still believe El Paso should be theirs and that Texans stole a considerable portion of New Mexico lands, especially along its eastern border.

In the late 1970s James, John, and I attended a meeting just a few miles north of El Paso. The New Mexico Folklore Society met in Alamogordo, and at that meeting James and John introduced me to C. L. "Doc" Sonnichsen, one of the grand men of the TFS. I met Sonnichsen where else but in a bar, a Holiday Inn watering hole. Doc was as impressive a man in person as he was in the voice speaking in the many books of history he authored. I will never forget the banquet speech he gave at the 1975 Houston TFS meeting, and it was obvious that James and John had an enormous amount of respect for him. He was a sort of intellectual godfather for them, and possibly for many in the cultural outpost of El Paso.

In the dark Alamogordo Holiday Inn bar where we spent a significant part of our time in that town, James told me how he and John had strong impulses to be active members of the New Mexico Folklore Society, which was the child of folklorist and English professor T. M. Pearce, whom I also met in Alamogordo. However, James told me, "We decided to cast our lot with the Texas Folklore Society," which to me says much about how strong is the lure of New Mexico out west where one is a long way from the Hill Country and Austin. There are many Texans who move to New Mexico and immediately renounce their hooligan Texas ways. Of course, James and John had many other reasons to become active in the TFS, both receiving their last degrees in the center of the state, John at the University of Texas and James at Baylor.

As I mentioned early in this essay, both James and John came more than once to visit the Harris family in Hobbs. James came alone one time soon after we moved into a house we had built north of Hobbs. One of the times John came he brought Jose Cisneros. That would have been in 2004, when the Lea County Museum, where I work, had a small exhibition of Jose's drawings and John gave a talk about the famous artist's life and work.

I have many memories of being at TFS annual meetings with the two men. When we met in El Paso in 1977, James and John brought two different states-of-mind together in the El Paso del Norte hotel by bringing the two state folklore societies together. Although they had a rich, four-hundred-year history on which to draw, the New Mexico Folklore Society members were struggling

An autographed photo given to James Day from John O. West, Mody Boatright, and Hudson Long (l-r)

to keep their organization alive, while the TFS had no trouble filling its annual programs. In addition, it is part of the popular culture in New Mexico that native New Mexicans are still uneasy breaking bread with the Texans next door.

At Galveston in 1987, Rudolfo Anaya gave the banquet speech, and James, John, and I drank beer in the Caribbean-themed hotel's bar called "Hemmingway's," irritatingly spelled with too many M's.

In 2001, at San Angelo, John O. (along with Martha Emmons and Ab Abernethy) was made a Fellow of the TFS. Of course, I have many fine memories of being with John's wife Lucy and his son Johnny. Mary and I were in the West home with the family several times, and John, Johnny, and I spent a couple of nights at my isolated desert camp in the Big Bend.

For the TFS members who have been around for a few years, there must be dozens of different memories, even strikingly different recollections, of these two men, but for me remembering James and John is a trip back to a time that already seems long ago. It's a time that will be no more in a city, or two cities, that will never be the same. I'd known El Paso and Juarez in history books, in novels, and in country-western songs, such as those of Marty Robbins. I saw the place up close through the eyes of James and John. One of the first times in the city with them, they drove me to the burial site of the dark angel of Texas, John Wesley Hardin. Beside the grave, we lingered in the shade of a concrete pillar holding up part of Interstate 10.

Now when I think of El Paso del Norte, I see buildings and humans out of Cormac McCarthy novels. In my mind, El Paso has changed that much. I miss spending a little time in the Kentucky Club. I miss James and John living on the concrete banks of the Rio Grande and giving the place specific meaning for me. And I miss James and John, TFS apostles out west, being there with me.

It's 11:00 a.m. on a Wednesday. James M. Day, John O. West, and I are sitting in the Kentucky Club in Ciudad Juarez. We represent three of the five early customers, and the bar still smells of the bleach dumped on the concrete floor, the morning mop leaving the place glistening in the sun slipping through windows made of ancient decorated glass. What we smell and see in the harsh light of our minds is a place that has the scent of heaven and grit honesty.

We have just ordered our first round of margaritas. They are served "up," which is to say cool without ice and with just a hint of triple sec and lime. Mostly, the squatty, steady glasses are filled with the best tequila in Mexico. In the Kentucky Club these drinks have the kick of an army mule. Even before the first drink, the space we occupy is all that was good when we were kids and all that we missed as adults.

The 1920 Kentucky Club, just two blocks south of America, may be the best bar in the world. It's where history is made and memories are built. It looks like it could have been constructed in the 1880s instead of the 1920s, the old black and white photos of century-old boxing matches, the 24" × 36" posters of famous Mexican bullfighters, now long dead, who performed a couple of miles away in the city's famous bullring. The Kentucky looks like a place Hemingway would have frequented in Havana in the 1920s or where Pancho Villa would have cooled down during his rampage through northern Mexico in 1914.

James and John, two good writers and storytellers, are in excellent spirits. Considering where they are and where they are going, why wouldn't they be?

They're away from the oppressive UT El Paso campus, and from the moment they climbed into James' lumbering Buick on the north side of the river John has been telling jokes, some of them vulgar, several of them with academic settings scatological, all of them from the multi-volume encyclopedia of humor he has carried in his head for much of his life. James and I have been laughing at him and with him as if each laugh adds hours to our lives.

But part of the joy of John's humor comes from the fact that the stories are an integral part of our collective lore, and they tell us where we are going, where we are, and where we have been. So we lift our glass to the future, to the here and the now, and to the sunny slopes of long ago.

ENDNOTE

1. Abernethy, Francis Edward. *The Texas Folklore Society 1943–1971, Volume II.* Publications of the Texas Folklore Society LIII. Denton: University of North Texas Press, 1994. 268.

The author speaking at a TFS meeting

EVERYTHING BUT THE KITCHEN SINK

GHOSTS, LEGENDS, LANGUAGE, AND OTHER LORE

The Dougherty house, built in the 1870s

GHOST STORIES AND LEGENDS OF OLD SAN PATRICIO

by J. Michael Sullivan

Last year as I walked into my Spanish class, I noticed pictures of big, creepy-looking houses, pictures that weren't usually in that classroom. As my attention was drawn toward one particular picture of a house, I realized I had been there many times. I told my teacher, "Mrs. Cornejo, umm, I have my family reunions at this house." She told me that that house was "Crazy Rachel's" house, and that she would be sharing with our class that story among other South Texas ghost stories and legends. I'm here to tell you that there are many ghost stories and legends of San Patricio, and no two of them are ever the same.

The ghost story that seems to be the most famous among residents of the area is the one Mrs. Cornejo told us in class that day about "Crazy Rachel." The legend says that if you go to the Dougherty house at night, you will see a woman sitting in an upstairs bedroom window rocking in a rocking chair or wandering around outside. The Rachel referred to as "Crazy Rachel" is Rachel Timon. The folk stories confuse her with Rachel Dougherty, my grandfather's grandmother, or my great-great-grandmother. Rachel Sullivan Dougherty and her husband Robert Dougherty built the house in the 1870s as a home for their family and a boarding school for boys, known as St. Paul's Academy. The family lived downstairs; the school was upstairs. The house sits on the shore of Round Lake, a lake of unknown origin just outside the town of San Patricio.

According to my mother, Rachel Timon was a great-niece to Rachel Sullivan Dougherty and did not live in the Dougherty house until after all of the original Doughertys had moved away or died. She lived in the house supposedly as caretaker, but my mother doesn't think Rachel Timon could be considered an actual caretaker. The family needed someone to live in the house, and Rachel needed a place to live. Although Rachel Timon wasn't actually crazy, she was an eccentric person and a recluse.[1] So, it's really not unthinkable that such stories of her could have started and grown, as they certainly have. Now, there have been other spiritual sightings at the house, but the "Crazy Rachel" stories are what have made the Dougherty house so popular among the youth of Orange Grove and surrounding communities.

Rachel Dougherty, the author's great-great-grandmother, who is often confused with "Crazy Rachel"

One night on the bus coming home from a baseball game, some of my friends were talking about wanting to go out to the cemetery in San Pat on Friday. In fact, tiny San Patricio has two cemeteries for kids to go to: the old cemetery on the hill, and the newer cemetery behind the church. From visiting the two cemeteries, especially the old one on the hill, I can see why some people might think that it is haunted. All the old headstones and the leafless trees give the cemetery an eerie look. While on the bus, someone asked me if I knew how to get to "Crazy Rachel's," and I told them that I have my family reunions at that house and that she is my kinfolk. They were surprised and asked, "Are you serious?"

I firmly answered, "Yes I am!"

I know from hearing other stories around school that often kids go sneaking out there to see if they can catch a glimpse of Rachel, or go out to the old San Pat cemetery to spot a ghost. In fact, a friend of mine went out to the Dougherty house one night and said he saw Rachel, but before he could try to get a closer look, the caretaker at the time came outside and started yelling and throwing rocks and waving a baseball bat, so he said he "hooked it out of there," and he actually has a scar running from his palm up to his forearm from when he jumped the barbed wire fence. When my older cousin Alainya was in school, kids were going out to the Dougherty house and the old cemetery. The first time my mother talked to Alainya about the house, before we started having family reunions, Alainya exclaimed, "Really? Crazy Rachel's house is our family home? Cool!" Up until that time, all she knew about the house was that it was supposed to be haunted with crazy ghosts all about.[2]

In fact, I have witnessed spirits at this house. Once when I was about ten years old, I was wandering around the house when I came across where there used to be a big, brick BBQ pit on the shore by the lake; now it is just bricks piled on top of one another. As I rounded the corner of the house, I started to hear voices and sounds of laughter. When I peered around the house toward where the voices were coming from, I saw a group of people having a BBQ on a brand new brick pit. I saw a few men standing around the pit, children running and playing, and the women and young

The remnants of a BBQ pit where the author saw a ghostly party

girls coming from in the house. It was all very clear, like it was actually happening. For a moment, it was as though I were in the 1940s. The pit is still there; it just is not as elaborate as it used to be. The piles of bricks that had fallen out of formation have since been hauled off to make the house more presentable to visitors, and personally, I think the ghosts wanted their house to look better, so they forced the caretaker to take care of the eyesore. The house is much less creepy now than it used to be; now it is painted, and pieces of the house aren't falling off anymore.

There is another legend of reported sightings of a Green Lady in the Round Lake area. In fact, one recent story is about when some men were working cattle in San Patricio and were to stay the night in the Dougherty house. Everyone was fine and comfortable, when all of a sudden from a bedroom fireplace, out walked "some green lady" as told by Richard Beall. He said, "so I ran outside and spent the rest of the night in my truck."[3] Another sighting of the green lady occurred from the porch of the McGloin house. The story goes that Mary Ann McGloin looked out over Round Lake and saw a "fairy-like lady dressed in green skimming

The Dougherty house today

so smoothly along that she might have been on solid ground."[4] When she told her husband Pat about the lady in green, he told her that his uncle Empresario James McGloin had once told Pat that when he lived in Ireland, a "Lass" was in love with him and "once was dressed in green." On the day he left her, she told him "that when she died she would haunt [him], and it would be on a lake and she'd be wearing her green dress and bonnet."[5]

There are many other ghost stories and legends of Old San Pat and the Coastal Bend that are still told in the area and considered legends of Old San Patricio. "Fort Lipantitlan was a Mexican army fort established in 1825 near San Patricio on the site of a Lipan Apache Indian camping grounds and an old presidio, on the bank of the Nueces River." There is a legend about this fort being haunted by "ghostly cries for mercy from a woman hidden in the mist wafting on the breeze."[6] The legend says that a young bride named Katie caught her husband leaving the house of another woman, Millie. Then Katie went to her friend Aggie's house and told her of what she had seen. Aggie told her to go back home and act like nothing had happened. Aggie got together with the other older women of the town, and they basically formed an angry, old person mob. The mob broke down Millie's door and dragged her outside and lynched her. The women left Millie hanging there until Katie's husband found her the next morning, cut her down, and buried her; then, he left Katie and Fort Lipantitlan, never to return. Millie's cries are *still* heard throughout Fort Lipantitlan.[7]

One legend is said to have actually taken place in Corpus Christi, which is about twenty miles from San Patricio. While County Judge Walter Timon was sitting in front of his fireplace, he looked up and saw the apparition of a man standing by the fireside. What made this figure so strange was that the circle of flames engulfed the entire apparition and disappeared just as quickly as it had appeared.[8] Other people have also seen the man in the circle of flames, and to this day no one has been able to figure out who the man is or why he appears in fire. But it also took place in San Patricio at the Bayou Ranch near Round Lake. Emelia Sullivan Timon saw the same apparition that the Judge did. "It is said that Mrs. Mary Dunn Magown saw the same ghost at the Bayou Ranch when she came once to stay with the Timon children when Emelia and Harry were away."[9]

I'm sure you've all heard of the Headless Horseman of Sleepy Hollow. Well, "there are those who live on the small ranches in the mesquite thickets around Alice and Ben Bolt, not far from San Patricio, who claim to have caught a glimpse of a headless rider, galloping through the moonlit night, and others who say they have seen him stopping at a willow-choked *resaca* to let his weary horse have a drink." Unlike Washington Irving's headless horseman, "The Headless One of Texas, or *El Muerto* as he is called, has his head, neatly covered with a wide-brimmed sombrero, and attached to his saddle horn by a long strip of rawhide where it swings eerily back and forth to the rhythm of the horse's moving feet."[10]

The legend goes that he was a horse thief named Vidal, and when he was finally caught, he was beheaded and strapped to a saddle on top of a wild mustang with his head hanging on the long rope, and the horse ran off. Since the horse was wild, it would have nothing to do with humans, so it would stay to the brush, and only a lonely explorer would find the horse and *El Muerto*. Any time other riders would see him, they would shoot at him, and the best marksmen would swear that they killed him, but the headless one would ride off with his chest up. When the wild pony was finally captured, still strapped firmly on his back was the dried-up corpse of Vidal, now riddled by scores of bullet holes, testifying to the correctness of the many marksmen who swore they had not missed. The body was buried in an unmarked grave near Ben Bolt, and the poor horse set free at last. And it is said that *El Muerto* will not die.[11]

The Old San Patricio Courthouse is said to be haunted by the ghost of Josefa Chipita Rodriguez, which is without doubt the most famous ghost story and legend of Old San Pat. Chipita is the only woman legally hanged in Texas, after she was accused of committing an axe murder. While the jury recommended mercy, the judge ordered her executed on November 13, 1863.[12] On the day of her execution, my great-great-grandmother, Rachel Sullivan (before she was married), gave Chipita the dress that she wore when Chipita was executed. I have been told that when Chipita's coffin was being carried off in a wagon to an unmarked grave, one of Rachel's brothers sneaked off and followed. When he heard a "thump and a moan" from inside the coffin, he ran off as fast as his legs would take him.[13] Many people claim to have seen her ghost, a woman with a rope around her neck wandering the streets of San Patricio, inside the Old Courthouse, and along the river where she had lived.

Not all stories have to deal with spirits and ghosts; I have found legends of buried treasure, as well. One of my favorite buried treasure stories takes place in the San Patricio area. John Henrichson had bought and sold ranches from Nuecestown to Sandia, all the way up the Nueces River Valley.[14] He didn't believe in banks, so he buried his riches on the ranches for his children. Henrichson buried the gold in iron pots, chests, and strong leather bags.[15] While on his death bed, he called for his son George because, up to this point, no one knew where he had buried it. He tried to tell George, but all he could get out was "Under the posts . . .

San Patricio, home to just over 300 residents

the posts . . . in the corral . . . the third . . . by . . . the gate" and those were his last words.[16] So the problem, was which corrals? Which ranch? Was it more than one set of corrals? According to the legend, the family never found the gold.[17]

Another buried treasure story is called, ironically, "Another Buried Treasure Story."[18] Back in the early 1800s, people who were traveling were often forced to bury their gold because it was such a heavy load. One day, Mustang Grey, whose real name was Pat Quinn, and his partner stole a large amount of gold from some Mexican soldiers and buried it under a mesquite tree at the bank of the Nueces River at El Paso de Piedras, or Old Rock Crossing, at Fort Lipantitlan. Years later, the partner asked John Timon to go with him to find the gold. They could not find the treasure, but they found where others had searched for the buried treasure. The treasure in question may still be buried there, or the tree and gold may have been washed in to the Nueces River. Who knows?[19]

These examples only scratch the surface of the countless number of ghost stories and legends in the San Patricio area. I hope to be able to share many more with you for years to come.

Endnotes

1. Campbell, Mary Margaret Dougherty. Personal interview. January 17, 2010.
2. Ibid.
3. Campbell, Cody. Personal interview. January 17, 2010.
4. Hebert, Rachel Bluntzer. *The Forgotten Colony: San Patricio de Hibernia*. Burnet, Texas: Eakin, 1981. 382.
5. Ibid. 383–84.
6. Coleman, Elaine. *Texas Haunted Forts.* Plano, Texas: Republic of Texas. 2001. 51.
7. Ibid. 52–54.
8. Williams, Docia Schultz. *Ghosts Along the Texas Coast.* Plano, Texas: Republic of Texas, 1995. 104.
9. Hebert. 389.
10. Fowler, Zinita Parsons. *Ghosts of Old Texas.* Austin: Eakin, 1983. 25.
11. Ibid. 26–27.
12. "Texas Hauntings." *San Antonio Paranormal Network.* www.ghost411 .com/texas hauntings. Accessed January 18, 2010.
13. Knight, Mary Elizabeth. Telephone interview. December 29, 2009.
14. Crofford, Lena H. *Pioneers on the Nueces.* San Antonio: Naylor, 1963. 42.
15. Ibid. 51.
16. Ibid. 49.
17. Ibid. 52.
18. Ibid. 63.
19. Ibid. 64.

A Hereford bull similar to the one the Widow Malvern lost
(Photo by Ron Mouser)

THE WIDOW'S REVENGE: THE GENESIS AND DEVELOPMENT OF A TALE IN BELL COUNTY

by Kenneth W. Davis

In a good year in Bell County, roasting ears are ready by June 19. Bulls don't know that June 'Teenth has festive connotations. They do know that fresh roasting ears are good, along with a bit of a salad from the tender leaves on corn stalks. The Widow Malvern's bull had only a good meal on his mind when he jumped out of his pasture and went to a nearby corn patch to eat his fill of forbidden fruit on June 19, 1943. This bull planned to have a feast and then return to his small harem of Herefords, over whose welfare he presided with a majesty befitting his English ancestry. But like the fox who ate the grapes, he found jumping back over the fence impossible because of the extra weight several hours of doing violence to a corn patch added to his rotund frame. If he made any other attempts to return to his wives and family dear, he soon gave up and sauntered out of the corn field to disappear for months in the pastures by the Salado Creek.

I learned of the bull's escape late in the afternoon. The Widow Malvern came up to our kitchen door from our bottom pasture and asked in delicate terms—so as not to offend my patrician mother "Has any of youall seen my male animal?" In those days, no one ever affronted the ears of a lady with the word "bull." My mother called my father from the supper table to ask him about the animal. He had not seen it, but promised to inquire in town the next day. He assured the widow that her creature would come home, but the widow was inconsolable; she suspected people down the road were trying to get the services of her bull for free.

The widow might have become hysterical, but my mother appeared with a soul-calming glass of iced tea laced with mint. She invited the Widow Malvern to have supper. The widow took the tea, but declined the meal with several "much obliged, nevertheless" statements. She protested that she had some pastures to scour before dark in her search for the bull, one of the few registered Herefords in the neighborhood. The word "scour" had two other meanings for me at the time: people used Brillo pads to scour pots and pans. And baby calves got the scours from too much rich milk. I didn't quite know what image to conjure up from the widow's plan to scour the pastures.

The next day, my father inquired about the widow's bull when we went to town and he was getting his monthly haircut. He first asked the spit-and-whittle boys who were sitting as usual under the sheet-iron awning in front of Buschland's Hamburger Stand and Café. They showed a powerful interest in the matter. By the time my father was in the barber chair, the June heat drove them into the relative coolness of the shop whose tall Emerson fan kept the air stirred up. Here, the many fascinating accounts of the bull's long absence began to develop.

My father asked the barbers where the bull might be. The tellers of tales then took over. A short, near-sighted man, a former dollar-a-year constable who thereafter was known as "Shurf Tawm," cleared his throat, a sure signal that he was about to pronounce great legal truths. He waited for the drawls of his cronies to stop, and then he began.

"Well, sir, I reckon the Widow Malvern ain't got no legal problems onless, and this is a important 'onless,' she didn't make shore and certain the gate to that air pasture were shut tight. Now, if she or some of them kids that sorry man of hers give her has left that gate open agin, she ain't got a case at all."

In this snippet the yarn acquires details totally unrelated to the original incident. The retired constable soon added that the Malvern woman was not really a "widow." To the assembled crowd he explained patiently yet again, that old Bob Ed Malvern up and left his wife when things were so difficult in the Depression just before "Mr. Roosevelt got us in the war to boost the economy." He went on to say that people called her "Widow Malvern" for the sake of politeness so that she would not have to explain that her man left her. This squinting sage would have gone on forever about the matter, but he was interrupted by a man built like a fifty-gallon gasoline drum. This man, probably a descendent of Chaucer's Miller, was a chain smoker before the government damned smoking. He had heroic emphysema.

"Tawm, you old mole," he wheezed, "you blind-as-a-bat old coot, you've told us that mess a hundred times. Why don't you tell it like it is? You know that the woman collected five hundred dollars on her old aunt's insurance and instead of buying a pickup that Bob Ed wanted, she bought that there bull and he filed papers for divorce but couldn't go through with it 'cause he didn't have no money to hire a smooth talkin' Temple lawyer to win the case." By then, this victim of nicotine's curse was red-faced and huffing in a grandly rhythmic pattern. The older barber spoke up. He was a man known for his sensible nature. When he cut hair, he was serious about it, and when he resolved to keep the dancer separate from the dance, he could be awesome.

He began: "I don't see what in the purple-starred Hell that pore woman's marital problems has to do with the undisputable fact that her bull has strayed. You know that the main issue here is that <u>the bull is lost</u>. Claude Davis tells the truth, and, anyway, he wouldn't lie about something as serious as a widow woman's bull. All you boys can think about is that pore woman's marriage shot all to Hell. It just don't make sense at all." The curly-headed younger barber kept silent. Rumors held that he and the supposed widow were "keeping company." His face was a frozen study, but maroon splotches appeared on his cheeks. His neck turned red as a beet in black dirt.

The yarn was now on its way to becoming fully developed. Doubtless, more details were added to it that day, but the old barber, nicknamed "Baldy," finished my father's haircut, and with a grand flourish snapped the cloth to remove all the clipped hair. As we left, the ancients promised to keep an eye out for the "widder's bull."

A few days later, the Widow Malvern came drooping to our back porch pitifully begging news of her prized male animal, whose name was Prince Hamlet. The widow had read only one play. Because her high school teacher told her *Hamlet* was the best play written, the widow saw no need to read further. With serene disregard for gender, she named all her animals after characters in *Hamlet*. She had a boar hog named Ophelia, an evil-tempered Leghorn rooster named Gertrude, and a milk-goat named Polonius. My father told her he would ask about the bull at the Taylor auction the next day. The tearful widow reaffirmed her fears that the sullen people down the road were keeping Prince Hamlet locked up with their heifers just to avoid paying "service" fees. My father offered to go with the widow to ask these notorious cheapskates about the bull, but the widow declined.

Next day, in Taylor, my father asked everyone about the bull. No one had information about the missing creature, but several of the regulars who never missed an auction or a dog fight added some ingredients to the developing yarn. A local dentist, whose secret ambition was to be an honest-to-God Paul Patterson-type cowboy, and who regularly slipped away from his office to be at the main part of the auction, said that he had a patient from Holland on the 20th or 21st of June who told him that the widow was offering a five-hundred-dollar reward for the bull's safe return, with no questions asked about how much "work" the bull had done for "free." My father smiled and noted that the only time in the widow's life she had had five hundred dollars was when her aunt providentially passed on and left the insurance money. He explained to the embarrassed dentist that the widow had bought the bull with the inheritance. The dentist nodded ruefully and noted: "They didn't teach us at the Baylor Dental School about what some folks will do to the facts."

Later in the afternoon, one of my father's friends hurried over to catch us before we were to leave.

"Well, sir," he began, "you can keep askin' around about that bull with some fool English name all you want to, but the truth of the matter is that the wider-woman probably has up and sold it and is just wanting people to feel sorry for her. Did I ever tell you about the time she done me out of $25 honest-fair-and-square money for some cabinets I built for her? She'd skin a flea for its hide and tallow."

My father was too eager to return home before dark to listen to this yarn again, so he merely waved at the lamenter and gunned the pickup's engine. We departed the Taylor auction barn in a cloud of blue smoke and dust. For a few days, we heard no more about the missing royalty, Prince Hamlet.

But on the following Saturday, we heard a new dimension to the tale. In Holland there was a pious, God-fearing cattle trader named John Roberson. So great was his reputation for uprightness that he was called "Mr. John" by everyone in the area. My father casually asked Mr. John about the widow's bull. The men sitting under the shade of the awning at Buschland's Hamburger Stand and Café perked up. Mr. John was known for seeing moral allegories in everything from a flat tire to the failure of Divinity candy on damp days.

"Well, Claude," he began. "As I see it, that bull's leaving home tells us something we need to remember in life's journey." I sagged. I had heard this man's impromptu sermons before; his homilies lasted longer than an ice-cold Delaware Punch could stay chilled even on a brisk autumn morning, much less on a hot July afternoon when sweat beads formed glistening diamonds on the pale foreheads of the worthies who awaited Mr. John's profound comments. "As I see it," he continued, "the Widow's bull is like Joseph in the Bible who sold his birthright and ended up sleeping with the hogs until he got the sense to come home and be welcomed with a banquet and the open arms of his daddy." The moral application droned on. I suspected that Mr. John had a couple of stories all mixed up in his mind, but what did I know? I was only eleven at the time, and although I was a bookish kid when I wasn't sneaking around with my friends racing horses like a drunken Comanche, I wasn't keen on biblical study. Not until years later, when I may have grown up, did I learn that Mr. John had studied for the ministry at a famous seminary in Texas and had been asked to leave before graduation. His mentors at that bastion of inerrancy felt uncomfortable about his enthusiasm for conflating several passages of holy scripture into a theme suited to his purposes.

Stories about Prince Hamlet's departure spread at meetings of ladies' aid societies at the several churches. The Episcopalian ladies discussed the matter in detail. One militantly chaste maiden lady, a mystery woman who supposedly inherited a fortune from her gambler father, was troubled by the reports of the widow's concerns over lost revenue from the bull's "services." Since she had turned twenty-one, this always elegantly dressed woman sometimes drove off in her Buick Roadmaster and disappeared for weeks. In her later years, her hearing was bad, so she was slow to figure out the substance behind the barrage of evasive words about the widow's lost revenue. When she did comprehend that the Widow Malvern was losing the fees charged for impregnating cows, she was outraged; she said, "But it's the man who pays . . . ." I acquired this information from my grandmother's housekeeper who sometimes took an afternoon off to work at the church to earn what she called that "good old Episcopalian money from them rich women."

What the pious ladies at the church circles couldn't add to the yarn, the ones who went to Mamie Jo's Beauty Parlor and Magazine Rack supplied. In most cultures, barbershops and beauty salons are seedbeds for splendid yarns—even gossip. Eudora Welty demonstrated this fact in her story "Petrified Man." Mamie Jo's customers got all the available details about Prince Hamlet's absence and then rearranged them the way some folks put a patchwork quilt together. The results were amazing. The ladies at Mamie Jo's concluded that the Widow Malvern got what was coming to her for giving a dumb animal such a highfalutin name.

The bull returned in late fall of 1943. He looked more like Pharaoh's lean kine than the fatted calf. The Widow Malvern came to tell us about this bovine prodigal. She wept as she described the once proud beast's fallen condition. She said, "My Prince Hamlet is so skinny you can use his hips to hang a hat on. My youngest is learning to count by looking across the road at that pore animal's ribs." The widow's youngest, by the way, through one of nature's miracles, was born a full year after old Bob Ed Malvern absquatulated. The child had a head of curly hair like that of the silent barber.

I thought the story had ended; the bull was home. But on the Fourth of July, 1944, the Davis and Ponder families had a reunion on the banks of the Salado Creek at the north of our small ranch. Many of my cousins were off in distant places such as North Africa, or the South Pacific, but uncles and aunts and assorted in-laws gathered for feasting on fried chicken, potato salad made from freshly dug Irish potatoes (we had an early crop that year), and Lord knows what else. Ice-cream made with real milk—the unpasteurized kind that can carry all sorts of diseases but which tastes better than any pasteurized, homogenized stuff—was plentiful, along with huge wedges of real cake, not the "generic supermarket" kind. When the meal was over and we were waiting until enough time had elapsed so that we could swim without fear of getting leg or stomach cramps, the story telling began. Aunt Grace, who played the best ragtime piano in three counties, led off with a new story she heard somewhere about a bull. Here is a brief version of her account:

> The Widow Malvern's old cow was in the pasture across the road from the Fergusons' corn patch. The Collyer girls were hoofing towards Belton, it being a pay-day for some of the soldiers at Camp Hood. Their dim-witted brother took after them in that '34 V8 he has to drive now that his daddy's drinking got his license lifted. Old Jim Collyer didn't want the girls to go into town for commercial reasons; so he told that son of his to bring them back. He didn't even believe that it was right for the widow to charge for the hire of her creature. Said it went against nature and the Bible. Those Collyer girls would run as fast as they could, but, of

> course, they couldn't outrun that Ford. And when they got out of breath, they'd run into the ditch to get away from Junior Collyer. He—like the flat-out nit-wit that he is—would take right after them. Got stuck in the ditch every time. Then, he'd start sweet talking the girls and promise a ride into town if they'd help him get the car on the road. They fell for it every time. All those Collyers are a bit feeble, you know. That's what comes from cousins getting married.

I must interrupt Aunt Grace here to say that she gazed sternly at a boy and girl about seventeen years old who were third cousins twice removed by marriage and who were the current scandal in the family because of their fervent attraction to each other. The fact that they were no blood kin mattered not to my aunt who, like Mr. John, found moral applications everywhere. The story resumes:

> The third or fourth time that idiot ran the car in the ditch, it was right by the widow's pasture. That time that Ford ended up with a broken radiator; steam shot up in the air for several yards. Junior was so mad he began to honk the horn for all it was worth; the cows in the pasture commenced running around in circles. Even the widow's bees flew out of their hives. Grady Ferguson saw it all and said the widow's cows would give blinky milk for a week, and that the bees' honey would turn to sugar ahead of time. That fancy male cow of hers was so upset by the commotion that he jumped the fence and hid out in the river bottoms until after first frost killed off all the green stuff; then, like the prodigal son, he came home from that far country. The Widow Malvern lost a lot of money on the deal, but she got her bull back.

Aunt Grace concluded by telling us that in the spring of 1944, there were more half-Hereford calves born in Bell County than at any time in recorded history. Where my aunt picked up her version of the yarn is a mystery. She didn't believe in going to beauty parlors for sets or shampoos and she was a deep-water Baptist. She hadn't heard it from our family, either.

I left Bell County in 1946. When I was there again years later in the same barbershop, I heard about a phantom Hereford bull—like the one in Irish mythology—that on moonlit nights in autumn fraternizes with registered Jersey and Guernsey cows. The results are calves worthless as breeding stock; all they are good for is to fatten as beef cattle.

The story, then, evolved until it had just about all the characteristics of good yarns. It went from facts to fantasy and even myth; the empirical facts were translated into a truth that we lovers of folklore appreciate.

The Widow Malvern lived to be more than ninety years old in the protective care of her many children, particularly that of her youngest, the curly-headed one. When she heard stories the spit-and-whittle crowd by Buschland's Café told of a ghostly bull, she smiled wisely and insisted the half-breed calves were a "widow's revenge." For her sake, and for the sake of that sometimes maligned bull, Prince Hamlet, I hope the widow was right. May their spirits rest, but may their stories live on.

[This article was previously published in *The Cross Timbers Review*. Cisco College, Spring 1985.]

A postcard featuring a "Legendary Longhorn"

TIP TO TIP—LEGENDARY TEXAS LONGHORNS

by Henry Wolff, Jr.

I saw my first Texas longhorn steer when an animal show came to my hometown of Ballinger, Texas, sometime shortly after World War II. Even though the steer did not have a horn spread that would compare with some of the more legendary Texas longhorns of the past or present, it did have a nice curved set of horns wide enough to impress a boy who had never seen anything like it. Living out in the country in the Runnels County farming community of Dry Ridge, we only had Jersey milk cows, along with the crossbred feeder calves that my dad bought each year to run on Sudan grass and maize stubble.

In the mid-1940s, longhorns were few and far between in Texas after having been virtually bred out of existence. The longhorned cattle that had evolved from the earlier Spanish mission herds would nearly become extinct in Texas except for a small number of herds of selected animals being kept by old-time ranchers interested in preserving the Texas cattle.

The federal government joined in the effort to save the longhorn when it was decided in the mid-1920s to build a typical herd at the Wichita Mountains National Wildlife Refuge in Oklahoma; another herd was built in 1936 at the Fort Niobrara Wildlife Refuge in Nebraska.

In 1948, folklorist J. Frank Dobie and one of the ranchers who had maintained a herd of longhorns, Graves Peeler of McMullen County, assisted in establishing a small state maintained herd in Fort Griffin State Park at Albany, Texas. More than two decades before, at the 1926 annual meeting in Austin, the Texas Folklore Society adopted a resolution submitted by Dobie to save the longhorn. He had written an article for The Cattlemen on "The Texas Longhorn's Dying Bellow."

Thanks to men like Dobie and Peeler, Will Barnes of the Wichita refuge, and Texas ranchers Milby and Henry Butler, E. H. Marks, Jack Phillips, M. P. Wright, II and Cap Yates, there are Texas longhorns, legendary and otherwise, to this day. There are longhorn breeders scattered throughout Texas, and the historic breed can be seen on numerous ranches in other states as well. It was years after seeing that first longhorn, however, before I would be equally impressed, and that was only a couple of times at the Brackenridge Park Zoo in San Antonio, where longhorns were an attraction along with exotic animals from other lands.

Longhorns would remain an oddity until the second half of the 20th Century when there was a renewed interest in the breed among Texas ranchers. When I wrote a newspaper article in 1966 on Walter B. Scott establishing a herd at Goliad from Graves Peeler stock, the *Victoria Advocate* headlined the story, "Legendary Longhorn Revived, History on the Hoof at Goliad." Significantly, it was at Goliad where many of the earliest longhorns once grazed the vast acreage of Mission Espiritu Santo, which historians have labeled the first great cattle ranch in Texas. The herd, once numbering in the thousands, was started prior to 1749 at an earlier location of the mission near present Victoria.

The renewed interest in these historic cattle resulted in the organization of the Texas Longhorn Breeders Association of America in 1964. The previously mentioned old-time ranchers contributed to the salvation of the breed and to what is known today as the "seven families of longhorns," referring to distinctive bloodlines within the breed. One of the ranchers, E. H. Marks, had a particular flair for showmanship, as did his son, Travis Marks. The younger Marks moved his longhorn operation to Goliad County in 1973, bringing with him a steer named Ranger that carried dignitaries for a number of years in the grand entry of the Houston Livestock Show and Rodeo.

On his father's ranch at Barker, Travis had become interested in training longhorn steers to ride while still in his teenage years and helped to ready a steer appropriately named Barker that Tex McDaniel rode to New York in 1932. McDaniel completed

2,500 miles to New York City and then headed toward Washington, D.C., where he had hoped to arrive in time to see Texan John Nance Gardner sworn in as Vice-President of the United States, but he did not reach the capitol city until the end of April. The steer had worn out twenty sets of steel ox shoes. Ranger died at the age of twenty-six in 1985, but another Marks-trained longhorn, Diamond, now owned by his daughter Suzanne Marks Steffens, continued to appear at Goliad as a "reinsteer" pulling Santa Claus in a one-steer open sleigh.[1]

There are a number of different things that can make a longhorn legendary, but the one thing that they all have in common is horns. While none of the previously mentioned steers had horns that would necessarily make them legendary, each was gifted with a nice spread. Perhaps it should be mentioned that it is the castrated male longhorn that grows the longest horns. While there are notable horn widths on some cows and bulls, it is the steers that are best known for their horns—the longer the better, and preferably with a nice curve.

Unfortunately, it is not always easy to compare horn widths of the most notable of the breed since varying methods have been used throughout the years to measure horns, the more acceptable being from tip to tip, though that is not always the case. Measurements are sometimes made all along the horn, and even when known this makes it difficult to compare with steers that were measured straight across.

One of the most impressive publicly displayed set of horns graces Old Tex, the stuffed steer at the Buckhorn Saloon and Museum in San Antonio that is promoted as having a spread of 8 feet and 9 inches. This is indeed a magnificent set of horns, though there has long been some question as to whether they were straightened by some method. The natural twist in horns can supposedly be straightened by steaming or boiling to give more length.

After visiting Old Tex in 1993, when the stuffed steer was still at the Buckhorn Hall of Horns at the Lone Star Brewery rather than at the present museum in downtown San Antonio, a docent

A postcard featuring Old Tex, in the Buckhorn Curio Store in San Antonio

privately admitted that the spread is "actually 8 feet and 1 3/8 inches." "I guess stretching the truth is a part of storytelling," Jack Posey noted.[2] The horns were originally from a steer named Old Broad that was killed by lightning on a ranch near Bandera; they were purchased by San Antonio bar owner Albert Friedrich for $5. When the horns were attached to the mounted body of another steer, the combination became Old Tex. It is said that Friedrich would remove the horns at night and place them in a safe.[3]

Another widely known exceptionally horned steer was Champion, referred to as "the best-known steer in the world" by Dobie in his book, *The Longhorns.* "For more than 40 years his likeness on postcards has circulated from Newark to El Paso," Dobie noted. "It has been published many times in magazines, newspapers, textbooks and trade books, and has served as a model for countless drawings. It has become the standard representation of Longhorn cattle."[4] The postcards are still being circulated among

A postcard, purportedly featuring Jim Dobie and Champion, who was confused with another legendary longhorn

collectors, nationally and internationally, and I paid a price that I won't mention for one showing Jim Dobie and four other men with the steer, likely when Champion was being exhibited in 1899 at the International Fair in San Antonio. Dobie is believed to be the man standing at the left behind the horn in the extensively retouched and hand colored photograph. The name of the steer is mistakenly given as "Jeronimo," apparently being confused with George West's famous lead steer Geronimo.

West was at the exposition with another steer described by J. Frank Dobie as being "worthy of consideration." Both Jim Dobie and George West were from Live Oak County, and Jim was an uncle of J. Frank Dobie. Jim Dobie had purchased the steer in the fall of 1892 from Nick Dunn of Nueces County in "a bunch of 200 steers at $12 around," and Dobie further notes in *The Longhorns* that the steer was only a "long-two," but had a six-year-old head. "I can see him yet," Dobie wrote, "between a pale red and brown in color, mighty-framed but narrow, the ponderous horns, which were reaching maturity by then, weighing his head low when he stood and wobbling it when he walked. To scratch the root of his tail with a horn-tip, he had but to turn his head slightly."[5]

While postcards give the steer's horn length as a wondrous 9 feet and 6 inches, New York and Chicago newspapers added an extra inch for good measurement. A South Texas cowboy and for a time world champion roper, Will Edison, who had worked for Jim Dobie, measured Champion's horns from tip to tip as 8 feet and 7 3/8 inches. In April 1900, the *Beeville Bee* reported that Champion had a spread of 7 feet and 8 inches and, in June, "a little less than 6 feet across" or 7 feet and 8½ inches following the curves.[6] The rival *Bee Picayune* reported a straight across spread of 6 feet and 3 inches. As Dobie commented in *The Longhorns*, anything over six feet was notable, which is true of horn spreads to this day.

According to an article on horns and measurements in the December 1992 *Texas Longhorn Journal*, Champion's horns are in the Smithsonian Institution. A former resident of St. Louis, Missouri, Jerry Stone purchased the horns from a gas station operator before moving to Texas and learning of the famous steer. He contacted the museum and the horns were verified as being from the famed Dobie steer. The steer George West had at the International Fair had a spread of 7 feet and 9 inches straight across and an upward curvature that put the tips over eight feet above his hoofs.

Not only can horn lengths vary by the method of measurement, but also in the telling, an example of the latter being the spreads of some oxen that the missionary Baptist Bill Grumbles described. A truthful man, according to Dobie, the good reverend claimed to have freighted between Port Lavaca and Austin with a couple of oxen with spreads of 13 feet and 6 ½ inches from tip to tip and 11 feet and 6 ½ inches. The trails must have been wider in those days than most of us can imagine.

Victoria County rancher Al McFaddin raised a steer with a spread of 8 feet and 9 inches, though the method of measurement is uncertain. The 88th anniversary edition of the *Victoria Advocate* in 1934 credited it as being "the longest horned steer in Texas." As late as 1960, the McFaddin steer was featured in a Ripley's *Believe It or Not* cartoon. McFaddin sold the steer sometime before 1934 to R. C. Sutton, and Louis A. Schreiner later purchased it for $1,000, it not being known if Schreiner got it from Sutton or some other party. "Its horns are said by old-time cattlemen to be more typical of the horns of the steers of the '70s and '80s than any now in existence," the *Victoria Advocate* noted in 1934. "It can now be seen on the Schreiner game preserve near Kerrville."[7]

An old, undated newspaper clipping in the Ripley files mentions that the steer "numbered among Charles Schreiner's show herd of Longhorn steers."[8] Assuming the above refers to Louis A. Schreiner's father who died in 1927, that would mean that the steer left Victoria County before the 1930s. I recall someone once saying the horns of the McFaddin steer were on display in "the Schreiner bank at Kerrville." Kathryn Lowery Livingston of the McFaddin Ranch family recalls the late Charles Schreiner III telling her that he had the horns in his home, but I have yet to verify where the steer or its horns ended up. It is also of interest that Schreiner donated seven head of Spanish longhorn cattle—"all with exceptional horns"—to the Brackenridge Zoo in San Antonio in June of 1937.[9]

Another notable set of horns from the Victoria area was a diamond-studded set in a head mount that Dennis O'Connor sent to President William McKinley in 1897, around the time of McKinley's inauguration and three years prior to the 25th U.S. President's assassination in 1901. They were a nice set of curved horns with a good width; Dobie described them as being "finely mounted, a Texas star set in one horn and a buckeye in the other."[10] I have yet to determine if this prized set of horns from the O'Connor Ranch is still in existence.

Presenting horns to notable Americans evidently had some appeal, as Dobie mentions that "a patriot" sent General Ulysses S. Grant a nine-foot set of horns that had come from Cushman's hide and tallow factory on the Texas coast in the early 1870s. In one of the "largest collections of horns in existence," collected by the late Earle A. Read of Big Spring, there is a mount in the Big Spring Heritage Museum with a point-tip spread of 10½ feet.[11]

"People call up and ask me if I am interested in buying a set of horns," Read said in an interview with Sam Blackburn for the *Big Spring Herald* in April 1965. "I ask, 'How big are they?' When they tell me seven feet, eight feet or nine feet, I just tell them I'm not interested."[12] While the 10½-foot set may be the longest horns in existence, the origin is not known since Read obtained horns from various sources, many from Mexico, and he and his father started the collection in 1929.

The Panhandle-Plains Historical Museum at Canyon has the horns of Old Blue, Plains cattleman Charles Goodnight's famous lead steer. A former wagon boss for Goodnight, Mitch Bell, recalled in an interview in 1938 with the *Amarillo Daily News* that "Old Blue knew every camp along the trail. . . . When he came to one he always pulled aside and made ready to stop," Bell recalled. "There was no moving until he got up, of his own free will and accord, and started on again."[13] In his old age, Old Blue continued to follow the chuckwagon on roundups in the spring and summer, accepting handouts along the way.

Another famous lead steer was Live Oak County ranchman George West's Geronimo, a mounted representation of which stands to this day in a covered and glassed-in enclosure on the courthouse square in the town of George West. In doing some research on Geronimo some years ago, I came to the conclusion there was not only one, but at least three steers that have contributed to the Geronimo legend. One often-told story has West leaving Geronimo in Kansas on his last drive and that within a year the steer had found its way home. The Geronimo in the glassed-in display is said to have died in 1927 at the age of twenty-two.

Nor do the horns on display come near to the 9 foot 6 inches sometimes mentioned, the measurement likely being confused with the Jim Dobie steer on the postcards. "During the steer's lifetime," J. Frank Dobie said of the George West steer, "newspaper stories gave the spread of his horns as being all the way from nine to 18 feet. Actually, it is a fraction over six feet."[14] After the last Geronimo's death, the steer was mounted and placed on the courthouse square where it has been ever since with exception of a trip to the Soviet Union as part of a U.S. Bicentennial Exhibition in 1976. At the time, Geronimo was virtually rebuilt and given a new hide.

The more notable of the legendary steers were generally acclaimed because of their horn lengths or for their abilities as lead steers. Today, we have no need for steers to guide herds northward, but we do have any number of Texas longhorns that stand up to some of the old-time steers in length of horn, an example being Amigo Yates, a steer owned by the late Fayette Yates of Tuscola near Abilene, that had a spread of 8 feet 9½ inches.

As mentioned in the April 2003 issue of *Texas Highways*, John Benda of The Ranch in Downtown Dallas, had a white longhorn named Bandit with a spread between 95 and 100 inches tip to tip, it having measured 7 feet and 11 inches two years before. Ralph Fisher of Swiss Alp in Fayette County had a very impressive horned steer named Milkbone with a spread along the horn of 9 feet and 6 inches, or 6 feet and 6 inches from tip to tip. Milkbone is an excellent example of how a steer with horns curving upward can have a wide difference in horn width by how the horns are measured. Tex, a world-class longhorn from Nueces County, owned by Billy Bedford and his son Billy Bob, measured 7 feet and 1 inch in 1999 when I saw him at the Texas Folklife Festival.

Another impressive steer of 7 feet or more, named Wow, is a Texas Longhorn Breeders multi-world champion from the Kimble Cattle Co. of Karnes County. There are others, and some of the measurements will change with a steer's age, but all the aforementioned can be counted among the magnificent of the breed.

A limited number of longhorn steers have become legendary for reasons other than their horns or abilities as lead steers. There is Bevo, for example, a fixture at University of Texas football games. The name has been shared by a dozen or more steers since a group of rival Aggies supposedly snuck into Austin in 1916 and branded a large "13–0"—the score of an A&M victory—into the side of the first mascot longhorn. The now oft-disputed legend of the naming has it that UT students transformed the brand by changing the 13 into a B and the dash into an E, and inserting the letter V before the O. Athletic director L. Theo Bellmont is said to have later barbecued the branded steer and the head was displayed in the athletic office until it was dehorned by A&M students in 1943. Another longhorn, a bull but worthy of mention, that made quite an impression during the time of the Texas Sesquicentennial celebration in 1986, was Texas, U.S.A., born on the Village Creek Ranch near Fort Worth with a large white spot on his face in the shape of Texas. The bull did have nicely shaped horns, but like other bulls and cows of the breed could not compare with steers in horn spread.

"They said that you could pack all the roasting meat a Texas steer carried in one of his horns," Dobie wrote in *The Longhorns.* "They said that when the black prairie lands cracked from the drought, the cattle would fall into them and be saved from going to the bottom only by their horns hanging over the banks."[15] From tip to tip, Texas has long been a land of legendary longhorns.

Endnotes

1. Sizemore, Deborah Lightfoot. *The LH7 Ranch in Houston's Shadow: From Longhorns to the Salt Grass Trail.* Denton: University of North Texas Press, 1991.
2. Posey, Jack. Letter to Henry Wolff, Jr., August 19, 1993.
3. Ibid.
4. Dobie, J. Frank. *The Longhorns.* Austin: University of Texas Press, 1990, reprinted by arrangement with Little Brown and Company.
5. Ibid.
6. Ibid.
7. *Victoria Advocate*, 88th Anniversary Edition. September 24, 1934.
8. Womack II, Jesse Y. Correspondence from *Ripley's Believe It or Not.* June 8, 1992.
9. *San Antonio Light.* June 10, 1937.
10. Dobie.
11. Shackelford, Kipp. *The Cattleman.* December 1965.
12. Blackburn, Sam. *Big Spring Herald.* April 25, 1965.
13. Johnson, Vance. *The Amarillo Daily News.* January 7, 1938.
14. Dobie.
15. Ibid.

The Aurora Cemetery historical marker, which mentions the legend of the spaceship crash

THE AURORA AIRSHIP CRASH OF 1897

by Jo Virgil

Sometimes, the draw of a legend is simply that we *wish* it were true. And sometimes that wishing muddies the water so thoroughly that it's hard to separate fact from, well, from An Enticing Legend.

But even a tale as bizarre as the Aurora Airship Crash of 1897 needs nuggets of truth to keep it alive for more than a century. The more deeply that historians and researchers dig into the story, the more evidence they unearth, both for proving the story to be a hoax, and for confirming that something very odd did happen that night.

As the story goes, the night sky of April 17, 1897, in the tiny Wise County, Texas, town of Aurora was filled with stars and the sound of crickets. While nearby Fort Worth had a booming population of almost 25,000 residents, the tiny town of Aurora had almost ceased to exist. The town's peak population of somewhere between 1,000 and 3,000 residents had begun to dwindle to just a handful of families after an epidemic of spotted fever, unrealized plans of a railroad through town, a boll weevil infestation, and a major fire that destroyed several buildings. The post office was about to shut down, businesses had closed doors, and people had moved on. That spring night in the tiny, barely surviving community was quiet and dark.

Until, that is, sometime just before dawn, when a tremendous explosion startled the nearby residents. According to the *Dallas Morning News* story by S. E. Haydon, a slow-moving, cigar-shaped aircraft crashed into a windmill on the property of Judge J. S. Proctor, bursting into pieces "with a terrific explosion, scattering debris over several acres of ground, wrecking the windmill and water tank and destroying the judge's flower garden."[1] Haydon tells readers that apparently the pilot of the ship was the only one on board, and "while his remains were badly disfigured, enough of the original has been picked up to show that he was not an inhabitant of this world."[2]

And so the story begins. This was 1897, six-and-a-half years before the Wright Brothers flew at Kitty Hawk and made headlines as the first heavier-than-air machine to achieve controlled flight with a pilot. And while at this point in the Aurora story many people roll their eyes and quit listening, the plot thickens.

During the months leading up to the spring of 1897, newspapers across the country, including North Texas, were full of accounts of mysterious moving lights in the night sky. In fact, the original story of the Aurora Airship Crash was just one of many that ran in the April 17 *Dallas Morning News*, although the other stories tended to be simply reports of moving lights. Some of the more dramatic (but also more outlandish) stories during that time appeared in newspaper articles across the country. In a *Dallas Morning News* posting called "Tolbert's Texas," Frank X. Tolbert, in an October 1970 column, tells these tongue-in-cheek stories from the era:

> Judge Samuel Foster was entertaining 7 guests on his front porch in Corsicana. The news story didn't mention what the judge was serving, but he and all his guests declared they saw "the flying machine roar over like a railway passenger coach at a rather fast speed against the firmament." In Dallas, M. E. Griffin, described as "a church man and a non-drinker," said he borrowed a powerful glass, climbed up to the top of the courthouse and the airship conveniently flew over to his "great delight" and he called it "a sublime sight." Fort Worth's leading witness was Joseph E. (Truthful) Scully, a railroad conductor who "never told a lie in his life."[3]

The Aurora story, though, allegedly had multiple witnesses, left physical debris, and involved the dead body of the pilot.

The story about the Aurora Airship Crash languished for a while, as was typical of that era, when people lived without the same fast and widespread communications as we have now. However, the story gained momentum in the mid-1970s with a story distributed by UPI, and then shortly thereafter by the Associated Press. As the tale gained momentum, the Mutual UFO Network (MUFON) picked up on the story and began an investigation that continues to this day.

Various research, investigations, and interviews have unfolded a tale that is both intriguing and suspicious. Because more than a hundred years have passed since the incident, we will probably never know how much of the story is fact and how much fiction, but whether the story is a hoax or truth is based on three different aspects of the case: metal debris found at the site, the burial of the body, and the witnesses' stories.

THE METAL DEBRIS

Bill Case, who in the 1970s was the State Director for MUFON and an aviation writer for the *Dallas Morning News*, along with other investigators, used sophisticated metal detecting equipment and found many pieces of metal near the crash site that, according to his report for MUFON, were in a pattern that strongly suggested an explosion. Although it would be impossible to determine without error which bits of metal found using the detector were simply scraps from the farming and ranching activities and which might have been the result of a 100-year-ago explosion, Case had some of the more unusual pieces of metal analyzed by various laboratories. In his report, he states:

> An electron-dispersion X-ray analyzer was used to identify the elements found in the sample. Only aluminum with a trace of iron could be detected. The sample was retrieved from a location about 100 feet west of the well site beneath four inches of soil. It was lodged directly against the face of the

> limestone rock and conformed to the exact configuration of the stone, indicating it was in a near molten state when it penetrated the earth and hit the rock where it cooled. The soft x-ray spectrographic analysis verified the high purity of the aluminum, the inclusion of iron, and the absence of copper. This also is an anomaly, because commercial aluminum alloys that contain iron usually contain copper.[4]

While not conclusive as to the origin of the metal, the lab report did raise questions.

Tom Gray, a physicist during the 1970s at North Texas State University (now the University of North Texas), examined some of the metal. Gray determined at the time that it was about 75 percent iron, but said it lacked some of the properties common to iron, such as the ability to be magnetized. Gray acknowledged that it was an unusual metal, but cautioned that he couldn't draw any definitive conclusions about its origins. A later test of metal pieces found around 2008 on the property was tested by the more sophisticated equipment in Gray's lab, again showing an unusually high iron content in the aluminum. Gray said that the type of metal does not match commonly used alloys now, and would have been prohibitively expensive to produce in 1897.[5]

Another twist to the legend was added in 1945, when Brawley Oates moved to Aurora to the property where Judge Proctor's windmill once was. He made use of the well that reportedly had the pieces of the spaceship thrown into it. A few years later he developed severe arthritis in his hands, disfiguring them with huge knots, and he blamed the condition on radiation from the contaminated well water. Oates had the well sealed with a 6" concrete slab.

Although debunkers of the Aurora Spaceship Crash claim that there never even was a windmill on Judge Proctor's property, a 2008 History Channel episode of *UFO Hunters* shows investigators removing the well house that had been built over the plugged well where the windmill once stood and using heavy equipment to unplug the sealed well. Wearing radiation suits, they physically dove into the well, bringing up rocks and sand that tested with significantly elevated levels of aluminum (although not radioactivity). In an interview on the same episode, Bill Oates, the son of Brawley, said that his father had had the well cleaned of lots of metal debris before he had it capped. No one knows exactly what became of the metal extracted from the well. The investigators also found four windmill stops near the well, though, confirming the past existence of the windmill.[6]

Investigators for the *UFO Hunters* episode also found a 200-year-old oak tree that made the metal detectors screech at a certain spot where a branch had long ago broken off. They would not cut down the historic tree to look for metal, but felt certain that the existence of imbedded metal in the tree was further evidence of an explosion nearby.[7]

The Body of the Pilot

The body of the pilot, according to interviews and city records, was gathered up and buried in the local cemetery. Today, a visit to the Aurora Cemetery confirms the legend of the Aurora Airship Crash and the burial of the alien on an Historical Marker at the entrance to the cemetery. The marker, which tells of burial sites for many victims of a "spotted fever" epidemic (now believed to be meningitis) and for veterans of several wars, also states, "This site is also well-known because of the legend that a spaceship crashed nearby in 1897 and the pilot, killed in the crash, was buried here."

As the investigation by MUFON, investigative journalists, and other researchers ramped up, the details and the authenticity of the burial story became cloudier. Although legend has it that the gravesite of the airship pilot had originally been marked with a stone bearing curious markings that resembled a delta and two circular figures, the headstone no longer is in the cemetery. Some say vandals stole it; others say the cemetery association hid it in an attempt to squelch MUFON's legal request to exhume the body; still others, of course, say the headstone never existed and is just part of a hoax. There are, however, photographs from the early 1970s or before that show the broken headstone in place. But since the grave marker is no longer available, no one knows for certain where the alleged burial site is.

As part of the *UFO Hunters* episode, however, investigators used the historical photos of the actual headstone to look for landmarks that might indicate where the burial spot was located. Focusing on trees and other markers, they determined approximately where the gravesite may be. Using Ground Penetrating Radar (GPR) equipment, they found a clearly rectangular plot of disturbed ground, most likely an unmarked grave, within inches of their estimation. Because of concerns of the respect and privacy of all families with relatives buried in the cemetery, the Aurora Cemetery Association will not give permission for an exhumation. So, although researchers are relatively certain that there is a gravesite at the spot where the headstone once was, who—if anyone—was buried there remains a mystery.

WITNESSES' STORIES

In any investigation, witness reports are both vital and questionable. So it is with stories of the Aurora Airship Crash. Bill Case, the MUFON State Director, interviewed surviving family members of several residents who claimed to have seen the crash or the aftermath. Mary Evans, who was about fifteen years old at the time of the crash, said that her parents would not allow her to see the body, but that they told her that the pilot, who was a very small man, had been torn up in the crash and that local men had taken his body to the cemetery. Another resident, Charlie Stephens, reported that his father had described the crash to him, saying that the airship hit the windlass over the water well and caused a chain-reaction explosion and a fire that was visible for more than three miles.

Haydon Hewes, founder of the International UFO Bureau, visited Aurora in 2005 to speak with descendants of residents who lived in the area in 1897. Some laughed and explained that everyone knew it was simply a publicity stunt put forth to bring attention—and possibly visitors and revenue—to the dwindling town. Others shared accounts that family members had told, confirming the cigar-shaped craft, the explosion from the crash into the windmill, the body of the alien, and its burial.

Some debunkers claim that the original story by S. E. Haydon in the *Dallas Morning News* was written by a known hoaxster and practical joker. Others say there is no evidence to support that theory, and that other stories by Haydon in the newspaper show no such tendency. A former mayor of Aurora, Barbara Brammer, did some of her own research and decided that the story was probably put forth to help revive a dying town by drawing attention to it. Those who disagree with that theory point out that, in 1897, stories traveled slowly and were not widespread enough to have made a noticeable difference in the reputation of the town. Many of the modern residents of Aurora prefer that the story be kept quiet or ignored. "They don't want a horde of wild-eyed fanatics coming in and digging up their yards," said Marilyn Maddox, who once worked at a tiny shop in Wise County called Area 114. The store, which no longer is in business, was fashioned after Roswell tourist stops that refer to "Area 51," and was named after the two-lane Highway 114 that runs through town. The shop sold such souvenirs as T-shirts, bumper stickers, and a candy called Shiny Mutant Pops.

THE STORY TODAY

MUFON and other investigators continue to research historical records and the physical scenes of the crash and gravesite to try to come up with a definitive answer as to the validity and the accuracy of the legend of the Aurora Airship Crash. However, they all agree that, after more than a hundred years, conclusive findings are not likely.

What research does know is that a windmill did once exist on Judge Proctor's property and it is no longer there. The well that sat below the windmill did have evidence of metal debris in the water that had been cleaned out. Metal debris was also unearthed all along the site of the alleged explosion, some of which would have been unusual—but not impossible—for people to have used around the turn of the century.

Tales of the burial of an alien body in the Aurora Cemetery are supported by family stories, photos of an unusual headstone, and the GPR findings of a burial plot where the now missing headstone once stood. But because legal battles have kept any exhumation from happening, who—or whether anyone—is buried at that spot is up to speculation.

Although newspaper stories from that time all across the U.S., particularly in the Midwest and North Texas, report sightings of mysterious moving lights and sometimes cigar-shaped objects, some are obviously tongue-in-cheek hoaxes. Others continue to intrigue researchers, particularly considering that such stories in those long-ago days would not easily be shared with other parts of the country. Stories handed down from Aurora residents tend to be divided. Some laugh at the idea that a hoax perpetrated by their ancestors more than a hundred years ago still lives on; others insist that the family stories confirm that something strange did happen that April night in Aurora.

We may never know the facts of the Aurora Airship Crash, but the legend, no doubt, will live on.

Endnotes

1. Haydon, S. E. "A Windmill Demolishes It." *Dallas Morning News.* April 17, 1897. 5.
2. Ibid.
3. Tolbert, Frank W. "Tolbert's Texas: Story of 'Spaceman's' Burial in Wise County." *Dallas Morning News.* October 3, 1970.
4. Case, Bill. Report to MUFON: "Investigation of Reported Crash of UFO in Aurora, Texas." http://www.mufon.com/FamousCases/Aurora%20Texas%20Crash%20Part%201%20MUFON%20Case%20File.pdf. June 1973.
5. Gray, Tom. Telephone interview by author. Reported in "Aurora 'airship' tale endures," *Fort Worth Star-Telegram Northeast Metro.* April 19, 1996. 19A.
6. "UFO Hunters" series. *The History Channel.* November 19, 2008.
7. Ibid.

Claire Campbell giving her "hidfolks" paper at the TFS meeting in Nacogdoches, 2009

THE HIDFOLK OF TEXAS

by Claire Campbell

Hearken to my tales of the hidfolk! Most of our folklore presentations describe places and things and people that we can see. I want to reveal a bit about the hidfolk of Texas: the "little people," fairies and elves, brownies, trolls, the little men of the Comanche Indians. Hidfolk are a part of cultures all over the world, and the people of those cultures have brought them to Texas.

If you think hidfolk are imaginary, that's alright. Einstein said, "Imagination is more important than knowledge." But if they're real we just have to live with them. You probably already do if you think about it. I know we do at our house. Whenever we can't find something or when something suddenly shows up that we've missed, we know it's the Borrowers—those little people who live under the floor—but they almost always bring things back. The hidfolk are like all folklore, a haunting blend of history and fantasy, and we can't be quite sure which part is real.

The diversity of the people of Texas has been compared to a patchwork quilt made of many patterned pieces. Each piece has its own spirit hidden in the stitches: the Czechs of Central Texas are careful to avoid their evil water-well spirits; the Poles in Panna Maria warn us of ghosts and werewolves; African Americans don't have fairies[1] but they know about "hants" and ghosts, and Anansi the spider can be anywhere; Italian hidfolk are sometimes hard to hide, because many of those that were brought from Sicily are ogres who tend to be BIG.

I don't want to forget the Chinese Texans who built the railroad. The Chinese say that the fox is the cleverest of animals, and so the fox fairy can change himself into a man or woman whenever he wants to.[2] We may have one among us at any time or place, for no one can tell them from everyday folk.

The hidfolk of Native Americans are the original fabric of our quilt. Five hundred years ago Cabeza de Vaca met early Pueblo Indians in Texas, the Jumanos.[3] Other Pueblo Indians came in the

1700s and settled near what is now El Paso. Because some of this paper may sound like storytelling to you, there is a Pueblo hidfolk tradition that is important to remember. Pueblo tradition says winter is storytelling time.[4] Stories may not be told between the last frost in spring and the first frost in fall because that is planting and growing time. People would listen rather than work; even animals would come close to hear stories and would forget to raise their young or to grow the winter coats they will need. So, if a Pueblo storyteller ignores that tradition the Spirit will become a bee and sting the tongue of the teller, or become a snake to wrap around his throat and thus stop the telling. This hidfolk belief is still very much observed by the older Pueblo tellers.

W. W. Newcomb, in his book *The Indians of Texas*, tells of Comanche spirits, "the little men." They were something like the elves of other cultures, but much more dangerous. These little creatures were almost a foot high and were armed with shields, bows, and stone-tipped arrows, arrows that always killed. Sometimes a daring shaman tried to acquire power for himself from these little men. That was a dangerous thing to do because the power could be easily misused and misdirected.[5]

We don't often hear about Mexican hidfolk. I once asked a cultural anthropologist in San Antonio. She knew, of course, of the brujas, the witches, and La Llarona, but nothing like "the little people." But I searched and I have found some that are known as the "pichilingis." In the old days they could be seen in every place imaginable. Anthony John Campos, author of *Mexican Folk Tales*, said when his great-grandmother was alive she would tell him of experiences she had as a young girl. "You could be walking along a road," she said, "and suddenly you would catch sight of one in a treetop. At night, while people were sleeping, the pichilingis would drag them off their sleeping mats so that when they woke up they were in a different place than where they had gone to sleep."[6] She said that when she and her mother went to the village to visit friends, they never knew what shape they would find their house in when they returned.

J. Frank Dobie learned much of his folklore information while sitting around the campfire listening to vaqueros sing and tell sto-

Blue Water (Esther Martinez), a Tewa Pueblo Indian Master Storyteller from San Juan Pueblo, New Mexico, who shared Pueblo hidfolk traditions with the author

ries. In his book, *Tongues of the Monte*, Dobie tells of one such night when the vaqueros sang a short and unusual song: "Lunes y martes y miercoles, tres! Lunes y martes y miereoles, tres!" (Monday and Tuesday and Wednesday, three). They seemed to enjoy singing this song over and over, so Dobie asked about it. One of the older vaqueros said:

> There was once a hunchback wood-cutter who came upon a whole crowd of dwarfs and elves and

> fairies in the forest. They were dancing madly around a huge fire, singing at the top of their lungs, "Lunes y martes y miercoles, tres; lunes y martes y miercoles, tres" over and over. After listening to this one line chanted over and over again at least forty times, the woodcutter stepped out where they could see him and added another line: "Jueves y viernes y sabado, seis" (Thursday and Friday and Saturday, six). The elves and fairies were happy that the hunchback had completed their song. The vaquero storyteller told Dobie they began dancing around the woodcutter, touched his humped back, and suddenly his back was straight! "He stood as erect as any soldier that ever saluted," said the vaquero.[7]

As you may guess, there's more to the vaquero's story—"y domingo, siete!" But, since it was a VERY long story as Dobie's stories can be, I'll let you read it in *Tongues of the Monte*. We now know there were fairies and elves in Mexico; I have no doubt they crossed the Rio Grande and there were met by early Texas colonists.

Stephen F. Austin wasn't the only empresario who brought folks to Texas. Sterling Robertson was busy in my part of the state, and he brought the Irish. In 1829, the Henry brothers, along with other Irishmen, built homes east of the Little Brazos River beside the Old Spanish Road. They named their settlement Staggers Point. Families from miles around were attracted by the churches they built, the general store, and the race track.[8] With all that building going on, it seems that the little people were involved in some of it. A story was told in 1846, and this is the way I heard it.

Lanty McCluskey, of old Staggers Point, had chosen a wife and needed a house to take her to. Now Lanty had his land; he looked it over and chose for the site for his house a clearing in the woods, a beautiful green circle. Some of his friends warned him that in the Old Country a green circle like that was the playground of the fairies. But Lanty was a headstrong Irishman, not much given to fear. He said, "I wouldn't give up such a pleasant spot to please all the fairies in Ireland—and besides, this is Texas! There are no fairies here!" So he built his house and the day Lanty brought his wife home he got a fiddler and invited friends to a housewarming dance. That night the fun was proceeding briskly, when a sound was heard like the crushing and straining of the rafters on the top of the house! Everyone stopped dancing and listened. That's what it was—heaving and pushing as if a thousand little men were working. They heard a voice say, "Come, men! Work harder! You know we must have Lanty's house down before midnight." This was an unwelcome piece of news for Lanty, for he knew who it must be. "They've come to Texas!" he said, as he walked out of the house. Lanty looked toward the roof and said, "Gentlemen, I humbly ask your pardon for building on any place belonging to you; but if you will be kind enough to let me alone this night, I promise I'll begin to pull the house down and remove it first thing tomorrow morning." There was a shout of "Bravo, Lanty! Now, build your house halfway between the two sweetgums above the spring." Then, with a rushing noise, they were gone.

The story, of course, doesn't end there. When Lanty was digging the foundation for his new house—above the spring, between the two big sweetgum trees—he found a full pot of gold! He was a richer man because he left the fairies their playground.

What about the Norwegians? Norwegians have lived in Texas almost from the beginning. Did they bring their hidfolk with them? One of the Norwegians was Cleng Peerson, a wanderer and a storyteller. Wherever he stopped on his travels, folks enjoyed his tales about the trolls of the Old Country. He knew some must have come to Texas from the moss-grown mountains of Norway. Today, modern members of the Norwegian Society of Texas agree. They say there definitely are some of the smaller trolls in the Society's meeting place, the Troll Hjem on Goldenrod Street in Fort Worth! Apparently, since there aren't many mountains in Texas, trolls will live in city buildings as well as caves and rocks.

Let me tell you a bit about trolls. Some of you may remember when your babies were little. Did any of you have one who cried and screamed all day and night? If he stayed naughty like that, your child may have been a changeling! You see, the troll hags look with envy on the good little human babies because theirs are always naughty and ugly. So, whenever a troll hag has a chance, she'll snatch a human infant from his bed and put one of her troll brats in its place. It will look like yours, but be oh, so naughty. There's just one way for you to get our own child back. You have to take the ugly changeling out behind the barn—if you have a barn—or behind the house; take him outside on a dark Thursday night and spank him soundly. Sometimes it takes three Thursdays in a row, but then, if the human mother is lucky, the changeling's howls will melt the stony heart of the troll mother and she'll come running. She'll throw the human child to his mother, grab her own, and run off. Of course if that doesn't work, you'll just have to live with a naughty troll in your house for the rest of your life.

No matter what good Christian German Texans may tell you, there *are* little people around. You find them in stories and songs, but also in an old habit of yours. You may not realize this is something you do because of the elves. When you hear someone sneeze, do you say "God bless you"? According to an old German elfin superstition, if a person sneezes three times while an elf is nearby and no one says "God bless you," that person belongs to the elf forever and will have to do whatever he says. So don't forget to say, "God bless you."

The hidfolk may not be talked about often, but I know they can be found all over Texas. There really are fairies at the bottom of our garden, and I often find myself looking past the stile for a red-peaked cap. But that's another story.

ENDNOTES

1. Puckett, N. N. *Folk Beliefs of the Southern Negro.* Chapel Hill: University of North Carolina Press, 1969. 45–147.
2. Carpenter, F. *Tales of a Chinese Grandmother.* Tokyo: Charles E. Tuttle Company, 1973. 89.
3. Newcomb, W. W. *The Indians of Texas.* Austin: University of Texas Press, 1955. 225.

4. Martinez, Blue Water. Personal interview by the author. San Juan Pueblo.
5. Newcomb. 188.
6. Campos, A. J. *Mexican Folk Tales.* Tucson: University of Arizona Press, 1977. 87.
7. Dobie, J. F. *Tongues of the Monte.* Austin: University of Texas Press, 1935. 8–19.
8. Baker, J. W. *A History of Robertson County, Texas.* Robertson County Historical Survey Comm. 1970.

Supposedly, a real Fox Fairy lives at the author's ranch

The author viewing a photo of herself at the Texas Folklife Festival

CURSES! ("!?*#ZX?@")

by Jean Granberry Schnitz

How things have changed! There was a time in Texas when people would not dare to say certain words or expressions. Nowadays, people seem to say whatever they want to—whenever and wherever they want to! If it is true that traditions, attitudes and behavior patterns reflect folklore, then these behavior and language changes are part of our Texas folklore.

Exclaiming and cursing are probably as old as mankind, but throughout history there have been major changes in what people say when they curse, swear, and exclaim. People react verbally to many things. The words used depend on what causes the reaction, as well as on a person's vocabulary, experience, and social training.

Earliest cursing was based on beliefs that supernatural power and/or witchcraft could be invoked to cause injury or evil to descend upon enemies. This usage of the word "curse" is common in literature throughout history. For purposes of this paper, referring to the use of profane, insolent or obscene words as "cussing" differentiates between "cursing" in the sense of invoking evil.

Early usage of profane language was associated with certain classes of people and/or certain professions. For example, an old and well-worn expression refers to "cussing like a sailor." I think it's fair to say that sailors were not the only ones cussing! According to J. Frank Dobie, cowboys used their share of language that was "too raw for gentle ears." Dobie also said, "In a society vigorously and exclusively masculine, a great deal of the song and talk . . . is downright obscene."[1] Cowboys? Obscene talk? Not John Wayne! Not Gene Autry! At least there was none on camera.

For purposes of comparison, let's "rewind" back as many years as you can remember. Think about what you heard people say, both for "cussing a cat" and for what was said for exclamation and comment. Think about what you and your friends said—for emphasis—as you were growing up. I did that, and this is what I remembered from sixty to seventy years ago. Bear in mind that I was raised in Texas during the 1930s and 1940s in a home where use of certain language was cause for having one's mouth washed out with soap. I learned to think twice before using a cuss word. It was even possible to have one's ears washed out with soap for simply having overheard somebody else's use of prohibited language.

The male elders in my family, being normal human beings, were prone to anger in certain situations, but never (in the presence of children, at least) would they utter a word considered to be loathsome, obscene, or vulgar. Grandpapa Scudder's favorite word to use in times of stress was, "Tarnation!" but sometimes he would say, "Blazes!" or "Doggies!" "Pshaw!" indicated extreme disgust. Grandpapa also apparently invented, "Tonsonnit!" for use in totally disgusting situations. What would you have said if you had a green parrot bite your upper lip and not let go? As he grabbed the parrot and threw him across the room, Grandpapa exclaimed, "Consarn you!"

Grandma and Grandpa Scudder's 60th Anniversary photo, 1951

I never heard either of my grandmothers exclaim angrily. Nothing seemed to provoke them to anger, though in times of stress, Grandmama Scudder might say, "Oh, Lordy!" or perhaps, "Fiddlesticks!" Can you imagine a Grandma nowadays with such a mild vocabulary?

My Daddy probably had the worst temper of anyone in the family. He was, however, skilled at mumbling when he was angry. It was possible to hear sounds that might be interpreted as "cuss" words, but it couldn't be proved. He was pretty good at expressing his anger by waving his arms, shaking his fists, grimacing, and kicking things. Mama's most fervent expression was, "Mercy!" or, "Horrors!" Well, most of the time. I can still laugh as I remember the time Mama stood screaming and dancing around on the toilet seat—trapped by a tiny mouse on the floor—while Daddy and I collapsed on the floor amid gales of laughter. "I hate you," she shouted, but we knew she wouldn't hate us once the mouse was gone.

Any word or expression that could be mistaken for using the Lord's name in vain was strictly taboo, but "Lordy mercy" was tolerated, as was "Oh, Lord." To say, "Jeez," "Gee," or "Gee whiz" was likely to cause wrath to descend upon the head (or rear) of the speaker. I never could figure out why it was okay to say "Lord" but not okay to say "God" or "Jesus Christ," but that's how it was. We tiptoed pretty close to trouble sometimes by saying, "My law!" or "Lawsy," but "Gosh-a-mighty" was mighty close to the edge of tolerance! However, "Gosh," "Heavens," "Heavens above," or "For Heaven's sake" were okay, as was "Good Heavens." "Land of Goshen!" was downright Biblical; however, "Gollee" when drawled out through clenched teeth has an ugly ring to it. (Goodness gracious, we even said, "Holy Cow" and "Holy Mackerel.")

We sometimes kept from using a verboten word such as "hell" by using "heck" or "hello" or something that sounded similar. The trick in using a sound-alike expression has always been to enunciate clearly so the hearer will not mistake the words used for something forbidden. It was okay to say, "Heck Fire!" or "Fire and brimstone!" We might even say, "Where in tunket (or tarnation) did that come from?" or "What in blazes (or tarnation) is that?" Uncle Kirby's frequent expression was, "Thunder!" as in "What in thunder is going on?"

Aunt Esther used some expressions which thinly masked the true meaning, such as "Pie!" (as in "You scared the pie out of me!"). As probably the most animated person in my family for the last several generations, Aunt Esther was pretty good at coining expressions that were socially acceptable, but expressive.

It was okay to use, "Darn" (or "Dern"), "Drat," or even "Dang," but woe to one who would say, "Damn!" "Dadgummit!" was my personal favorite, but "Doggone it!" was a close second. Some people even had a scale of tolerance for the "d" words, with "Darn" being the most tolerated and "Dern" being at the low end, just before the pits—"Damn!"

"Baloney!" "Man alive!" "My stars!" "Jeepers!" All these expressions were popular. Popeye, a comic strip character, popularized the expression, "Well, blow me down!" Other comic strip characters contributed to the language. Little Orphan Annie exclaimed, "Glorioski, Zero [her dog's name]!" Comic books contributed favorites such as "Shazam!" "Bless my soul!" and "Lo and Behold!" along with "Yikes!" and "Zowie!"

"Oh, Boy!" For years I actually thought that "What the . . . ?" or "Who in the . . . ?" constituted the entire question, as frequently written in the funny papers or spoken in movies, because nobody ever uttered an audible third or fourth word. My eldest son uses the expression, "Well, I'll be." Same thing. It took many years for it to dawn on me why the question was never finished. I finally figured out that everybody mentally added their favorite word to the question—and left it unsaid. In April of 2007, a San Antonio television station had a feature of its morning news entitled, "What the . . . ?" They introduce the feature by describing something strange—something "that would make you say, 'What the . . . ?'"[2]

"I'll be a monkey's uncle," was permissible, as was "I'll be switched," or "I'll be doggone(d)!" A person might be called a "son of a sea-cook" or "son of a gun," but it was not okay to be called a mother dog's son! Some circles would tolerate the "SOB" initials—if the words were left unsaid. In fact, those initials sometimes took on a life of their own, without ever saying or even knowing what they "stood for." I know that is true because for awhile I heard and even used that expression a couple of times before I found out what it meant.

Fifty years ago a person would be told where to go and what they could do by an angry person without saying any bad words. You might be told to "Go jump in the lake," or "Go fly a kite," or to "Drop dead." Nowadays, you would likely be told in much more explicit terms what an angry person wants you to do.

During the 1940s it became customary to use the expression, "Blankety blank" in place of a curse word. The way to write "blankety blank" is to use weird symbols, like "!?*#ZX?" Sometimes a very brave kid would scribble such symbols on the blackboard when he was mad at the teacher. Usually, the teacher would simply erase them with no comment. But the point wasn't lost on the rest of us! Maybe that was the idea that started the gang symbols of the 1990s, though I know there is more to gang symbols than that.

When I was in grade school in the 1930s, I thought the funniest joke I ever heard was about the little boy whose sister pestered him all the time. One day, he asked his father, "Is there a place in Holland called Rotterdam?" "Yes," came the answer. "Is it okay to say 'Rotterdam'?" "Yes." "Well," said the little boy, "my sister ate my candy and I hope it will Rotterdam teeth out." I never got my mouth washed out with soap for that one, and we all laughed, though Mama would frown menacingly.

My husband, Lew, remembers when he was in grade school in the 1930s that it was popular to say, "Go to Helena, Montana, and tell 'em my hat got damaged by a fire." Certain voice inflections could make this sentence and/or parts of this sentence sound pretty bad! Obviously, these parts were emphasized!

In about 1939, the children at school were passing around a poem. What I could understand of that poem was very funny, but there were numerous words such as "s-dash-dash-dash" and "h-dash-dash-dash." I didn't know what that part was all about, but the rest of it was funny enough to take a copy home to Mama. She turned pale, took me to the bathroom, and washed my mouth and ears thoroughly with vile tasting soap amid stern warnings to never bring anything like that into the house again. So, I found out that what you didn't know *could* hurt you. After that I figured that anything containing a word that wasn't spelled out was intrinsically bad. No more blanks! I found that poem in Mama's cedar chest more than fifty years later, and found out why she turned pale. By today's standards, though, it wasn't all that bad.

Consequently, children growing up in the 1940s and 1950s learned to say other perfectly good words instead of "cuss" words. We might say, "Curses!" or "Rats!" When I was in high school in the 1940s, a friend could mutter "Guatemala!" in five extremely foul sounding syllables. My own favorite word was, "Formaldehyde!" with emphasis on the "mal" syllable. A later favorite was, "Crimea!" It was pretty mild to say, "Caramba!" or "Phooey!" I knew a girl who could make "Fie!" sound wicked. A cousin of mine would exclaim, "Well, forevermore!" and make it sound bad. Another cousin regularly used the expression, "Gee cow!" instead of a certain Spanish expression.

The so-called "s" word was not tolerated at my house, but it was okay to say, "Shoot!" or "Shucks!" I know several people who exclaim, "Sugar!" while dragging out the first syllable for maximum effect. Grandpapa even did that! But the real thing was the word of choice for Papa Schnitz, who came from Germany when he was four. Sometimes he would say it in German, but usually he said it in English, compounded by the name of the animal from whence it came. The way to tell his degree of anger was to evaluate the sort of manure to which he referred. If it came from a horse or dog, he wasn't very mad, but if it was chicken you-know-what, it was the pits! It didn't get any worse than that.

I still laugh when I remember the young lawyer from New York City that I worked with in San Antonio in 1975. Someone took him to The Farmer's Daughter, a western-style dance hall, and he was explaining to another New York lawyer about the song they sang called "Cotton Eyed Joe." He noticed some ladies were present, and he told his friend, "They were shouting, 'Bull-blank!' 'Bull-blank!'"

The author's mother, Lena Scudder Granberry (right), and her Aunt Esther (left), along with her beloved Uncle Hollis, who said, "Phooey on having your picture taken!", circa 1920

People invented their own expressions. A lawyer I know said, "Crud ball!" Ed Raines said, "Cob fine!" or "Cob fuzzy!" Ken Taylor muttered, "Pot." Sometimes the voice inflection expressed more feeling than the words themselves. I'll bet every one of you in the audience has a favorite word you use in times of anger or crisis.

For many years it seemed to me that real cursing was done only by males, but in the early 1950s I met a young girl who could swear with the best of them—and she didn't care who heard her. Her cussing shocked many people in that small town, but since she came from a well-known family, she was tolerated. It was highly unusual in the 1940s or 1950s for a girl to swear like that. I met her son recently and wondered if he knew his mother was the most outstanding "cusser" I had ever heard. I suspect he could quote—or even out-cuss—her!

Now, let's all "fast forward" to the latter years of the 20th century and "Y2K." Big changes have occurred in what people say when they cuss or swear—or exclaim. Sometimes the same words are used to express anger and amazement, awe, or disgust, though the demeanor of the person speaking usually leaves little doubt about what is meant!

Many formerly "nice" English words have been corrupted by usage to the point where they are either obscene or the meaning has totally changed. If my heart were young and "gay" today, it might not be the same thing it was in the 1920s. And some modern expressions are pretty descriptive without being obscene or even ugly.

Conversely, how did we ever talk without saying, "Get used to it," or "Don't go there!"? "Gross!" "Awesome!" "Cool!" Cussing? No, that's not cussing—but it is using words that have been around for a long time in a new way.

Have you noticed that dictionaries now define all words, including obscene words? There was a time when it was not possible to find out the meaning of certain words by looking in a dictionary, because they were not included. It is also true that every year many new words are added to dictionaries through changes in usage or the coining of completely new words.

These changes in language and usage are symptomatic of changes in attitude, tradition, and culture—in short, changes in our folklore. Some words formerly considered obscene have lost much of their shock value because they are so commonly used and heard. Overuse is causing some words to become almost—but not quite—humorous. I have overheard situations in which a certain obscenity was used as a noun, verb, adverb, adjective, and/or participle—in the same sentence! Amazing! Fifty years ago a person would have been socially ostracized forever for having said that word one time, let alone time after time!

Recently, I ran across a television show on prime time which was so heavy on the expletives that there were few "normal" words in the dialogue. I didn't watch that one for very long except out of amazement. Besides being offensive, it was hard to understand what the actors were trying to say. It seemed they were having some kind of contest to see who could use the most offensive words the most often. There were more "bleep-outs" than words! Another time I came upon a television show with a fellow doing a rap song in which the tune was totally obliterated by such constant bleep-outs! Some celebrities seem to play a sort of game in which they manage to sneak expletives past the censors.

In the April 2007 edition of *Texas Monthly* magazine, the editor attempts to explain why it was necessary to disregard that magazine's longstanding policy of not printing obscene language, pointing out that to adequately represent their interviews with certain members of the Bandidos and with rock star celebrities, such language was necessary. He also pointed out that prior to these articles the artful use of dashes following an "f" assumed that no one thought that that meant "farm." See there! What I learned so long ago about "blanks" is still true! Evan Smith, Editor, writes:

> My mother wasn't a longshoreman. My father wasn't a mob boss. They weren't church choir directors, either, but they certainly didn't raise me to drop the F-bomb in conversations as liberally as you might sprinkle salt on french fries. . . . Two stories you're hopefully about to read . . . are, at least in parts, more R-rated than our usual fare. But they need to be, because the people we're writing

> about talk a certain way, and that way defines who and what they are as much as anything possibly can. We would not be doing them or you justice if we sugarcoated or papered over the reality. So consider this a heads-up. . . .[3]

He goes on to list twenty-nine (29) profanities and/or obscenities that were quoted or otherwise used in the two described interviews.

If you don't think obscene language is commonly used by lots of people, try listening to a rock radio station or a rap song on television without hearing them. Try going to a popular movie. Try walking down a crowded street or in a shopping mall. Try watching television during family hour. Try floating down the Comal River on an inner tube. Sooner or later (unless you are living in a cave)—probably sooner—you'll hear obscene language. I guarantee!

Apparently, uttering forbidden words provides some people with the feeling that they have uttered the vilest possible word—which seems to increase the level of their satisfaction. Poor communication seems to be the basic problem. Plus, we tend to reflect what we hear. If a person constantly hears cussing, in time it will seem normal to cuss.

Maybe I do not know any words worse than what people are already saying—and they may exist—but I wonder what people are going to say "for toppers" after they have said all the existing profanities. I'm not sure I WANT to know!

What are future generations going to say? Don't worry. They will think of something, and you can bet your boots it won't be mild! It will very likely be different and it will no doubt reflect the traditions, attitudes, and behavior patterns of future Texans.

ENDNOTES

1. Dobie, J. Frank, "Cowboy Songs" from "Ballads and Songs of the Frontier Folk," *Texas and Southwestern Lore*. Publications of the Texas Folklore Society Number VI. Southern Methodist University Press, Dallas, 1927. 154–156.
2. "First News First." KABB-TV, San Antonio, Texas. March 2007.
3. Smith, Evan. "The Profanity Defense" from "Editor's Letter." *Texas Monthly*. April 2007. 28

J. Rhett Rushing, 2010

MONSTERS IN TEXAS

by J. Rhett Rushing

Are there monsters in Texas?

In the interests of time and avoiding fistfights, this paper will not cover elected officials, high school math teachers, or the Houston Astros relief pitchers.

It will cover a wide range of bogies and boogers, some real and some imagined, plus enough beasties, nasties, and ghoulies to keep you sleeping with the light on tonight.

I am going to define "monster" as an aberration—to civilization, to morality, to Judeo-Christian ethics, to Mom and apple pie, bluebonnets, baseball, and chicken fried steak. Monsters exist to define societal boundaries—to embody those traits that ordered society cannot abide or allow. They are frequently inversions, existing in our Folklore as opposites and object lessons of how NOT to behave.

Monsters have withstood the test of time, passed down narratively from person to person in the best tradition of Folklore. They serve as our Boogey Men, Cucuis, and things going "bump" in the night to warn us away from behaviors that our home culture doesn't want us messing in.

You've told the kids to go to bed and they're still wrasslin' around upstairs? Bring on the Boogeyman that lives under their bed and eats the feet of children who dare to get out after hours. You've got a wayward husband? Bring on La Llorona. You've got frisky, adventurous, curfew-stretching teens? Bring on La Lechusa or the Donkey Lady, or the Hook. For every kid-crime there is a narrative monster warning in the Folkloric arsenal.

But Texas Monsters serve other functions for us as well. For the emerging adult they are tests of maturity—proof positive that the childhood belief is no longer scary. They serve as targets of human thrill-seeking—things to be conquered through direct contact, or perhaps captured and sold on eBay. They serve as tourist attractions, Chamber of Commerce claims, endless fodder for bad "B" movies, and sometimes, yes, sometimes, those Monsters just may be real.

Texas' earliest monster stories came from the earliest Texans. While the Apache tell of a dragon in the Guadalupe Mountains, the Caddo tell of water monsters in the Sabine River—one that turned over canoes paddled noisily and another stretching for miles down the river whose presence warned of an impending flood.

Early Spanish settlers coming into Texas told of a Dragon-Serpent whose breath could suck wandering souls straight down into hell, and of the famous basilisk—the dreaded serpent-monster born of an egg laid by a rooster. Everyone from North Africa through Spain and into the New World knew that it was instant death if the basilisk's eyes met yours.

In 1837, settlers around the Navidad River claimed to spot a wild woman covered in hair and faster than a horse. Of course, settlers along the Red River and the Neches River claimed a few wild folks as well. Still do.

It is no great stretch to imagine a wild man or wild woman as the possible source for a Bigfoot sighting, but believe me, we've got Bigfoot in Texas. According to the Texas Bigfoot Research Center, Bigfoot has been in Texas—and especially East Texas—for a very long time. There are literally thousands of sightings, news accounts, one top-flight museum exhibit, and even a couple of movies to attest to this, and hundreds of dutiful believers out shaking the trees and setting camera traps and whatnot in attempts to prove the creature's existence.

After twenty-plus years as a fieldworking Folklorist, it is in my professional opinion that there cannot be many a Bigfoot between the Sabine and the Neches simply because my relatives would've eaten or married them a long time ago.

There was a flurry of activity around Lake Worth in the late 1960s when a monster—half goat, half fish-man—jumped onto the hood of a car full of teenagers "minding their own business" in the wee hours of the morning. There were other reported sightings of the fishy man-goat, or Lake Worth Monster, but most fell away to the mists of time.

Texas has vampires as well. Among the early Czech settlers stories of the *upir* and the *mura* abound. The *upir* comes out of the ground to suck people's blood like any good vampire. The *mura* is described as a live man or woman whose soul comes out at night, leaving the body looking dead. It sometimes affects sleepers by sitting on their chest, causing bad dreams, and keeping them from waking up. He may also suck a person's blood.

The Czechs also brought us the *Hastrmane* or *Vodnik*—an imp-like water sprite that dragged passing children down into the well. The *Vodnik* could also appear in the form of a white horse, dog, wolf, or other animal. Czech children were taught a rhyme to sing as they went to the well to fetch water, thereby protecting them from the *Vodnik*:

> Hastrmane, buffoon, come out of the water
> Give us your skin for a drum
> We will beat the drum until you come out.

Of course there are werewolves. The Bell Plains Cemetery guardians are known to be giant wolf creatures that walk on two legs and have glowing red eyes. These werewolves will howl at nights and have been very successful in keeping people out of the cemetery after dark. Down near Port Arthur and Sabine Lake many of the older Cajun fishermen and drillers still speak of Le Loup Garou—the werewolf that patrols the swamps and preys upon folks that get lost.

Perhaps now is a good time to bring up the Ottine Swamp Monster. Ottine is a little town near Luling that has always been known for its very own swamp monster. Some have described it as human-like and covered with hair, some have given it more alien features, but most agree that it is invisible. Many have encountered it—that eerie feeling that something is watching you in the palmetto swamp, that spooky certainty that something is behind you in the river bed, those sounds of brush being crunched beneath huge hairy feet just ahead of you—but no one has caught it yet.

La Lechusa is another interesting boogey-monster. Descriptions range from a human figure with bat-like wings and a wraith-like appearance to an oversized owl. La Lechusa is territorial and often preys upon the poor soul out wandering alone. If society wants happy people surrounded by the safety of friends and family, then La Lechusa exists to swoop down and gobble up those soulful, lonely outcasts.

"La Lechuza," an original block print by Matthew Diaz

And we cannot forget the chupacabra! Originally the goat-sucker from Puerto Rico, the chupacabra has been spotted all across the state in a variety of guises. Supposedly standing on its hind legs, the beady-eyed varmit would slash and bite livestock, draining them of blood and leaving the carcasses untouched. One was shot near Boerne but it turned out to be a coyote. One was shot recently near Elmendorf but it was a coyote with mange. Then they shot one under a house in Lufkin and it had the indecency to turn out to be a coyote with mange as well.

However, the chupacabra has been found on the pages of Ben Rehder's novel *Flat Crazy*, on an episode of the *X-Files*, and now on everything from school lunch boxes to T-shirts to coffee mugs.

We cannot forget the Big Bird of McAllen back in the mid-'70s with huge wings and red eyes and a grey gorilla-like head. It appeared to a number of teachers, school children, and more than a few drunks in 1976, but its heyday peaked just as the Yankees and birdwatchers descended upon McAllen for the annual winter bird watching.

One of many "chupacabras" found and reported on in newspapers all over Texas

As for the really big monsters, we have to think about "Old One Eye" up in Lake Granbury. Described as a Texas Nessie, this creature is supposed to be scaring the bejeezus out of bass fishermen and sunbathers alike. Hailed as a modern-day dinosaur, Old One Eye seems best suited for selling burgers and tabloids near the marina.

Not the case in 1872 aboard the barque *St. Olaf.* Steam-sailing from Newport to Galveston, the *St. Olaf* and her crew were just two days out of Galveston when:

> Report of Captain A. Hassel, of barque *St. Olaf,* from Newport to Galveston, Texas—
>
> Two days before arrival at Galveston, and about 4:30 P.M. on May 13, weather calm, smooth sea, lat. 26 52", long. 91 20", I saw a shoal of sharks passing the ship. Five or six came under the vessel's stern, but before we could get out a line they went off with the rest. About two minutes after, one of the men sang out that he saw something on the weather bow, like a cask on its end. Presently another one called out that he saw something rising out of the water like a tall man. On a nearer approach we saw it was an immense serpent, with its head out of the water, about 200 ft. from the vessel. He lay still on the surface of the water, lifting his head up, and moving the body in a serpentine manner. Could not see all of it; but what we could see, from the after part of the head, was about 70 ft. long and of the same thickness all the way, excepting about the head and neck, which were smaller, and the former flat, like the head of a serpent. It had four fins on its back, and the body of a yellow greenish colour, with brown spots all over the upper part and underneath white. The

> whole crew were looking at it for fully ten minutes before it moved away. It was about six feet in diameter. One of the mates has drawn a slight sketch of the serpent, which will give some notion of its appearance.—A. Hassel, master of Norwegian barque *St. Olaf.*—Witness to signature, J. Fredk. Walthew.[1]

Monsters frighten us and keep us in line because we bring them on ourselves. Psycho-socially, we can actually control our contact with monsters simply by behaving the way our Mommas taught us to. And without a doubt, sometimes it's a little exciting to flirt along that behavioral edge and see just how close we can get to that monster around the corner.

ENDNOTE

1. A.C. Oudemans. *The Great Sea Serpent: An Historical and Critical Treatise.* JZN, 1892. 64–65.

Acayla Haile giving her paper on plant lore in Galveston, 2006

THE FOLKLORE OF PLANTS: GROWING UP IN THE HILL COUNTRY

by Acayla Haile

I have long been interested in the plants of my Texas home. As a child, one of my favorite games involved gathering interesting looking plants and grinding them between two rocks and presenting them to my family as "medicine." As I grew older my father used to point out plants to me and explain their uses as our family went on walks on our property in the Hill Country. He would later quiz me on their names. It is from him that I inherited my love of botany and gardening. There is nothing like going out to your garden and picking beans, peppers, and strawberries in a basket you wove out of basket grass gathered from the nearby creek. But it is the plants that grow wild that hold the most intrigue.

The Hill Country is ecologically very diverse, with many plants and animals found nowhere else in the world, along with many very useful plants that have been used by the settlers and the Native Americans since ancient times. With a little knowledge they are still useful today. One of my favorites is the admittedly common pecan trees that grow in the bottoms. Wild pecans are generally smaller than the cultivated varieties, but sometimes you will find a tree of the Cherokee or Lipan varieties that produce larger nuts. I think the smaller wild varieties are more flavorful, and therefore worth the extra effort of cracking and peeling them. A mature pecan tree can produce up to two tons of pecans a year, and I feel like I could eat them all.

I have loved gathering pecans as long as I remember, at my grandparents' house in Quihi, or along the banks of the Medina River in Bandera. In fact, just last year my mother and father and I gathered nearly forty pounds of pecans in the space of a few hours. We have a special tool we use just for pecan picking—a twenty-five-foot bamboo pole cut from a vacant lot we use to knock the pecans loose onto a blanket laid out below to catch them. We keep pecans by the bucketful to crack in the wintertime. As productive as they are, it is no wonder they are Texas' state tree.

Cattails are another common plant with myriad uses that I remember being taught as a child. The roots of the cattail can be dug up and eaten; they are very starchy, with a texture a little like a potato. One must be very careful to cook them thoroughly first, as they can cause vomiting if eaten raw in large amounts, especially if you gathered them from an area of polluted water. A very interesting method for cattail preparation involves the seeds, which are laid out on a flat surface and lit while still attached to the fluff. The fluff burns off almost instantly, leaving the seeds separated and cooked in one simple step, ready to be eaten warm or ground into a flour, as it was often used by the pioneers. The fluff is very useful as tinder since it lights so easily. At the Folklife Festival in San Antonio I was shown how the pioneers dipped the cattails in wax to make long-burning candles. My sister and I came home every year with a cattail candle each. I have also been told that the fluff on the seedpod can be spun into thread and woven, or used for stuffing pillows or rag dolls. Cattail leaves and stalks are used for stiffer weaving, such as room partitions or chair caning.

Another particularly useful plant I remember well from my early years is Mullein, also called skunk cabbage or lambs ear. A tea of mullein is most often used for coughs or sore throats by boiling the leaves for ten minutes or so. But don't drink it just yet. The plant is covered with small hairs that should be strained before drinking. The bruised and slightly boiled leaves are applied directly to burns to soothe and help heal them. The Navaho used mullein tea to treat mental illness. The leaves and flowers produce a strong yellow dye that Roman women used to dye their hair, because in their society yellow hair was the ideal beauty. Like the cattail, the dried flower stalks were dipped in wax to make torches. I remember the large soft leaves as wonderful bedding and blankets for my dolls, or as sails for their ships. The growing flat plants I used as a pillow when I was tired out from playing and needed a nap. But I remember mullein best for another reason . . . in a pinch they are a perfect toilet paper substitute.

The velvety leaves of a mullein plant (Photo by Janet Simonds)

A form of entertainment that amused me as a child is something we called spear grass. Texas Winter Grass is its actual name, and it provided for me and my family endless afternoons of entertainment. The seeds of the grass are barbed at one end, with a long stalk on the end to balance it, and when pulled from the stem they resemble small spears two to three inches long. If thrown correctly they stick to clothing and prick the skin. Often our family walks deteriorated into all-out spear grass wars. My sister and I would gang up on our parents, until the alliances shifted and we would all turn on one person and shower him or her with tiny spears until the unlucky victim resembled a cactus pad.

Walks with my father are where I learned most of what I know about plants. He taught me to identify them, and he'd tell if they were edible or poisonous. We would walk along talking about plants. He made the learning like a game, and I was always eager to show off if I had learned anything new. From my father I learned how to make a meal of dandelion, wild onions, Yucca, or greenbrier tips. I often munched on greenbrier whenever we went on school field trips, to the amazement of my friends. I was safe though; I only ate from plants I was absolutely sure were harmless, and certainly did not offer anything even remotely unsafe to my friends. Greenbrier, easily identifiable and safe, was rather popular among my friends.

I put this knowledge to good use a few summers ago, when I helped out as a counselor at the Treetops in the Forest Summer Camp for the Texas Folklore Society children in East Texas. The greenbrier vines grew wild in abundance all around the central house and along the roads. As we hiked around one day, I showed the children what greenbrier looked like, how to identify it from the surrounding foliage, and how much of the tips were edible. Armed with this knowledge we set out, gathering at least a basketful throughout the walk. When we arrived back at the house I fried them in butter and served them with salt and pepper as a side dish so everyone could try some. The tips taste somewhat like asparagus, and were more accepted by the older kids than the little children, but all in all the experience worked out well for everyone.

Every year our family would make a pilgrimage out to Big Bend National Park between Christmas and New Years and stay for about five days. It was there I encountered plants like candellaria, named because a clear-burning wax can be extracted from it. From the 1930s through the 1950s, candellaria wax was a big industry in the Big Bend area and through Mexico. The wax was used in the production of a multitude of things, from chewing gum and shoe polish to phonograph players, and in World War II, it was used extensively to waterproof the army's tents. Piñon pine trees are also common in the region, and cover the Chisos Mountains where we would often camp. They were our favorite destination in the park; my sister is even named for them. When we were there at the right time of year, we were happy to pick up any cones that had fallen near our camp, because the delicious piñon pine nuts can be removed from the pine cones and eaten raw or cooked for a handy snack while you hike the mountains.

A blossoming century plant

I have tried my hand at using Agave, or century plant, another West Texas native, after I was shown what it is useful for. As we were walking along playing our usual plant game, we came across an agave plant by the trail. We stopped our hike and Dad proceeded to show me how to strip out the long fibers from a leaf while still leaving one end attached to the needle point. This functioned as a very sturdy needle and thread. I later learned that the

Apache Indians used this sturdy fiber to make fishing lines and nets. We use the inner stalk of the century plant for flipper dinger balls, parts of an old folk toy used by the pioneers, because the pith is very lightweight. We even had the dried top of a century plant for our Christmas tree one year. We transplanted some Agaves to our home in Tarpley, a bit out of their normal range, and they took off. We now have an Agave that looks like something out of the Cretaceous period; twelve feet tall and big enough to cast shade on the chair we put by it.

Sotol, a similar looking plant that is unrelated and grows in the Hill Country, was used by the Native Americans for food and the leaves for weaving. The inner sotol leaves and bulb can be cooked and eaten; they taste good with salt and butter. In fact, Native Americans were thought to have scooped out large pits in which the sotols were cooked in large amounts, leaving the blackened rock mounds as evidence. In addition to the sotols, we also had Yuccas growing wild around our house. The petals of a Yucca flower, which grow in clusters on a stalk, are not only beautiful, but can be eaten raw, added to salads, or fried in butter. My mother told me this story of when she was in college in 1978, the first year she dated my dad. She and her roommate were working on an art project when in waltzed Dad with a huge bouquet of flowers. It was a whole Yucca stalk. As they stood there admiring the bouquet, he proceeded to wash, dry, and sauté the bouquet which they later ate with butter, salt, and cheese. You can use the seeds from shepherd's purse, or peppergrass, for a peppery seasoning for the Yucca snack. The roots have a more unusual purpose. They are high in sopatids and when crushed, will lather and can be used as a soap. Indians used Yucca root to wash their hair.

I remember every spring gathering from the abundance of fruit around us. We gathered dewberries from vines that grew wild around our house to eat and to make pies. Dewberries are a deep purplish color, very sweet and always a spring favorite for me. When we went to my grandmother's house in Hondo my sister and I would gather the bean pods from a mesquite tree growing in their front yard. I have loved the taste of the mesquite beans ever since I was four, when Dad showed me how to crack open the pods and get at them. My grandfather told me they were a major food source for the Indians of the area and that they could be ground and eaten that way. The only problem was getting to the seedpods without impaling your foot on the especially long and sharp needles, which have some poison on the end and will cause swelling. This calls for some agile footwork in the tree, and a sharp lookout when gathering the pods that have fallen to the ground below.

My father also showed me the tart but wonderful berries of a flaming sumac. These berries are actually poisonous if you swallow them, but we would just suck the flavor off the outside, then spit them out. We would also soak them in cold water for about ten minutes and then strain the berries and bits of bark from the liquid, sweeten it a bit, and then drink it. It made one of the best tart drinks I have ever had, although if you plan on trying this at home, be very careful not to crush the berries when they are in the water, and never swallow them when they come straight from the trees.

Later in the year there were ripe Texas persimmon fruit which I would pick and eat with relish. My hands and lips would turn a deep brownish black from the thick juice. Native Americans would string necklaces from the dried seeds that were very beautiful. I was determined once to make dried persimmon leather, so upon gathering several small buckets full we smashed and strained them, sweetened the gooey mix and dried it in pans. When we tried to cut it into squares it would not cut. When we tried to scrape it out, it would not scrape. Even boiling water and soap had no effect. As I recall we had to throw one of the pans away, persimmon candy still faithfully attached. At the end we had one-and-a-half pans that could be used. I rolled it into small balls, which looked exactly like chewed tobacco, but tasted good. If you want a lesson from that story, don't use your best pans if you are planning on making persimmon leather.

We gathered agarita for pies and goodies, as well, when they were ripe. We laid sheets under agarita bushes and beat them for the berries to avoid the spiked leaves. We used these for jelly. Once, without Mom's expertise, my dad and I tried to make jelly. We ended up with eighteen jars of liquid agarita syrup instead. Some of them are still sitting in our cupboard. We also gathered prickly pear tunas to eat. I am told that on August 21, 1988 (the day before I was born), my mom and her aunt Eloise, gathered, prepared, and canned twenty-five quarts of prickly pear jelly from 7:00 a.m. until 8:00 p.m. That's what caused Mom to go into labor with me. Mulberries and ground plums grew wild through the Hill Country, too. Berry picking was always a wonderfully social outing with friends and neighbors.

Wild mustang grapes grew along the rivers where we swam during the summer, and I remember many times climbing up a tree to get to the bunches of small purple grapes. I did not think they tasted particularly good, but we ate them anyway, in small amounts. If you squished them just right, the clear, jelly-like, inner grape would come out of the purple skin with a pop. I would eat the inner grape and discard the skin, which was much too acidic for my tastes, although I have seen other people eat mustang grapes whole. All of the grapes were so full of acid your hand would begin to itch, burn, and turn red if you did not wash off the juice quickly. There is a redeeming factor, though. I have tasted wonderful jelly made from mustang grapes, though I have never made any myself.

Another important food of note is the acorn. Acorns are very nutritious, and although high in tannic acid and therefore bitter, the bitterness can be lessened by preparing them correctly. Native Americans of the Hill Country used caliche to leech the tannic acid from the crushed acorns, which were then ground and used for a variety of foods. They will not keep well in their natural state if it has been a damp year. The tannic acid is also very useful in softening leather hides, and as a mordant to set dye.

In fact, many of these foods I have mentioned doubled as dyes. Dewberries, blackberries, and mulberries made shades of purple or blue. Cochineal, though not actually a plant but an insect found on prickly pear cactus, made shades of maroon to red. Cochineal was shipped from the Americas back to Europe and was the dye used on the uniforms of the British Redcoats in the American Revolution. Agarita wood and roots made bright yellow; onion peel, another common food, gave a deep orange dye. I have used walnut husk quite effectively for a deep brown on cotton and skin. Peppergrass will produce a green or yellow, mustang grapes a purple or blue, and the fruit of the flaming sumac a reddish brown. The sap of a mesquite tree when boiled will give a deep brownish black, but mesquite sap, like cedar sap will stick to you for ages. The only way I have found to get rid of it is with rubbing alcohol, and a lot of time.

I, like many children, knew all the little rituals associated with flowers. Pick a dandelion, make a wish, and blow. If you can scatter the seeds in one breath, your wish will come true. And, like many little girls, I picked the petals from flowers—he loves me, he loves me not. . . . I knew to hang mistletoe and holly at Christmas, and to sleep with flowers in your hair in the summer for good luck. Even simple childhood rhymes such as "ring around the rosies, pockets full of posies" give you clues to how plants were viewed. During the plague in Europe, posies were carried around by people to ward off the Black Death. Also, people were condemned for having parsley growing in their yard, because it was well known then that parsley could only be grown by witches. These are the sort of traditions and trivia every child should learn just for the fun of knowing.

Of the many things I have learned, I cannot stress enough how important is the need to be careful. Seemingly innocent, enticingly beautiful plants can harbor very strong poisons. I have only had two very bad experiences (ones that required trips to the emergency room). I have been well warned not to eat things I do not absolutely know are safe. However, while playing one day when I was little, I ground up the root of a bladderwort, a tiny plant with tall stems, few leaves, and tiny yellow flowers. At first everything was fine. But a couple of hours later my hands began to swell; soon I could not close my fingers, and there was a bright red blistered line across the bridge of my nose and one cheek where I had wiped some sweat from my face. Mother took me to the hospital where they treated my hands with sulfur. I had second-degree chemical burns from just touching this tiny plant; they took a month to heal.

Another time my sister and I were out walking and playing, as we often did, and picked some tall plants with a straight stalk branching into three and three again at the top, with light green and white flowers. The plant was called snow-on-the-mountain, and we proceeded to peel the outer bark and leaves from the stem. They made excellent fencing swords. The next morning when I woke up, I could not open my eyes. Both of us had eyes that were red, swollen shut, and watery. We must have rubbed our eyes sometime during the walk after we had peeled the stems. To the hospital again to be treated for this new scrape I had gotten into. I was lucky. Both times there was no serious damage.

However, others are not so lucky. A few years ago a girl from the city was walking with one of her friends along the Medina River near where I live. They thought all natural things were good for you. They were never told that some of the strongest poisons in the world come from plants. They were grazing as they walked and mistook the leaves of a young poison hemlock for some carrot or parsley. The girl died, and her friend, who had only eaten a little, went into a coma. Anyone who forages for meals should be careful; there are many harmful plants growing wild out there, just as there are helpful ones.

I was taught to be cautious and to identify many of the deadly plants on our property. Milkweed, and anything else with milky white sap, I was taught to avoid. Lantana and bluebonnets, locoweed and Jimson weed should not be eaten. Mountain laurel, with its beautiful purple flowers and red beans is deadly. Even the laurel blossoms, which I consider one of the most beautifully scented flowers, and the smell of which brings back memories of happy times spent in the hills, can overpower you. My father picked a big bunch of the blossoms once, and put them in the car with the windows rolled up. On his way home he began to get dizzy and lightheaded. He stopped the car and opened the windows to air it out until he felt better, and now we know to never keep the flowers with us in places where the ventilation is not good.

Experiences passed down from generation to generation are the basis of much of our knowledge. I am so very grateful to my father and mother and everyone else for what they have taught me. Doubtless it has saved my life a few times, and my knowledge of the natural world around me has truly enriched my life. There is so much more to learn, and I feel as though I have barely scratched the surface of what is out there, even just in my Hill Country home.

Gene Young teaching folklore at Sam Houston State University

HIGH ART VERSUS THE ORAL TRADITION

by Gene Young

I teach English—mostly American literature and Southwestern Literature, plus an annual installment of a course called "Texas Crossroads," which examines the intersections between Texas history, literature, and various segments of Texan culture. I've been doing this gig for a long time now, from the University of Tennessee, to Texas A&M, in Kentucky, and now at Sam Houston State University. I came to Sam from Kentucky in 1992 to be the chair of the Department of English and Foreign Languages. Anyhow, one of my ideas during that time was to propose that we split our English 363 course, titled "Mythology and Folklore," into two courses, simply "Mythology" and "Folklore," the reason being that the fellows teaching the course were cramming the kids' pointy little heads with lots of Mythology (of the Joseph Campbell variety) but not a bit of Folklore. In 1998, we put through the proposal, and two years later (two years being the gestation period for an academic course in the State of Texas), we took the wraps off our brand spanking new course, English 364, Folklore.

I won't go into the logic of placing such a course in the English Department. Big schools have whole departments of folklore. Over at Texas A & M, my folklorist buddy Sylvia Ann Grider, from by-God Pampa, Texas, just retired from the Department of Anthropology. Not all regional universities of our size—16,000—have folklore courses, but the ones that do tend to place them in the English Department, which is where the High Art versus Low Art aspect of this presentation comes in.

Our hated purple Lumberjack rival up to the north has real folklorists, and so did we, for a while. We lucked into a young woman with a folklore degree from the University of Indiana, which to folklore studies is like Nashville is to a country singer wannabe. She was wonderful. She did radicalize great bunches of the good country (and city) folk who attend our fair university, but—truth be told—that wasn't so bad for them. Unfortunately, she left for higher altitudes (Utah). Hiring another folklorist to teach one course wasn't in the works, so we mothballed Folklore for a while. However, in keeping with the "use-it-or-lose-it" mindset of our sainted governing board, a course has to be taught at least once every three years. As you have by now guessed, the person who caused the spawning of this Child of Satan is the one to whom fell the awesome responsibility of teaching folklore to English majors. I've done it once now, and that's what this presentation is all about.

I won't go deeply into my background as a folklorist, mainly because there ARE no depths to my background as a folklorist. Basically, I'm from that population most loathed by professional folklorists. In other words, I am an amateur who still has the temerity to call himself a folklorist. I once presented a paper at the American Folklore Society (on elements of folklore in John Steinbeck's *The Grapes of Wrath*), and I have presented a few times at the annual meetings of the Texas Folklore Society. (Truth be told, my presentations here have been insubstantial meanderings crudely hitched to the work of my wife, Marynell, who has a deservedly national reputation as a collector and preserver of American fiddle tunes. As a good friend and colleague in Huntsville is wont to say, "Gene Young is widely known as the second most authoritative voice on American fiddle music in his own family.") But the fact is, I have no claim to a shred of authority as a folklorist, much less a teacher of the subject. However, since I have never been known to be one easily encumbered by modesty, humility, or good sense, I agreed to take on the course.

Now, before I get into the story of what happened, let me spend a little time talking to you about the discipline of English and about the typical English majors who populate it in our universities. The kids who come to Sam (as we affectionately call Sam Houston State University) are a splendid mix of the urban and the rural. About half come from Harris County, meaning Greater

The author and his wife, Marynell Young, performing at the Texas Independence Day Celebration

Houston, and about half come from rural east and southeast Texas. They—even those from the Big City—are by no means urban sophisticates, but they do bring to the table certain hard-won dispositions about language and literature.

I can best illustrate this by references to American Poetry of the 20th Century, which, for purposes of our discussion here, epitomizes High Art. This has to do with one of the great paradoxes of education in America. You see, every child in America (and throughout the world, for that matter) is born into the world hard-wired with a love of poetry, or at least the elements of language which go together to make up poetry. They cherish and practice with abandon all those elements, not just rhyme and rhythm, but also the play of words, the bending of linguistic rules, vivid imagery, the compression of poetic language, that go together to make poetry. This is manifest in the sing-song rhymes they chant on the playground, playing jacks, or at hopscotch. These ingrained dispositions are easily demonstrated in any class—or any room, for that matter. Pick any two females at random, and they can play one of those slap-hands rhythmic games ("Little Miss Mack, Dressed in Black"). Boys are less adept at these games, but that is not the subject of this paper. Besides, they have their own rhymes and rhythms. Kids also love the poetry common to the folk, such as the Mother Goose rhymes, Shel Silverstein, folk parables, you name it. Most importantly, they make their own rhymes, and they do it all the time. Well, that's on the first-grade playground. Let's fast-forward to high school graduation. As they come off the stage, let's ask them this question: "You're eighteen years old, and you just finished twelve years of school. What do you think about poetry?" The answer will be almost universal: "I hate it."

The reasons this paradox exists are complex, but I am going to reduce it to its least common denominators: English teachers and T. S. Eliot. T. S. Eliot may be responsible for the musical *Cats* (which a sardonic friend of mine describes as a "meandering banality"), but he is also responsible for, among other poetic works, *The Waste Land*. When *The Waste Land* was published, in 1922, it ushered in the Modernist era in American letters and the Formalist era in 20th-century literary criticism. It stopped the world in its tracks. The poetic world, that is. The real world went on about its business as though nothing had happened. To make a long (and much more complicated) story short, what happened over time—despite the resistance of poets such as Robert Frost, Langston Hughes, and William Carlos Williams—was that the chief standards for the quality of poetry became, pretty much, difficulty, abstruseness, elusiveness, and learnedness. In other words, if a poem were not difficult and elusive (if it didn't give you a migraine headache), it simply didn't qualify as a "real" poem.

Of course, much of this difficult poetry (including *The Waste Land*) rightly stands as the standard against which other works are judged. What is not so fortunate, though, is that this formula infected practically everyone—poets, critics, editors, college professors, and—ultimately—their students, particularly the ones who ended up teaching poetry in the schools. Now, don't misunderstand me. I have spent much of my career in higher education helping prepare good teachers for public schools. My wife is a high school teacher, as were my mother and two of my sisters. An older brother was a high school superintendent. I have deep respect and admiration for the people who teach in the public schools. However, it is true pretty much beyond dispute that we university English teachers share complicity with our high school colleagues in privileging a kind of poetry that—unlike folk rhymes, folk poetry, and folk poems—is not readily accessible to ordinary folk. Thus ends this segment of the long tale leading to the nearly universal depredation: "I hate poetry."

Despite the fact that college English majors are regular kids from regular families, and no matter how much they may dip snuff, listen to country and western music on the radio, or go four-wheeling on the weekends, when they come to the subject of English literature and language, they bring to the table those attitudes reflected in a little story about my 5th grade grammar teacher. This teacher, whom I call "Miss Fitchett," though that was not her real name, was the original Grammar Nazi. She drilled us recalcitrant West Texas children of the soil like foot soldiers, and the subject was—endlessly—English grammar. We had our pointy little heads crammed with all the rules of proper English usage as practiced among the gentry, but one anecdote of her war on ignorance will suffice.

She always kept the door to her room closed, and when one of us returned from some dutiful sojourn, we were required to knock on the portal and request entrance. She would say, in the most schoolmarmish squawk imaginable, "Who is it?" We were admitted only after either Hell froze over or we uttered that most unnatural execration for a growing West Texan—"It is I." I believe some of my schoolmates must have considered enlisting in the Foreign Legion rather than saying such a thing, but nothing deterred her.

While few of my English majors will rise to such an unholy level of practice as my Miss Fitchett, they will adopt a certain superiority about grammar, spelling, and punctuation. There is nothing wrong with that, in and of itself, but these stringencies translate readily to other aspects of language and letters including folklore and the oral tradition. I discovered early on that I needed to bring about a little attitude adjustment if I wanted these students to put their High Art orientations in the background and to engage folklore in the way that Mody Boatwright described it in an article appearing in the 2005 TFS volume on learning through folklore. Boatwright says he wrote "on the assumption that the processes which create folklore do not cease when a society becomes literate. . . ."[1] In order to give nourishment to that assumption in my first folklore class, I discovered very early that I had to do battle against certain assumptions my students brought to the enterprise. The first of these had to do with the stability of a text, and the other has to do with attitudes toward narrative, toward language and dialect, and toward research.

Boatwright insisted that "the oral and written traditions are not most fruitfully conceived as separate and distinct. Each is continually borrowing from the other as the processes of adaptation and creation continue."[2] This is implicit in the work of most poets and fiction writers (or the ones worth a damn, anyway). Robert Frost, John Steinbeck, William Faulkner, and Flannery O'Connor, for instance, all exhibit studied understandings of folklore and folkloric processes. All artists, especially poets and dramatists, know that their work (their words) are damaged when read silently. No serious poet writes without an acute understanding of the connection between sound and sense. Shakespeare certainly did not write his plays to be studied, as we often do in English classes, as mute texts. To read Robert Frost silently is to read Robert Frost only half. This, in combination with the fluid nature of folkloric texts, is an important consideration in a folklore class.

Very often, our literature anthologies include folk songs alongside "more serious" works. This is a good thing, but the problem is that these songs (and for some reason the default selection is either of two ballads: "Barbara Allen" or "Sir Patrick Spens") are represented in a single version. The first problem is that the representation of these ballads as mute texts dramatically diminishes their power. The other problem points out an essential difference between the literate and oral traditions. To print "Bonny Barbara Allen" in a text such as this suggests that this is THE version of the ballad. Our English majors are conditioned to look upon poems as being represented in only one version—the one the poet crafted and revised and then settled on as "the" poem. When they see Frost's poem "The Witch of Coos," it is THE poem, the only one there is. Even in poetry, it's more complicated than that, but in the oral tradition it is a flat misrepresentation. A printed single version of "Barbara Allen," as everyone in the Texas Folklore Society knows, is only one snapshot of hundreds of variants that occur in a fluid stream stretched out over long time. My English majors, though, so wedded to the idea of mute, printed, final-version texts, did not understand this. They needed to come to grips with how different things are in the oral tradition.

The same is true of the whole notion of narrative, which we English majors consider our province. The very nature of the narrative (the story) in the oral tradition is profoundly different from the (again) more rigid structure of narrative in the literary tradition. For my folklore class, besides the basic text (Jan Harold Brunvand's *The Study of American Folklore*), I used two literary narratives, both of which featured embedded folkloric elements. The first was Zora Neale Hurston's *Mules and Men* and the second was Cormac McCarthy's *The Crossing*.

What happened with the latter novel is instructive. *The Crossing*, the second in McCarthy's Border Trilogy, can be viewed as an essentially folkloric document, particularly in three respects: (1) the existence and perpetration of animal myths, in this case the Mexican wolf; (2) the process of how a folk-hero ballad, in this case a Mexican *corrido*, comes into being; and, (3) the nature of story as an element fundamental to human existence. To a large degree, McCarthy's novel can be viewed as an account of how the exploits, misadventures, and escapades of Boyd Parham become the basis for a *corrido*, part truth and part myth, much like the Corrido of Gregorio Cortez as articulated by Américo Paredes in his monumental work, *With His Pistol in His Hand*. This is a long, slow book, and much of the reason is that McCarthy privileges the story and the story teller. At one point, Billy Parham, who is on a journey to somewhere, sits and listens to the story of a hermit. The story, which contributes to the idea of Story but has little to do with the plot, runs for a full thirty-five pages, which may explain why novelists like Cormac McCarthy do not find much favor in a world of page-turner readers. Consider this statement about story, taken from *The Crossing*:

> The man pushed back slightly from the table and the cat stepped down into his lap and curled up and subsided and turned its head and gravely regarded the boy across the table in the manner of a consultant. A cat of counsel. The man placed one hand upon it as if to secure it there. He looked at the boy. The task of the narrator is not an easy one, he said. He appears to be required to choose his tale from among the many that are possible. But of course that is not the case. The case is rather to make many of the one. Always the teller must be at pains to devise against his listener's claim—perhaps spoken, perhaps not—that he has heard the tale before. He sets forth the categories into which the

> listener will wish to fit the narrative as he hears it. But he understands that the narrative is itself in fact no category but is rather the category of all categories for there is nothing which falls outside its purview. All is telling. Do not doubt it.[3]

In another place a character says, "Rightly told, all stories are one." And in another, a character is advised to "Listen to the old corridos of your country. They will tell you."[4]

This novel is a laboratory for folklore and folkloric processes, but what I discovered was that—despite my ranting and precautions—the students wanted to read it like a literary text. I told them again and again, "Do not read this as a novel. Read it as a cultural and folkloric document." Most of them came around, but you can't imagine how many times I was asked, "What do you think this symbolizes?" Quit it. It is what it is. It symbolizes nothing. This is a hard sell to hardcore English majors, but I made some headway. I daresay that some of them even felt liberated in a sense by reading a text for what it is rather than for how it is "interpreted."

The same perceptions and behaviors are true of language and usage in the classroom versus the real world. If you want to see a gritty, down-to-earth representation of this, read the section on "Language and Study" in the 2005 TFS edition; this includes Jack Duncan's piece on "Popular English Usage in Texas." Nowhere is the gulf between High Art and the Oral Tradition wider than in the subject of language. The tendency of English teachers is to see language (like those literary texts) as fixed, solid, immovable, and impermeable—written in stone. Consider the incredibly long life and durability of the prohibition against splitting an infinitive or ending a sentence with a preposition—the latter of which Winston

Churchill discombobulated with the following: "That is a rule up with which I will not put." Arbitrary rules about grammar and syntax are more durable than most Child ballads.

The folklorist sees language and dialect in an entirely different light. They understand the truth in the following story, related by Steven Pinker (in *The Language Instinct*) about the psycholinguist Martin Braine. Braine was simply trying to correct a usage his young daughter had fallen into:

> Child: Want other one spoon, Daddy.
> Father: You mean, you want THE OTHER SPOON.
> Child: Yes, I want other one spoon, please, Daddy.
> Father: Can you say "the other spoon"?
> Child: Other . . . one . . . spoon.
> Father: Say . . . "other."
> Child: Other
> Father: "Spoon"
> Child: Spoon
> Father: "Other . . . spoon."
> Child: Other . . . spoon. Now give me other one spoon?[5]

If an introduction to folklore does anything, it should introduce English majors (and especially those who are going to be teachers or linguists) to the notion that language is more flexible than we like to admit—and that the world is not going to Hell in a handbasket if people use double modals or end sentences with prepositions.

The final element I want to speak about is that other English major bugbear, research. For this class, I required several small collection projects and then one large end-of-the-semester project. At the outset, I had them collect jokes and stories, as well as variants of songs and sayings. The major collection project was an exercise in material folklore. At the beginning, my English majors were all tied up in knots. How am I going to find this in the library? Answer: You're not. By the end of the semester they largely had come to accept some ideas that are critical to folklore (and that should be more a part of traditional research): that all the answers are not found in the library or in written form, and that interviews with quilters or songsters or great-grandmothers who had talked to Civil War veterans are invaluable—and maybe preferable—sources of knowledge. In addition, the folkloric collection process brought home other important lessons for my English majors, that flexibility and fluidity are good alternatives to the rigidity of my fifth-grade grammar teacher and that sometimes our attention belongs on processes rather than product.

I hope that an introduction to folklore and the processes of folklore broadened my students' horizons, and I dearly hope that it will make better teachers out of those who choose that profession. I think they learned a good deal, but I know I did. I can't wait for my next try at teaching English 364, in the fall semester of 2007.

ENDNOTES

1. Boatright, Mody C. "Folklore in a Literate Society." *Inside the Classroom (and out): How We Learn Through Folklore.* Publications of the Texas Folklore Society LXII. Kenneth L. Untiedt, ed. Denton: University of North Texas Press, 2005. 9
2. Ibid.
3. McCarthy, Cormac. *The Crossing.* New York: Alfred A. Knopf, 1994. 155.
4. Ibid. 230.
5. Pinker, Steven. *The Language Instinct.* New York: Harper Collins, 1994. 281.

A Cusco shaman

THE HISPANIC SHAMAN

by Charles B. Martin

The word "shaman," especially in Asian countries, refers to a person or priest who tries to contact the good and evil spirits in the world to help solve people's problems, which can be both physical and spiritual. Similar forms of primitive spiritualism were practiced by native Indians in America. The word "curandero" denotes a priest-like person in the community engaged in physical healing. This second term, which comes from the Spanish verb "curar" (to cure), is more common in America. Curanderos sometimes engaged in more spiritual tasks; hence, the two words are often interchangeable. "Witch doctor," a common synonym, is sometimes substituted for both words, but seems to have more pejorative connotations.

There may be various specialties practiced by a shaman or curandero. A "yerbero" practices herbal medicine; a "partera" is a mid-wife; a "sobador" (from "sobar," to rub) massages aching body parts; a "huesero" (from "hueso," bone) fixes broken or fractured bones; a medium contacts spirits, and a sorcerer ("brujo") casts spells. New World shamanism has been influenced from several directions: Judeo-Christian religion, Arabic and Greek medicine, Medieval witchcraft, Native American herbal lore, and Caribbean voodoo.

My first example of a shaman comes from the descendents of the Inca Indians of Peru. The best known monument to Incan culture is Machu Picchu, the ancient city which was abandoned some time in the 1400s and not discovered until 1911. Many people in local villages in the surrounding mountains still dress in traditional clothing, and the llama is the most common beast of burden and source of wool. Another popular Incan city was Pisac, at 9,000 feet, with terraced hillsides for growing foodstuffs and a temple at the top. Various traveling groups come to this temple to feel the magnetic energy that supposedly comes together at this juncture in the mountains, a force that has been sought both by the Incan shaman and by modern New Age spiritualists and Feng Shui followers.

The largest city in Peru, after Lima, is Cusco, a town of 300,000 people nestled in the mountains at an elevation of 11,000 feet. It was here that our small group of fourteen Overseas Adventure Travelers were introduced to a shaman who conducted a ceremony of blessing especially for us with all the necessary items and rituals. The local market even had a section where shamans could buy such items as llama embryos or a blood-red sap which can be squeezed from the bark of a certain tree and used to cure cancer.

The shaman first made an offering to Pachumama, Mother Earth, on a white cloth altar on which were placed a piece of cotton representing clouds, a tiny biscuit representing the sun, an orange doll representing Mother Earth, and other similar symbolic objects. Wine was poured out from the cup nearby. He then put

An offering made to Pachumama

some leaves in the center, one at a time, after blowing on them to call the spirits to come to the mountains. He placed a sea shell, representing Mother Ocean, near the leaves, along with a condor feather (perhaps representing a rainbow) and some small pieces of bread. Various other items were added from the unfolded paper nearby: a tiny starfish, a few grains of corn and lima beans, pieces of a conch shell, some llama fat, coca seeds, raisins, peanuts, rice, sugar, some incense, a piece of silver foil, a piece of string, a few alphabet noodles, some confetti, and some figs. He sprinkled these items with water from a bottle on the ground.

We handed him the coca leaves we had been given, he blew on them and put them in a pile to be wrapped up with the other items on the cloth, all the while offering prayers in the local language. He called anyone who wanted to participate to stand up while he "swept" the package up and down our backs and fronts. He asked us to make three wishes. Then he took the bundle to the nearby fire, held it up in the smoke from the fire, and returned for a final prayer to the spirits of Mother Earth for love, peace, and prosperity. I have to confess that all three of my wishes came true, so it evidently worked.

My second example comes from Chiapas state in southern Mexico. My wife and I visited the tiny town of San Juan Chamula, near San Cristobal de las Casas, where the Zapatista uprisings took place in the 1990s. Although the Zapatistas were unlucky in overthrowing an oppressive Mexican government, they did succeed in cleaning out the Catholic Church in Chamula and converting it to their own form of worship. The tile floor was carpeted with tiny, fresh pine branches. Tables around the sides were crammed with candles in glass containers or standing alone in a clump of wax. Here and there were individuals or whole families seated near lighted candles, some with a shaman saying prayers for them in the local Maya language. Occasionally, a single shaman was praying for a family who had paid him to offer prayers. One woman had her shaman and a couple of fresh eggs lying in front of her on the floor by the candles. Eggs, because they contain the seed of life within them, are an important part of many healing ceremonies. Another woman had a live chicken, which she would presumably sacrifice at some point in her ritual.

San Cristobal de las Casas, the largest town in this part of the mountains (population 100,000), has an excellent Museum of Maya Medicine with life-size tableaux representing the specific areas of medicine practiced by these natives, including the following. The pulse reader determines the patient's illness by examining the blood flow. He determines the cause of sickness (fright, envy, bad spirits, nature) and then prescribes a cure. The mountaintop prayer healer prays on a sacred hill using candles and incense whenever there is a crisis in the community, a poor harvest, or an interfamilial conflict. A mural on the wall represents the village and Mother Earth. The lake in the mural contains a fetus, signifying that Mother Earth gives us life.

The herbalist knows the properties of medicinal plants and how to ask their permission to cut them, and performs a ceremony before cutting them. In a nearby tableau, an herbalist was making "pilieo," a compound of wild tobacco and limestone placed in a gourd to be kept with the person to protect him or her when walking at night or when suffering from stomachache or nausea. The midwife works with women during pregnancy, and later with the newborns, administering appropriate herbs. She is seen in another tableau with a man and his pregnant wife who is ready to deliver. A bone healer treats fractures, sprains, swelling and pain through massage, whistling to frighten evil spirits, and blowing to send bad spirits away. He uses herbs, candles, and incense. The museum also has a lifesize candle maker in the process of dipping candles, which are an important part of healing in that they liberate the spirit of the sick person and serve as food for the gods.

In a living chapel within the museum natives may pray to various favorite saints or to Christ, though Christ is often seen as a figure in a glass coffin in many churches in Chiapas. (In the Temple of San Cristobal, high on a hill overlooking the city, the painting over the main altar is one of John the Baptist.) In a room near the chapel, a resident curandero was on call. We could hear him chanting as he went through a healing ceremony. A booklet printed by the museum describes the typical cleansing service this way: Candles of a particular color are chosen to match the illness, the healer prays in a loud voice to contact the spirits and saints, and then he "sweeps" the body of the patient from head to toe with basil or pine needles. He may even pass an egg or a chicken over the ailing part of the body and then he "spits posh (a kind of local liquor) over the patient, in front, behind, and on all sides, in order to scare away bad spirits and bad winds, and to purify the person."[1] Outside the chapel was an herb garden with various medicinal herbs labeled. Near the entrance to the museum we saw a young woman waiting to see the healer, holding an ill child in her arms and a pine branch and plastic bag containing a raw egg in her hand.

My third example of shamanism comes from South Texas, where the curandero is still a vital part of Mexican-American life along the border with Mexico. According to Robert Trotter and Juan Chavira, the curanderos are involved in treating people at three different levels: material, spiritual, and mental. The material level is practiced the most through the use of physical objects like herbs, spices, candles, and crucifixes, and with the reciting of various ritual invocations to favorite saints or spirits. For example, an egg or a pine branch might be "swept" up and down the patient's body to absorb negative influences in the patient, or incense might be used in houses or businesses to drive away negative influences.

At the spiritual level the folk healer, more often called a shaman, tries to contact someone in the spirit world, usually through some kind of trance through which his spirit leaves his body and is possessed by a different spirit who directs positive and negative forces toward the patient to improve his condition. Even group sessions may be held at a "center" devoted to healing and communication with the dead.

The mental level is the least common level and has "the fewest rituals and the least visible behavior,"[2] as the curandero probes the patient's mind and tries to solve his problem, somewhat like psychological analysis in modern medicine.

W. D. Smithers' photographic study of the Big Bend cites numerous examples of folk healing, even cases where the author himself was healed by a curandera from yellow jaundice, typhoid fever, sunstroke, and various cuts and scratches.[3] Ironically, many of our modern drugstore pills are made from the same plants used by curanderos for hundreds of years.

Can the curandero find a place in twenty-first-century medicine? Local hospitals and doctors are unlikely to invite him or her to be on their boards or to attend their medical meetings. However, the local culture has not given up on them. Trotter and Chavira in their last chapter, "The Future of Curanderismo," tell the story of an Hispanic man who had a gall bladder operation in a local hospital. He came home in good condition but began a long bout with depression. Finally his wife called a curandero, who came to his house for three different "cleansing" sessions. The man's spirits soon revived and he went back to work. When asked what the curandero gave him that the doctor didn't, he said, "Animo," which means "spirit" or "enthusiasm." Thus, the two types of medicine can exist together and complement each other. Trotter and Chavira suggest that curanderismo "combines self-reliance with cultural relevance and family systems and gives some Mexican-Americans a sense of stability and continuity in the face of socially disrupting urban-technological change. It provides a linkage of past and future in a therapeutic system."[4]

The title "Hispanic Shaman" may be a bit restrictive in that the people studied, especially the Incas of Peru and the Mayan descendents in Chiapas, Mexico, are of Indian origin living in a basically Hispanic community, whereas in Texas curanderos are Mexican Americans albeit Hispanicized mestizos. Perhaps "New World Folk Healers" would have been more precise. But whatever term we use, we cannot escape the fact that curandismo has long been an important part of Texas folklore and Texas folk medicine.

ENDNOTES

1. Photocopied booklet by the Organization of Indigenous Medics in the State of Chiapas (OMIECH).
2. Trotter II, Robert T. and Juan Antonio Chavira. *Curanderismo: Mexican American Folk Healing*, 2nd ed. Athens, GA: Univ. of Georgia Press, 1997. 149.
3. Smithers, W. D. *Chronicles of the Big Bend*. Rotan, TX: Madrona Press, 1985.
4. Trotter. 174.

Francis Edward Abernethy, Distinguished Regents Professor Emeritus of English at Stephen F. Austin State University, was Secretary-Editor of the Texas Folklore Society from 1971 to 2004, editing or co-editing over twenty volumes of TFS publications in his thirty-three years of leading the organization.

Ken Baake is an associate professor of English at Texas Tech. Born and raised in Maryland, he moved to Texas in 1987 after a stint teaching for the U.S. Peace Corps in Kenya. He spent ten years as a reporter and business editor at the *El Paso Herald-Post.* After receiving a Ph.D. in rhetoric and professional communication at New Mexico State in 2000, Ken and his family moved to Lubbock where he took a job teaching in the area of technical communication and rhetoric at Texas Tech. His courses range from the Rhetoric of Scientific Literature, Classical Rhetoric, and Technical Report Writing, to courses that consider types of writing about historical topics, such as World War I. Ken has recently developed an undergraduate course titled "Booms, Busts, and Dust: Writings about Texans and their Land," which examines various historical and present-day writings about Texas culture and its environment, particularly relating to the oil industry, water issues, and agriculture. He has published a book (*Metaphor and Knowledge: The Challenges of Writing Science*, 2003) about metaphor and science writing. Ken increasingly has become fascinated with folklore, folk music, and narrative as means by which people understand their environment. His hobbies include playing with varying degrees of success the banjo, guitar, and piano to accompany folk songs.

Scott Hill Bumgardner is a real estate consultant, retired Houston cop, grandpa, rancher, writer, and professional storyteller. He has served several terms as president of the Houston Storytellers Guild, and has been a member of the Houston Rodeo Speakers

Committee since 1991. His foundation in historical tales and cowboy poetry has taken a turn for the outlandish. Funny, far-fetched tales keep falling out of his head. The lighter side of his nature keeps the audience on the edge of their seats as his fun, action-packed tales come roaring by.

Claire Campbell says, "Long ago there was always time for a story," and she still believes in carrying on that tradition. Claire has been a Texan since 1963. She graduated from Texas A&M University in 1988, and she and her husband, Al Campbell, have been members of the Texas Folklore Society since 1990. Claire began storytelling professionally in 1984 at the Texas Renaissance Festival. The following twelve years she told stories to a wide range of audiences: kindergartners and college students, libraries and festivals, and at the National Storytelling Festival as the teller representing five Southwestern states. She particularly enjoyed her years as teller at the Texas Folklife Festival in San Antonio, and in Albuquerque at Storyfiesta. Those years introduced her to a great variety of hidfolk! In 1997, Claire retired from her storytelling travels to write family histories, be a ranch wife, and be a Grandmama. She and her husband live at Querida Ranch in Robertson County.

Paul H. Carlson lives with his wife Ellen along the upper reaches of the Brazos River near Lubbock. He is Professor Emeritus of history at Texas Tech University. He has published several books and dozens of professional articles and essays. He is a Fellow of the Texas State Historical Association, former president of the West Texas Historical Association, and a member of the Philosophical Society of Texas.

Kit Chase is the senior staff writer and photographer for *The Weekly News of Cooke County* in Gainesville, Texas. She is married to Tom Chase and they have four children and two grandchildren, Hannah and Amelia. Kit enjoys the challenges her career presents, and best of all the opportunities to write about local Cooke County history. Kit has been a journalist in Cooke County for fifteen years. She is a member of the "Telling Our Stories" program directed by Dr. Jerry Lincecum in Sherman, Texas.

Kenneth W. Davis, a Fellow of the Texas Folklore Society, is a past-President of the Society and of the American Studies Association of Texas, the Southwest/Texas Popular Culture Association, and the West Texas Historical Association. He is also a past-sheriff of the Lubbock Westerners' Corral. He is Professor Emeritus of English at Texas Tech University. He remains interested in the grand oral traditions of storytelling in the American South and Southwest.

Robert J. (Jack) Duncan has taught at Collin College and Grayson County College and has worked in staff positions at Collin College and Richland College. He was President of the Texas Folklore Society in 1980, and is a life member of the Texas State Historical Association. Jack is a widely published freelance writer, in both scholarly and popular periodicals, including *Reader's Digest.* For the past dozen years, he has worked as a writer/editor/researcher for Retractable Technologies, Inc., a manufacturer of safety needle medical devices in Little Elm. A lifelong learner, Jack continues to frequently take graduate courses at UNT in a variety of disciplines. He has lived in McKinney most of his life. He is married to his high school sweetheart, the former Elizabeth Ann Harris; they have two sons and five grandsons. Jack and Elizabeth have been active members of the Texas Folklore Society for more than forty years.

Carla Ellard is the Curator for the Southwestern & Mexican Photography Collection at the Wittliff Collections at Texas State University-San Marcos and has worked there since 2000. She is originally from the Rio Grande Valley; she was raised in Edinburg, Texas, and graduated with a B.S. in photography from East Texas State University (now TAMU-Commerce) and a MSLIS from UT Austin. Carla is a new member of the Texas Folklore Society.

Mike Felker and Liz Brandt. Mike Felker taught at Texas Tech for eight years and at South Plains College for twenty-two-and-a-half years, serving as chair of the department of English for eighteen of those years. He retired from full-time teaching in December 2010. Liz Brandt taught English at Tech for two years, and spent twenty-five years in the Special Education department at Ropes High School, where she taught sixth through twelfth grade, all subjects, content mastery. At night, "in her spare time," she taught world literature at South Plains College. She retired from Ropes in May of 2008, but, like Mike, continues to teach part-time for SPC. Mike's 1990 TFS presentation, "Ghosts, Goblins, Virgins, and Other Supernatural Creatures," was included in the Texas Folklore Society's 2005 publication, *Inside the Classroom and Out*, and Mike and Liz, along with the late Warren S. Walker, are co-authors of three catalogs of the folk motifs and types of folk tales in the Archive of Turkish Oral Narrative at Texas Tech. Both hold the two Legendary Ladies of Texas who are the subject of this article "near and dear to their hearts."

Lora B. Davis Garrison was born and raised a Texas ranch girl, with no electricity, no running water, and an outhouse in the corner of the garden. She learned to cook on a wood stove, chopped wood, hauled water when the cistern was dry, and was educated in a three-room school house. She is a native of Uvalde County and a descendent of some of the first settlers in Texas and the Texas Hill Country. She has been collecting oral histories from pioneer families since 1979. These histories appeared in her columns in the *Uvalde Leader News.* She was voted Woman of the Year by Texas Press Women in 1984. Her stories have appeared in magazines, newspapers, and in the Texas Folklore Society publications. She has served as President of the Daughters of the Republic of Texas, and President of the Texas Folklore Society. She served on the Board of Directors for the Alamo for eight years, and on the Board of the French Legation's museum in Austin for four years, as well as on the Board of the Republic of Texas Museum for two years. She has an educational background in art, fashion design, anthropology, folklore and creative writing. She was a storyteller at the Texas Folklife Festival in San Antonio for more than ten years. She now spends most of her time writing and telling pioneer stories. She tells that in another life she taught in a Fashion Design School in Virginia and designed hats for Lady Bird Johnson, Alice Roosevelt Longworth, Mrs. Arthur Fiedler, and many senators' wives.

Acayla Morenci Haile was born in 1988, and has been a member of the Texas Folklore Society since then. She was raised in Tarpley, Texas, in a house the family built—from tree to house—by themselves. She graduated with honors from Schreiner University and now lives in San Marcos, Texas. She is a storyteller and a puppeteer, and enjoys gardening, painting, and hearing and telling interesting stories. This is her second paper for the Folklore Society.

Jim Harris is a past-President of the Texas Folklore Society. He and his wife Mary and his son Hawk have been members of the TFS since the 1970s. He is a writer, photographer, runner, cyclist, and fisherman. He is the executive director of the Lea County Museum in Lovington, New Mexico. Jim and Mary spend a lot of their leisure time at two remote camps in the Big Bend Country.

John Igo was born in San Antonio in 1927. He had storytelling uncles on both sides—one comic, one imaginative. John spent forty-six years teaching college English, and twenty-two years in radio (on grammar). He has published or produced eleven books of poetry (two of which won awards), two textbooks (one folkloric), two folkloric essays (for the TFS), one memoir, one short urban history, one novella (folkloric), and one ballet scenario (folkloric). He has also published pen-and-ink graphics, several one-act plays (two of which won awards), and he earned one Emmy in 1985 for writing/editing a one-hour documentary. He spent seventeen years as a weekly theatre critic in newspapers, and ten years as a talking head theatre critic, PBS, KLRN, on "Art Beat." He has other finished works "in the oven," including a biography of New Yorker's Mendez Marks, a collection of folktales from Helotes,

Texas, one heavy drama, one full-length farce, and one comic novel, as well as shelves of notebooks (for more information see http://johnigo.com/About.html). John has been a TFS member since 1953.

James Ward Lee is a past-President and now a Fellow of the Texas Folklore Society. He is author of a hundred or more articles, reviews, and short stories and is author or editor of ten books, the most recent being *Texas Country Singers* and *Elmer Kelton: Essays and Memories.* His collected stories, *A Texas Jubilee*, is forthcoming from TCU Press. Lee, inducted into the Texas Literary Hall of Fame in 2010, has been a member of TFS since 1958. He lives in Fort Worth.

Jerry B. Lincecum, a sixth-generation Texan, is Emeritus Professor of English at Austin College. He holds the B.A. in English from Texas A&M University and M.A. and Ph.D. degrees from Duke University. A past-President of the Texas Folklore Society, he has presented many papers at annual meetings of the Society and co-edited *The Family Saga: A Collection of Texas Family Legends* for the TFS in 2003. Since 1990, he and Dr. Peggy Redshaw have directed "Telling Our Stories," a humanities project at Austin College that aids older adults in writing their autobiographies and family histories. He also serves as a trainer and editor for the Legacy program at Home Hospice of Grayson County, which collects the life stories of Hospice patients and publishes them in booklet form.

Al Lowman, in business since 1935, is now retired but marches on as Stringtown's foremost sedentary lifestyle activist. He is past-President of the Texas Folklore Society, the Book Club of Texas, and the Texas State Historical Association. Most recently he is founder and honorary curator of the Al Lowman Printing Arts Collection in the Cushing Library at Texas A&M University. He is also a member of the Philosophical Society of Texas, the Book Club of California, and the Grolier Club of New York City.

Charles B. Martin retired in 1999 after teaching English language and literature for thirty-five years at the University of North Texas in Denton. He grew up in New Mexico and attended UNM for a Bachelor's degree, and then the University of Florida for a Master's and the University of Missouri for a Ph.D. He spent two years in Spain, one on a Fulbright lectureship (1967–68) and one as an exchange professor (1985–86). He has traveled widely in Spain and Mexico and has given several papers on Hispanic folklore at the TFS meetings, where he served as Vice President and President of the Society.

Archie P. McDonald retired from teaching history full-time at Stephen F. Austin State University after forty-four years, and then served SFASU as the University/Community Liaison until his death in August of 2012. He had served as director of the East Texas Historical Association and editor of the association's *Journal* for thiry-seven years, and was a past-president of the Texas State Historical Association, past vice-chair of the Texas Historical Commission, and author/editor of more than twenty books on historical topics—and one book of humor titled *Helpful Cooking Hints for House-Husbands of Uppity Women.*

Dr. Manuel F. Medrano holds a doctorate degree from the University of Houston and is currently a professor in the History Department at the University of Texas at Brownsville, specializing in Mexican-American history and culture. He is a member of the Humanities Texas Board and its Distinguished Speaker's Bureau. He has authored three published historical/cultural poetry books about the border, including *In Body and Mind, Imagenes,* and *In the Shadow of My Soul*; he also co-authored a history book with Dr. Milo Kearney titled *Medieval Culture and the Mexican American Borderlands.* Since 1993 he has produced and directed, in conjunction with the UTB/TSC Media Services, twenty-three Los del Valle oral history profiles of people and events in the Rio Grande Valley, including legendary folklorist Américo Paredes and acclaimed Tejano writer Rolando

Hinojosa. In 2005, Medrano received the Chancellor's Teaching Excellence Award, and he received the Houston Endowed Chair for Civic Engagement at the University of Texas at Brownsville in 2008. In 2009, he co-authored with Dr. Anthony Knopp and Ms. Pricilla Rodriguez, *Charro Days in Brownsville*, published by Arcadia Press. In 2010, his biography about scholar and folklorist Américo Paredes titled *Américo Paredes, In His Own Words*, was published by the University of North Texas Press.

Lori Najvar, a native Texas-Czech, grew up hearing her parents speak and sing in Czech, and it wasn't until the eighth grade that she learned the English word for *pupek* was navel. Now, as an Austin resident and visual artist, she seeks out American cultural traditions as director of PolkaWorks, a non-profit organization that explores and documents traditions through multimedia projects. Texas Czechs and auctioneers are two entertaining subcultures she's explored extensively and shares with the world through film and exhibitions. "Czech Links: 800 Pounds of Tradition," "Moravia, Texas U.S.A.," "Going, Going, Gone! Story of the Texas Auctioneer," and the latest, "The Grove, Texas," are all documentaries that include three generations of storytelling, humor, and Texas pride.

J. Rhett Rushing is a proud father and Aggie who has been a TFS member for twenty-nine years. Rhett has contributed several articles to TFS publications, and served as TFS President in 2004–2005.

Jean Granberry Schnitz was born in Spur, Texas, on October 11, 1931. She graduated from Raymondville High School in 1948, and from Texas College of Arts and Industries (now Texas A&M University–Kingsville) in 1952. She and Lew Schnitz were married in 1953. They have three sons and four grandchildren. A retired legal secretary, she lives near Boerne. Jean served two separate terms on the Texas A&I Alumni Board—in 1968–1971 and

1991–1993. She has served on Boards for several United Methodist Churches in several Texas towns, and on the Board of the Wesley Community Center in Robstown, Texas, for five years. She was President of the Nueces County Legal Secretaries Association in Corpus Christi in 1980. Since 1990, she has presented ten papers to the Texas Folklore Society, most of which were published in TFS annual volumes. She became a Director on the Board of the Texas Folklore Society in 2002, and was elected Vice-President for 2005–2006. She presided as President at the 91st annual meeting of the Texas Folklore Society in San Antonio, Texas, in April of 2007. She was a participant in the Texas Folklife Festival in San Antonio for the 30th year in 2011.

J. Michael Sullivan, a seventh-generation Texan, is a freshman Energy Commerce major at Texas Tech University. In 2004, he attended his first TFS meeting when he was in the 5th grade. Through the years, J. Michael has participated in various TFS youth activities during and outside the annual meetings. He is a 2011 graduate of Orange Grove High School where he was active in football, basketball, baseball, track, and FFA. In 2010, he participated with the Society of the Historical Interpreters of Texas in its living history representation of Texas trail drivers, assuming the character of the young trailblazer George W. West, at the George West Storyfest. He presented his San Patricio ghost stories paper at the 2010 TFS meeting in Abilene as a high school junior.

Jo Virgil has served as Community Outreach and Information Coordinator for the Texas Governor's Committee on People with Disabilities since January 2009. She holds a Master of Journalism degree from the University of North Texas and a Bachelor of Arts degree in English from Texas Tech University, as well as teacher certification in English and journalism. Her background includes a position as Community Relations Manager for Barnes & Noble and, before that, as a reporter and columnist for the *Fort Worth Star-Telegram*. She is a fourth-generation Texan and comes from a family of avid storytellers. Jo currently serves on the Board of the Central Texas Storytelling Guild and is active in Story Circle Network, an organization that encourages women to write their life stories, and the Writers' League of Texas.

Henry Wolff, Jr. is a long-time Texas journalist whose career embraced some fifty years. He retired in 2009 from the *Victoria Advocate*, Texas' second oldest existing daily newspaper, where his "Henry's Journal" column appeared for three decades. During that time he wrote more than 6,000 columns about the people, places, history, and culture of Texas, particularly of South Texas and the Texas Coastal Plains. Henry is a former President of the Texas Folklore Society and of the South Texas Historical Association. He has served on the boards of the South Texas Zoological Society and the German-Texan Heritage Society, and was also a long-time vice-chairman of the Victoria County Historical Commission.

Linda Wolff is a native of Wichita, Kansas, and has lived in Texas since 1983, when she became a staff writer and bureau chief for the *Victoria Advocate* at Port Lavaca. In 1993, she left the *Victoria Advocate* and accepted a position as consultant to the Texas Parks and Wildlife Department providing staff support for the Governor's Task Force on Nature Tourism. In more recent years she served the Golden Crescent Regional Planning Commission in Victoria as coordinator of economic development and as environmental resources coordinator. She also served as executive director of Texas Settlement Region, a coalition of seventeen Texas counties promoting heritage tourism. Linda is Vice-President of the Texas Folklore Society, a former chair of the Victoria County Historical Commission, and she has served as a member of the board of directors of the South Texas Historical Association. She is the author of "Indianola and Matagorda Island, 1837 to 1887," a local history and visitor's guide to the historic seaport and nearby barrier island on the Texas Gulf Coast. Linda and her husband, retired *Victoria Advocate* columnist Henry Wolff, Jr., reside in Victoria.

Gene Young was born in San Angelo and grew up in various towns in West Texas and the Panhandle. He has degrees from Borger (Texas) Senior High School, West Texas State University (B.A. and M.A.), and the University of Tennessee (Ph.D. in American literature). He served five years as an Air Force officer and B-52 navigator in Southeast Asia before returning to finish his master's and Ph.D. He has taught American literature, Texas and Southwestern literature and culture, folklore, and a variety of other subjects at Texas A&M, Morehead (KY) State University, and since 1992, at Sam Houston State University. He is currently a professor of English and Director of the Honors College at Sam Houston. He plays fiddle and guitar in three traditional old-time acoustic bands, along with his wife Marynell, who teaches Spanish and ESL at Centerville High School. His bands play a variety of "re-enactment" venues, such as the Texas Independence Day Celebration at Washington-on-the-Brazos, the Texas Folklife Celebration in San Antonio, the Liendo Plantation Civil War re-enactment, and Texian Market Days at the George Historical Ranch. He and Marynell have three children and a growing number of grandchildren, all living in Austin. He hopes that when he dies, his tombstone will read "Here lies a damned good fiddler."

INDEX

A

B

C

D

E

F

G

H

I

J

K

L

M

N

O

P

Q

R

S

T

Y

Z